LIVES OF GIRLS
WHO BECAME FAMOUS

BY

SARAH K. BOLTON

Author of "Lives of Poor Boys Who Became Famous"

REVISED AND ENLARGED EDITION

ILLUSTRATED

NEW YORK
THOMAS Y. CROWELL COMPANY
PUBLISHERS

PRINTED IN THE UNITED STATES OF AMERICA

PUBLISHERS' NOTE

In presenting a new, revised edition of Mrs. Sarah K. Bolton's famous book on "Famous Girls," it is interesting to glance back at editions which have gone before. It was first brought out in 1886, as a companion volume to "Poor Boys Who Became Famous," and has had a success quite as great. Edition after edition has appeared. More than a hundred thousand copies of the two books have been sold, and the demand continues steadily year by year.

Who can measure the good that these two books have accomplished? How many other ambitious boys and girls have been spurred on to high endeavor by these stories of what other boys and girls have done? There is a satisfaction in publishing such books, which far outweighs any monetary consideration.

"Lives of Girls Who Became Famous" is now entirely revised and reset. A few of the subjects, who were living when Mrs. Bolton laid down her pen, have since passed away. Their biographical sketches have been completed. Some new material has been added, including: Jenny Lind, Jane Addams, Alice Freeman Palmer, Clara Barton, Frances E. Willard, Helen Keller, Anna Howard Shaw, Elizabeth Blackwell, Susan B. Anthony, Lady Astor and Madame Curie. There are now twenty-eight life stories in all, each full of inspiration for other girl readers.

PREFACE TO FIRST EDITION

ALL of us have aspirations. We build aircastles, and are probably the happier for the building. However, the sooner we learn that life is not a play-day, but a thing of earnest activity, the better for us and for those associated with us. "Energy," says Goethe, "will do anything that can be done in this world"; and Jean Ingelow truly says, that "Work is heaven's best."

If we cannot, like George Eliot, write *Adam Bede,* we can, like Florence Nightingale, visit the poor and the prisoner. If we cannot, like Rosa Bonheur, paint a "Horse Fair," and receive ten thousand dollars, we can, like Mrs. Stowe and Miss Alcott, do some kind of work to lighten the burdens of parents. If poor, with Mary Lyon's persistency and noble purpose, we can accomplish almost anything. If rich, we can bless the world in thousands of ways, and are untrue to God and ourselves if we fail to do it.

Margaret Fuller said, "All might be superior beings," and doubtless this is true, if all were willing to cultivate the mind and beautify the character.

S. K. B.

CONTENTS

LIVES OF GIRLS WHO BECAME FAMOUS

ELIZABETH BARRETT BROWNING

EVER since I had received in my girlhood, from my best friend, the works of Elizabeth Barrett Browning, in five volumes in blue and gold, I had read and re-read the pages, till I knew scores by heart. I had longed to see the face and home of her whom the English call "Shakespeare's daughter," and whom Edmund Clarence Stedman names "the passion-flower of the century."

I shall never forget that beautiful July morning spent in the Browning home in London. The poet-wife had gone out from it, and lay buried in Florence, but here were her books and her pictures. Here was a marble bust, the hair clustering about the face, and a smile on the lips that showed happiness. Near by was another bust of the idolized only child, of whom she wrote in *Casa Guidi Windows:*—

"The sun strikes through the windows, up the floor;
 Stand out in it, my own young Florentine,
Not two years old, and let me see thee more!
 It grows along thy amber curls to shine
Brighter than elsewhere. Now look straight before
 And fix thy brave blue English eyes on mine,
And from thy soul, which fronts the future so
 With unabashed and unabated gaze,
Teach me to hope for what the Angels know
 When they smile clear as thou dost!"

I

Here was the breakfast-table at which they three had often sat together. Close beside it hung a picture of the room in Florence, where she lived so many years in a wedded bliss as perfect as any known in history. Tears gathered in the eyes of Robert Browning, as he pointed out her chair, and sofa, and writing-table.

Of this room in Casa Guidi, Kate Field wrote in the *Atlantic Monthly,* September, 1861 : "They who have been so favored can never forget the square ante-room, with its great picture and piano-forte, at which the boy Browning passed many an hour; the little dining room covered with tapestry, and where hung medallions of Tennyson, Carlyle, and Robert Browning; the long room filled with plaster casts and studies, which was Mr. Browning's retreat; and, dearest of all, the large drawing-room, where *she* always sat. It opens upon a balcony filled with plants, and looks out upon the old iron-gray church of Santa Felice. There was something about this room that seemed to make it a proper and especial haunt for poets. The dark shadows and subdued light gave it a dreamy look, which was enhanced by the tapestry-covered walls, and the old pictures of saints that looked out sadly from their carved frames of black wood. Large bookcases, constructed of specimens of Florentine carving selected by Mr. Browning, were brimming over with wise-looking books. Tables were covered with more gayly bound volumes, the gifts of brother authors. Dante's grave profile, a cast of Keats' face and brow taken after death, a pen-and-ink sketch of Tennyson, the genial face of John Kenyon, Mrs. Browning's good friend and relative, little paintings of the boy Browning, all attracted the eye in turn, and gave rise to a thousand musings. But the glory of all, and that which sancti-fied all, was seated in a low armchair near the door.   A small table, strewn with writing materials, books and newspapers, was always by her side."

Then Mr. Browning, in the London home, showed us the room where he wrote, containing his library and hers. The books are on simple shelves, choice, and many very old and rare. Here are her books, many in Greek and Hebrew. In the Greek, I saw her notes on the margin in Hebrew, and in the Hebrew she had written her marginal notes in Greek. Here also are the five volumes of her writings, in blue and gold.

The small table at which she wrote still stands beside the larger where her husband composed. His table is covered with letters and papers and books; hers stands there unused, because it is a constant reminder of those companionable years, when they worked together. Close by hangs a picture of the "young Florentine," Robert Barrett Browning, now grown to manhood, an artist already famed. He has a refined face, as he sits in artist garb, before his easel, sketching in a peasant's house.

The beloved poet who wrote at the little table is endeared to all the world. Born in 1809, in the county of Durham, the daughter of wealthy parents, she passed her early years partly in the country in Herefordshire, and partly in the city. That she loved the country with its wild flowers and woods, her poem, *The Lost Bower*, plainly shows.

"Green the land is where my daily
    Steps in jocund childhood played,
Dimpled close with hill and valley,
    Dappled very close with shade;
Summer-snow of apple-blossoms running up from
    glade to glade."

Elizabeth Barrett wrote poems at ten, and when seventeen, published an *Essay on Mind, and Other Poems*. The essay was after the manner of Pope, and though showing good knowledge of Plato and Bacon, did not find favor with the critics. It was dedicated to her father, who was proud of a daughter who preferred Latin and Greek to the novels of the day.

Her teacher was the blind Hugh Stuart Boyd, whom she praises in her *Wine of Cyprus*.

More fond of books than of social life, she was laying the necessary foundation for a noble fame. The lives of Elizabeth Barrett Browning, George Eliot, and Margaret Fuller, emphasize the necessity of almost unlimited knowledge, if woman would reach lasting fame. A great man or woman of letters, without great scholarship, is well-nigh an impossible thing.

Nine years after her first book, *Prometheus Bound and Miscellaneous Poems* was published in 1835. She was now twenty-six. A translation from the Greek of Æschylus by a woman caused much comment, but like the first book it received severe criticism. Several years afterward, when she brought her collected poems before the world, she wrote: "One early failure, a translation of the *Prometheus of Æschylus,* which, though happily free of the current of publication, may be remembered against me by a few of my personal friends, I have replaced here by an entirely new version, made for them and my conscience, in expiation of a sin of my youth, with the sincerest application of my mature mind." "This latter version," says Mr. Stedman, "of a most sublime tragedy is more poetical than any other of equal correctness, and has the fire and vigor of a master-hand. No one has succeeded better than its author in capturing with rhymed measures the wilful rushing melody of the tragic chorus."

In 1835 Miss Barrett made the acquaintance of Mary Russell Mitford, and a life-long friendship resulted. Miss Mitford says: "She was certainly one of the most interesting persons I had ever seen. Everybody who then saw her said the same. Of a slight delicate figure, with a shower of dark curls falling on either side of a most expressive face, large tender eyes, richly fringed by dark eyelashes, a smile like a sunbeam, and such a look of youthfulness, that I had some difficulty in persuading a friend, in whose carriage we went together to Cheswick, that the translator of the *Prometheus of Æschylus,* the author of the *Essay on Mind,* was old enough to be introduced into company, in technical language, was out. We met so constantly and so familiarly that, in spite of the difference of age, intimacy ripened into friendship, and after my return into the country, we corresponded freely and frequently, her letters being just what letters ought to be,—her own talk put upon paper."

The next year Miss Barrett, never robust, broke a blood-vessel in the lungs. For a year she was ill, and then with her eldest and favorite brother, was carried to Torquay to try the effect of a warmer climate. After a year spent here, she greatly improved, and seemed likely to recover her usual health.

One beautiful summer morning she went on the balcony to watch her brother and two other young men who had gone out for a sail. Having had much experience, and understanding the coast, they allowed the boatman to return to land. Only a few minutes out, and in plain sight, as they were crossing the bar, the boat went down, and the three friends perished. Their bodies even were never recovered.

The whole town was in mourning. Posters were put upon every cliff and public place, offering large rewards "for linen cast ashore marked with the initials of the beloved dead; for it so chanced that all the three were of the dearest and the best: one, an only son; the other, the son of a widow"; but the sea was forever silent.

The sister, who had seen her brother sink before her eyes, was utterly prostrated. She blamed herself for his death, because he came to Torquay for her comfort. All winter long she heard the sound of waves ringing in her ears like the moans of the dying. From this time forward she never mentioned her brother's name, and later exacted from Mr. Browning a promise that the subject should never be broached between them.

The following year she was removed to London in an invalid carriage, journeying twenty miles a day. And then for seven years, in a large darkened room, lying much of the time upon her couch, and seeing only a few most intimate friends, the frail woman lived and wrote. Books more than ever became her solace and joy. Miss Mitford says, "She read almost every book worth reading, in almost every language, and gave herself heart and soul to that poetry of which she seemed born to be the priestess." When Dr. Barry urged that she read light books, she had a small edition of Plato bound so as to resemble a novel, and the good man was satisfied. She understood her own needs better than he.

When she was twenty-nine, she published *The Seraphim and Other Poems.* The *Seraphim* was a reverential description of two angels watching the Crucifixion. Though the critics saw much that was strikingly original, they condemned the frequent obscurity of meaning and irregularity of rhyme. The next year, *The Romaunt of the Page* and other ballads appeared, and in 1844, when she was thirty-five, a complete edition of her poems, opening with the *Drama of Exile.* This was the expulsion of Adam and Eve from Eden, the first scene representing "the outer side of the gate of Eden shut fast

ELIZABETH BARRETT BROWNING

with cloud, from the depth of which revolves a sword of fire self-moved. Adam and Eve are seen in the distance flying along the glare."

In one of her prefaces she said: "Poetry has been to me as serious a thing as life itself,—and life has been a *very* serious thing; there has been no playing at skittles for me in either. I never mistook pleasure for the final cause of poetry, nor leisure for the hour of the poet. I have done my work, so far, as work,—not as mere hand and head work, apart from the personal being, but as the completest expression of that being to which I could attain,—and as work I offer it to the public, feeling its shortcomings more deeply than any of my readers, because measured from the height of my aspiration; but feeling also that the reverence and sincerity with which the work was done should give it some protection from the reverent and sincere."

One person among the many who had read Miss Barrett's poems felt their genius, because he had genius in his own soul, and that person was Robert Browning. That she admired his poetic work was shown in *Lady Geraldine's Courtship,* when Bertram reads to his lady-love:—

"Or at times a modern volume,—Wordsworth's solemn-thoughted idyl,
Howitt's ballad verse, or Tennyson's enchanted reverie,
Or from Browning some *Pomegranate,* which, if cut deep down the middle,
Shows a heart within blood-tinctured, of a veined humanity."

Mr. Browning determined to meet the unknown singer. Years later he told the story to Elizabeth C. Kinney, when she had gone with the happy husband and wife on a day's excursion from Florence. She says: "Finding that the invalid did not receive strangers, he wrote her a letter, intense with his desire to see her.   She reluctantly consented to an interview.   He flew to her apartment, was admitted by the nurse, in whose presence only could he see the deity at whose shrine he had long worshipped. But the golden opportunity was not to be lost; love became oblivious to any save the presence of the real of its ideal.   Then and there Robert Browning poured his impassioned soul into hers; though his tale of love seemed only an enthusiast's dream.   Infirmity had hitherto so hedged her about, that she deemed herself forever protected from all assaults of love.   Indeed, she felt only injured that a fellow-poet should take advantage, as it were, of her indulgence in granting him an interview, and requested him to withdraw from her presence, not attempting any response to his proposal, which she could not believe in earnest.   Of course, he withdrew from her sight, but not to withdraw the offer of his heart and hand; on the contrary, to repeat it by letter, and in such wise as to convince her how 'dead in earnest' he was. Her own heart, touched already when she knew it not, was this time fain to listen, be convinced, and overcome.

"As a filial daughter, Elizabeth told her father of the poet's love, and of the poet's love in return, and asked a parent's blessing to crown their happiness.   At first he was incredulous of the strange story; but when the truth flashed on him from the new fire in her eyes, he kindled with rage, and forbade her ever seeing or communicating with her lover again, on the penalty of disinheritance and banishment forever from a father's love.   This decision was founded on no dislike for Mr. Browning personally, or anything in him or his family; it was simply arbitrary.   But the new love was stronger than the old in her,—it conquered."   Mr. Barrett never forgave his daughter, and died unreconciled, which to her was a great grief.

In 1846 Elizabeth Barrett arose from her sick-bed to marry the man of her choice, who took her at once to Italy, where she spent fifteen happy years. At once, love seemed to infuse new life into the delicate body and renew the saddened heart. She was thirty-seven. She had wisely waited till she found a person of congenial tastes and kindred pursuits. Had she married earlier, it is possible that the cares of life might have deprived the world of some of her noblest works.

The marriage was an ideal one. Both had a grand purpose in life. Neither individual was merged in the other. George S. Hillard, in his *Six Months in Italy*, when he visited the Brownings the year after their marriage, says, "A happier home and a more perfect union than theirs it is not easy to imagine; and this completeness arises not only from the rare qualities which each possesses, but from their perfect adaptation to each other. . . . Nor is she more remarkable for genius and learning, than for sweetness of temper and purity of spirit. It is a privilege to know such beings singly and separately, but to see their powers quickened, and their happiness rounded, by the sacred tie of marriage, is a cause for peculiar and lasting gratitude. A union so complete as theirs—in which the mind has nothing to crave nor the heart to sigh for—is cordial to behold and soothing to remember."

"Mr. Browning," says one who knew him well, "did not fear to speak of his wife's genius, which he did almost with awe, losing himself so entirely in her glory that one could see that he did not feel worthy to unloose her shoe-latchet, much less to call her his own."

When mothers teach their daughters to cultivate their

minds as did Mrs. Browning, as well as to emulate her sweetness of temper, then will men venerate women for both mental and moral power. A love that has reverence for its foundation knows no change.

"Mrs. Browning's conversation was most interesting. She never made an insignificant remark. All that she said was *always* worth hearing; a greater compliment could not be paid her. She was a most conscientious listener, giving you her mind and heart, as well as her magnetic eyes. *Persons* were never her theme, unless public characters were under discussion, or friends were to be praised. One never dreamed of frivolities in Mrs. Browning's presence, and gossip felt itself out of place. Yourself, not herself, was always a pleasant subject to her, calling out all her best sympathies in joy, and yet more in sorrow. Books and humanity, great deeds, and above all, politics, which include all the grand questions of the day, were foremost in her thoughts, and therefore oftenest on her lips. I speak not of religion, for with her everything was religion.

"Thoughtful in the smallest things for others, she seemed to give little thought to herself. The first to see merit, she was the last to censure faults, and gave the praise that she felt with a generous hand. No one so heartily rejoiced at the success of others, no one was so modest in her own triumphs. She loved all who offered her affection, and would solace and advise with any. Mrs. Browning belonged to no particular country; the world was inscribed upon the banner under which she fought. Wrong was her enemy; against this she wrestled, in whatever part of the globe it was to be found."

Three years after her marriage her only son was born. The Italians ever after called her "the mother of the beautiful child." And now some of her ablest and strongest work was done. Her *Casa Guidi Windows* appeared in 1851. It is the story of the struggle for Italian liberty. In the same volume were published the *Portuguese Sonnets,* really her own love-life. It would be difficult to find anything more beautiful than these.

"First time he kissed me he but only kissed
The fingers of this hand wherewith I write,
And ever since, it grew more clean and white,
Slow to world-greetings, quick with its 'Oh, list,'
When the angels speak. A ring of amethyst
I could not wear here, plainer to my sight,
Than that first kiss. The second passed in height
The first, and sought the forehead, and half-missed,
Half falling on the hair. O beyond meed!
That was the chrism of love, which love's own crown
With sanctifying sweetness, did precede.
The third upon my lips was folded down
In perfect, purple state; since when, indeed,
I have been proud and said, 'My love, my own!'
.   .   .   .

How do I love thee? Let me count the ways,
I love thee to the depth and breadth and height
My soul can reach, when feeling out of sight
For the ends of being and ideal Grace.
I love thee to the level of every day's
Most quiet need, by sun and candle light.
I love thee freely, as men strive for Right,
I love thee purely, as they turn from Praise.
I love thee with the passion put to use
In my old griefs, and with my childhood's faith.
I love thee with a love I seemed to lose
With my lost saints—I love thee with the breath,
Smiles, tears of all my life!—and, if God choose,
I shall but love thee better after death."

Mrs. Browning's next great poem, in 1856, was *Aurora Leigh,* a novel in blank verse, "the most mature," she says in the preface, "of my works, and the one into which my highest convictions upon Life and Art have entered." Walter Savage Landor said of it : "In many pages there is the wild imagination of Shakespeare. I had no idea that any one in this age was capable of such poetry."

For fifteen years this happy wedded life, with its work of brain and hand, had been lived, and now the bond was to be severed. In June, 1861, Mrs. Browning took a severe cold, and was ill for nearly a week. No one thought of danger, though Mr. Browning would not leave her bedside. On the night of June 29, toward morning, she seemed to be in a sort of ecstasy. She told her husband of her love for him, gave him her blessing, and raised herself to die in his arms. "It is beautiful," were her last words as she caught a glimpse of some heavenly vision.

The Italians, who loved her, placed on the doorway of Casa Guidi a white marble tablet, with the words :—

"Here wrote and died E. B. Browning, who, in the heart of a woman, united the science of a sage and the spirit of a poet, and made with her verse a golden ring binding Italy and England.

"Grateful Florence placed this memorial, 1861."

GEORGE ELIOT

Going to the Exposition at New Orleans, I took for reading on the journey, the life of George Eliot, by her husband, John Walter Cross, written with great delicacy and beauty. An accident delayed us, so that for three days I enjoyed this insight into a wonderful life. I copied the amazing list of books she had read, and transferred to my note-book many of her beautiful thoughts. To-day I have been reading the book again; a clear, vivid picture of a very great woman, whose works, says the *Spectator*, "are the best specimens of powerful, simple English, since Shakespeare."

What made her a superior woman? Not wealthy parentage; not congenial surroundings. She had a generous, sympathetic heart for a foundation, and on this she built a scholarship that even few men can equal. She loved science, and philosophy, and language, and mathematics, and grew broad enough to discuss great questions and think great thoughts. And yet she was affectionate, tender, and gentle.

Mary Ann Evans was born November 22, 1819, at Arbury Farm, a mile from Griff, in Warwickshire, England. When four months old the family moved to Griff, where the girl lived till she was twenty-one, in a two-story, old-fashioned, red brick house, the walls covered with ivy. Two Norway firs and an old yew-tree shaded the lawn. The father, Robert Evans, a man of intelligence and good sense, was bred a builder and carpenter, afterward becoming a land-agent for one of the large estates. The mother was a woman of sterling character, practical and capable.

13

For the three children, Christiana, Isaac, and Mary Ann, there was little variety in the commonplace life at Griff. Twice a day the coach from Birmingham to Stamford passed by the house, and the coachman and guard in scarlet were a great diversion. She thus describes the locality in *Felix Holt:* "Here were powerful men walking queerly, with knees bent outward from squatting in the mine, going home to throw themselves down in the blackened flannel, and sleep through the daylight, then rise and spend much of their high wages at the alehouse with their fellows of the Benefit Club; here the pale, eager faces of handloom weavers, men and women, haggard from sitting up late at night to finish the week's work, hardly begun till the Wednesday. Everywhere the cottages and the small children were dirty, for the languid mothers gave their strength to the loom."

Mary Ann was an affectionate, sensitive child, fond of out-door sports, imitating everything she saw her brother do, and early in life feeling in her heart that she was to be "somebody." When but four years old, she would seat herself at the piano and play, though she did not know one note from another, that the servant might see that she was a distinguished person! Her life was a happy one, as is shown in her *Brother and Sister Sonnet:*—

"But were another childhood's world my share,
I would be born a little sister there."

At five, the mother being in poor health, the child was sent to a boarding-school with her sister, Chrissy, where she remained three or four years. The older scholars petted her, calling her "little mamma." At eight she went to a larger school, at Nuneaton, where one of the teachers, Miss Lewis, became her life-long friend. The child had the greatest fondness for reading, her first book, a *Linnet's Life,* being tenderly cared for all her days. Æsop's *Fables* were read and re-read. At this time a neighbor had loaned one of the Waverley novels to the older sister, who returned it before Mary Ann had finished it. Distressed at this break in the story, she began to write out as nearly as she could remember, the whole volume for herself. Her amazed family re-borrowed the book, and the child was happy. The mother sometimes protested against the use of so many candles for night reading, and rightly feared that her eyes would be spoiled.

At the next school, at Coventry, Mary Ann so surpassed her comrades that they stood in awe of her, but managed to overcome this when a basket of dainties came in from the country home. In 1836 the excellent mother died. Mary Ann wrote to a friend in after life, "I began at sixteen to be acquainted with the unspeakable grief of a last parting, in the death of my mother." In the following spring Chrissy was married, and after a good cry with her brother over this breaking up of the home circle, Mary Ann took upon herself the household duties, and became the care-taker instead of the school-girl. Although so young she took a leading part in the benevolent work of the neighborhood.

Her love for books increased. She engaged a well-known teacher to come from Coventry and give her lessons in French, German, and Italian, while another helped her in music, of which she was passionately fond. Later, she studied Greek, Latin, Spanish, and Hebrew. Shut up in the farm-house, hungering for knowledge, she applied herself with a persistency and earnestness that by-and-by were to bear their legitimate fruit. That she felt the privation of a collegiate course is undoubted. She says in *Daniel Deronda:* "You may try, but you can never imagine what it is to have a man's force of genius in you, and yet to suffer the slavery of being a girl."

She did not neglect her household duties. One of her hands, which were noticeable for their beauty of shape, was broader than the other, which, she used to say with some pride, was owing to the butter and cheese she had made. At twenty she was reading the *Life of Wilberforce,* Josephus' *History of the Jews,* Spenser's *Faërie Queen, Don Quixote,* Milton, Bacon, Mrs. Somerville's *Connection of the Physical Sciences,* and Wordsworth. The latter was always an especial favorite, and his life, by Frederick Myers in the *Men of Letters* series, was one of the last books she ever read.

Already she was learning the illimitableness of knowledge. "For my part," she says, "I am ready to sit down and weep at the impossibility of my understanding or barely knowing a fraction of the sum of objects that present themselves for our contemplation in books and in life."

About this time Mr. Evans left the farm, and moved to Foleshill, near Coventry. The poor people at Griff were very sorry, and said, "We shall never have another Mary Ann Evans." Marian, as she was now called, found at Foleshill a few intellectual and companionable friends, Mr. and Mrs. Bray, both authors, and Miss Hennell, their sister.

Through the influence of these friends she gave up some of her evangelical views, but she never ceased to be a devoted student and lover of the Bible. She was happy in her communing with nature. "Delicious autumn," she said. "My very soul is wedded to it, and if I were a bird, I would fly about the earth, seeking the successive autumns. . . . I have been revelling in Nichol's *Architecture of the Heavens and Phenomena of the Solar System,* and have been in imagination winging my flight from system to system, from universe to universe."

In 1844, when Miss Evans was twenty-five years old, she began the translation of Strauss' *Life of Jesus.* The lady who was to marry Miss Hennell's brother had partially done the work, and asked Miss Evans to finish it. For nearly three years she gave it all the time at her command, receiving only one hundred dollars for the labor.

It was a difficult and weary work. "When I can work fast," she said, "I am never weary, nor do I regret either that the work has been begun or that I have undertaken it. I am only inclined to vow that I will never translate again, if I live to correct the sheets for Strauss." When the book was finished, it was declared to be "A faithful, elegant, and scholar-like translation . . . word for word, thought for thought, and sentence for sentence." Strauss himself was delighted with it.

The days passed as usual in the quiet home. Now she and her father, the latter in failing health, visited the Isle of Wight, and saw beautiful Alum Bay, with its "high precipice, the strata upheaved perpendicularly in rainbow,—like streaks of the brightest maize, violet, pink, blue, red, brown, and brilliant white,—worn by the weather into fantastic fretwork, the deep blue sky above, and the glorious sea below." Who of us has not felt this same delight in looking upon this picture, painted by nature?

Now Ralph Waldo Emerson, as well as other famous people, visited the Bray family. Miss Evans writes: "I have seen Emerson,—the first *man* I have ever seen." High praise indeed from our "great, calm soul," as he called Miss Evans. "I am grateful for the Carlyle eulogium (on Emerson). I have shed some quite delicious tears over it. This is a world worth abiding in while one man can thus venerate and love another."

Each evening she played on the piano to her admiring

father, and finally, through months of illness, carried him down tenderly to the grave. He died May 31, 1849.

Worn with care, Miss Evans went upon the Continent with the Brays, visiting Paris, Milan, the Italian lakes, and finally resting for some months at Geneva. As her means were limited, she tried to sell some of her books at half-price, so that she could have money for music lessons, and to attend a course of lectures on experimental physics, by the renowned Professor de la Rive. She was also carefully reading socialistic themes, Proudhon, Rousseau, and others. She wrote to friends: "The days are really only two hours long, and I have so many things to do that I go to bed every night miserable because I have left out something I meant to do. . . . I take a dose of mathematics every day to prevent my brain from becoming quite soft."

On her return to England, she visited the Brays, and met Mr. Chapman, the editor of the *Westminster Review,* and Mr. Mackay, upon whose *Progress of the Intellect* she had just written a review. Mr. Chapman must have been deeply impressed with the learning and ability of Miss Evans, for he offered her the position of assistant editor of the magazine,—a most unusual position for a woman, since its contributors were Froude, Carlyle, John Stuart Mill, and other able men.

Miss Evans accepted, and went to board with Mr. Chapman's family in London. How different this from the quiet life at Foleshill! The best society, that is, the greatest in mind, opened wide its doors to her. Herbert Spencer, who had just published *Social Statics,* became one of her best friends. Harriet Martineau came often to see her. Grote was very friendly.

The woman-editor was now thirty-two; her massive head covered with brown curls, blue-gray eyes, mobile, sympathetic mouth, strong chin, pale face, and soft, low voice, like Dorothea's in *Middlemarch*,—"the voice of a soul that has once lived in an Æolian harp." Mr. Bray thought that Miss Evans' head, after that of Napoleon, showed the largest development from the brow to ear of any person's recorded.

She had extraordinary power of expression, and extraordinary psychological powers, but her chief attraction was her universal sympathy. "She essentially resembled Socrates," says Mathilde Blind, "in her manner of eliciting whatsoever capacity for thought might be latent in the people she came in contact with; were it only a shoemaker or day laborer, she would never rest till she had found out in what points that particular man differed from other men of his class. She always rather educed what was in others than impressed herself on them; showing much kindliness of heart in drawing out people who were shy. Sympathy was the keynote of her nature, the source of her iridescent humor, of her subtle knowledge of character, of her dramatic genius." No person attains to permanent fame without sympathy.

Miss Evans now found her heart and hands full of work. Her first article was a review of Carlyle's *Life of John Sterling*. She was fond of biography. She said: "We have often wished that genius would incline itself more frequently to the task of the biographer, that when some great or good person dies, instead of the dreary three-or-five volume compilation of letter and diary and detail, little to the purpose, which two-thirds of the public have not the chance, nor the other third the inclination, to read, we could have a real 'life,' setting forth briefly and vividly the man's inward and outward struggles, aims, and achievements, so as to make clear the meaning which his experience has for his fellows.

"A few such lives (chiefly autobiographies) the world possesses, and they have, perhaps, been more influential on the formation of character than any other kind of reading. . . . It is a help to read such a life as Margaret Fuller's. How inexpressibly touching that passage from her journal, 'I shall always reign through the intellect, but the life! the life! O my God! shall that never be sweet?' I am thankful, as if for myself, that it was sweet at last."

The great minds which Miss Evans met made life a constant joy, though she was frail in health. Now Herbert Spencer took her to hear *William Tell* or the *Creation*. She wrote of him: "We have agreed that we are not in love with each other, and that there is no reason why we should not have as much of each other's society as we like. He is a good, delightful creature, and I always feel better for being with him. . . . My brightest spot, next to my love of *old* friends, is the deliciously calm, *new* friendship that Herbert Spencer gives me. We see each other every day, and have a delightful *camaraderie* in everything. But for him my life would be desolate enough."

There is no telling what this happy friendship might have resulted in, if Mr. Spencer had not introduced to Miss Evans, George Henry Lewes, a man of brilliant conversational powers, who had written a *History of Philosophy,* two novels, *Ranthorpe,* and *Rose, Blanche, and Violet,* and was a contributor to several reviews. Mr. Lewes was a witty and versatile man, a dramatic critic, an actor for a short time, unsuccessful as an editor of a newspaper, and unsuccessful in his domestic relations.

That he loved Miss Evans is not strange; that she admired him, while she pitied him and his three sons in their broken home-life, is perhaps not strange. At first she did not like him, nor did Margaret Fuller, but Miss Evans says: "Mr. Lewes is kind and attentive, and has quite won my regard, after having had a good deal of my vituperation. Like a few other people in the world, he is much better than he seems. A man of heart and conscience wearing a mask of flippancy."

Miss Evans tired of her hard work, as who does not in this working world? "I am bothered to death," she writes, "with article-reading and scrap-work of all sorts; it is clear my poor head will never produce anything under these circumstances; *but I am patient. . . .* I had a long call from George Combe yesterday. He says he thinks the *Westminster* under *my* management the most important means of enlightenment of a literary nature in existence; the *Edinburgh,* under Jeffrey, nothing to it, etc. I wish *I* thought so too."

Sick with continued headaches, she went up to the English lakes to visit Miss Martineau. The coach, at half-past six in the evening, stopped at "The Knoll," and a beaming face came to welcome her. During the evening, she says, "Miss Martineau came behind me, put her hands round me, and kissed me in the prettiest way, telling me she was so glad she had got me here."

Meantime Miss Evans was writing learned and valuable articles on *Taxation, Woman in France, Evangelical Teaching,* etc. She received five hundred dollars yearly from her father's estate, but she lived simply, that she might spend much of this for poor relations.

In 1854 she resigned her position on the *Westminster,* and went with Mr. Lewes to Germany, forming a union which thousands who love her must regard as the great mistake of a very great life.

Mr. Lewes was collecting materials for his *Life of Goethe.* This took them to Goethe's house at Weimar. "By the side of the bed," she says, "stands a stuffed chair where he used to sit and read while he drank his coffee in the morning. It was not until very late in his life that he adopted the luxury of an armchair. From the other side of the study one enters the library, which is fitted up in a very make-shift fashion, with rough deal shelves, and bits of paper, with Philosophy, History, etc., written on them, to mark the classification of the books. Among such memorials one breathes deeply, and the tears rush to one's eyes."

George Eliot met Liszt, and "for the first time in her life beheld real inspiration,—for the first time heard the true tones of the piano." Rauch, the great sculptor, called upon them, and "won our hearts by his beautiful person and the benignant and intelligent charm of his conversation."

Both writers were hard at work. George Eliot was writing an article on *Weimar* for *Fraser,* on *Cumming* for *Westminster,* and translating Spinoza's *Ethics.* No name was signed to these productions, as it would not do to have it known that a woman wrote them. The education of most women was so meagre that the articles would have been considered of little value. Happily our present-day colleges are changing this estimate of the sex. Women do not like to be regarded as inferior; then they must educate themselves as thoroughly as the best men are educated.

Mr. Lewes was not well. "This is a terrible trial to us poor scribblers," she writes, "to whom health is money, as well as all other things worth having." They had but one sitting-room between them, and the scratching of another pen so affected her nerves, as to drive her nearly wild. Pecuniarily, life was a harder struggle than ever, for there were four more mouths to be fed,—Mr. Lewes' three sons and their mother.

"Our life is intensely occupied, and the days are far too short," she writes. They were reading in every spare moment, twelve plays of Shakespeare, Goethe's works.

Wilhelm Meister, Götz von Berlichingen, Hermann and Dorothea, Iphigenia, Wanderjahre, Italianische Reise, and others; Heine's poems; Lessing's *Loacoön and Nathan the Wise;* Macaulay's *History of England;* Moore's *Life of Sheridan;* Brougham's *Lives of Men of Letters;* White's *History of Selborne;* Whewell's *History of Inductive Sciences;* Boswell; Carpenter's *Comparative Physiology;* Jones' *Animal Kingdom;* Alison's *History of Europe;* Kahnis' *History of German Protestantism,* Schrader's *German Mythology;* Kingsley's *Greek Heroes;* and the *Iliad* and *Odyssey* in the original. She says, "If you want delightful reading, get Lowell's *My Study Windows,* and read the essays called *My Garden Acquaintances* and *Winter."* No wonder they were busy.

On their return from Germany they went to the seashore, that Mr. Lewes might perfect his *Sea-side Studies.* George Eliot entered heartily into the work. "We are immensely excited," she says, "by the discovery of this little red mesembryanthemum. It was a *crescendo* of delight when he found a 'strawberry,' and a *fortissimo* when I, for the first time, saw the pale, fawn-colored tentacles of an *Anthea cereus* viciously waving like little serpents in a low-tide pool." They read here Gosse's *Rambles on the Devonshire Coast,* Edward's *Zoölogy,* Harvey's sea-side book, and other scientific works.

And now at thirty-seven George Eliot was to begin her creative work. Mr. Lewes had often said to her, "You have wit, description, and philosophy—those go a good way towards the production of a novel." "It had always been a vague dream of mine," she says, "that sometime or other I might write a novel . . . but I never went further toward the actual writing than an introductory chapter, describing a Staffordshire village, and the life of the neighboring farm-houses; and as the years passed on I lost any hope that I should ever be able to write a novel, just as I desponded about everything else in my future life. I always thought I was deficient in dramatic power, both of construction and dialogue, but I felt I should be at my ease in the descriptive parts."

After she had written a portion of *Amos Barton* in her *Scenes of Clerical Life,* she read it to Mr. Lewes, who told her that now he was sure she could write good dialogue, but not as yet sure about her pathos. One evening, in his absence, she wrote the scene describing Milly's death, and read it to Mr. Lewes, on his return. "We both cried over it," she says, "and then he came up to me and kissed me, saying, 'I think your pathos is better than your fun!'"

Mr. Lewes sent the story to Blackwood, with the signature of "George Eliot,"—the first name chosen because it was his own name, and the last because it pleased her fancy. Mr. Lewes wrote that this story by a friend of his, showed, according to his judgment, "such humor, pathos, vivid presentation, and nice observation as have not been exhibited, in this style, since the *Vicar of Wakefield.*"

Mr. John Blackwood accepted the story, but made some comments which discouraged the author from trying another. Mr. Lewes wrote him the effects of his words, which he hastened to withdraw, as there was so much to be said in praise, that he really desired more stories from the same pen, and sent her a check for two hundred and fifty dollars.

This was evidently soothing, as *Mr. Gilfil's Love Story* and *Janet's Repentance* were at once written. Much interest began to be expressed about the author. Some said Bulwer wrote the sketches. Thackeray praised them, and Arthur Helps said, "He is a great writer." Copies of the stories bound together, with the title *Scenes of Clerical Life,* were sent to Froude, Dickens, Thackeray, Tennyson, Ruskin, and Faraday. Dickens praised the humor and the pathos, and thought the author was a woman.

Jane Welch Carlyle thought it "a *human* book, written out of the heart of a live man, not merely out of the brain of an author, full of tenderness and pathos, without a scrap of sentimentality, of sense without dogmatism, of earnestness without twaddle—a book that makes one feel friends at once and for always with the man or woman who wrote it." She guessed the author was "a man of middle age, with a wife, from whom he has got those beautiful *feminine* touches in his book, a good many children, and a dog that he has as much fondness for as I have for my little Nero."

Mr. Lewes was delighted, and said, "Her fame is beginning." George Eliot was growing happier, for her nature had been somewhat despondent. She used to say, "Expecting disappointments is the only form of hope with which I am familiar." She said, "I feel a deep satisfaction in having done a bit of faithful work that will perhaps remain, like a primrose-root in the hedgerow, and gladden and chasten human hearts in years to come." " 'Conscience goes to the hammering in of nails' is my gospel," she would say. "Writing is part of my religion, and I can write no word that is not prompted from within. At the same time I believe that almost all the best books in the world have been written with the hope of getting money for them."

"My life has deepened unspeakably during the last year: I feel a greater capacity for moral and intellectual enjoyment, a more acute sense of my deficiencies in the past, a more solemn desire to be faithful to coming duties."

For *Scenes of Clerical Life* she received six hundred dollars for the first edition, and much more after her other books appeared.

And now another work, a longer one, was growing in her mind, *Adam Bede,* the germ of which, she says, was an anecdote told her by her aunt, Elizabeth Evans, the Dinah Morris of the book. A very ignorant girl had murdered her child, and refused to confess it. Mrs. Evans, who was a Methodist preacher, stayed with her all night, praying with her, and at last she burst into tears and confessed her crime. Mrs. Evans went with her in the cart to the place of execution, and ministered to the unhappy girl till death came.

When the first pages of *Adam Bede* were shown to Mr. Blackwood, he said, "That will do." George Eliot and Mr. Lewes went to Munich, Dresden, and Vienna for rest and change, and she prepared much of the book in this time. When it was finished, she wrote on the manuscript, *Jubilate.* "To my dear husband, George Henry Lewes, I give the MS. of a work which would never have been written but for the happiness which his love has conferred on my life."

For this novel she received four thousand dollars for the copyright for four years. Fame had actually come. All the literary world were talking about it. John Murray said there had never been such a book. Charles Reade said, putting his finger on Lisbeth's account of her coming home with her husband from their marriage, "the finest thing since Shakespeare." A workingman wrote: "Forgive me, dear sir, my boldness in asking you to give us a cheap edition. You would confer on us a great boon. I can get plenty of trash for a few pence, but I am sick of it." Mr. Charles Buxton said, in the House of Commons: "As the farmer's wife says in *Adam Bede,* 'It wants to be hatched over again and hatched dif-

ferent.' " This of course greatly helped to popularize the
book.

To George Eliot all this was cause for the deepest gratitude. They were able now to rent a home at Wandworth,
and move to it at once. The poverty and the drudgery
of life seemed over. She said: "I sing my magnificat in
a quiet way, and have a great deal of deep, silent joy;
but few authors, I suppose, who have had a real success,
have known less of the flush and the sensations of triumph
that are talked of as the accompaniments of success. I
often think of my dreams when I was four or five and
twenty. I thought then how happy fame would make
me. . . . I am assured now that *Adam Bede* was worth
writing,—worth living through those long years to write.
But now it seems impossible that I shall ever write anything so good and true again." Up to this time the
world did not know who George Eliot was; but as a
man by the name of Liggins laid claim to the authorship,
and tried to borrow money for his needs because Blackwood would not pay him, the real name of the author had
to be divulged.

Five thousand copies of *Adam Bede* were sold the first
two weeks, and sixteen thousand the first year. So excellent was the sale that Mr. Blackwood sent her four
thousand dollars in addition to the first four. The work
was soon translated into French, German, and Hungarian.
Mr. Lewes' *Physiology of Common Life* was now published, but it brought little pecuniary return.

The reading was carried on as usual by the two students. The *Life of George Stephenson;* the *Electra* of
Sophocles; the *Agamemnon* of Æschylus, Harriet Martineau's *British Empire in India;* and *History of the Thirty
Years' Peace;* Béranger's *Modern Painters,* containing
some of the finest writing of the age; Overbech on Greek
art; Anna Mary Howitt's book on Munich; Carlyle's *Life*

of Frederick the Great; Darwin's *Origin of Species;* Emerson's *Man the Reformer,* "which comes to me with fresh beauty and meaning"; Buckle's *History of Civilization;* Plato and Aristotle.

An American publisher now offered her six thousand dollars for a book, but she was obliged to decline, for she was writing the *Mill on the Floss,* in 1860, for which Blackwood gave her ten thousand dollars for the first edition of four thousand copies, and Harper & Brothers fifteen hundred dollars for using it also. Tauchnitz paid her five hundred for the German reprint.

She said: "I am grateful and yet rather sad to have finished; sad that I shall live with my people on the banks of the Floss no longer. But it is time that I should go, and absorb some new life and gather fresh ideas." They went at once to Italy, where they spent several months in Florence, Venice, and Rome.

In the former city she made her studies for her great novel, *Romola.* She read Sismondi's *History of the Italian Republics,* Tenneman's *History of Philosophy,* T. A. Trollope's *Beata,* Hallam on the *Study of Roman Law in the Middle Ages,* Gibbon on the *Revival of Greek Learning,* Burlamachi's *Life of Savonarola;* also Villari's life of the great preacher, Mrs. Jameson's *Sacred and Legendary Art,* Machiavelli's works, Petrarch's Letters, *Casa Guidi Windows,* Buhle's *History of Modern Philosophy,* Story's *Roba di Roma,* Liddell's *Rome,* Gibbon, Mosheim, and one might almost say the whole range of Italian literature in the original. Of Mommsen's *History of Rome* she said, "It is so fine that I count all minds graceless who read it without the deepest stirrings."

The study necessary to make one familiar with fifteenth century times was almost limitless. No wonder she told Mr. Cross, years afterward, "I began *Romola* a young woman, I finished it an old woman"; but that, with *Adam Bede* and *Middlemarch,* will be her monument. "What courage and patience," she says, "are wanted for every life that aims to produce anything!" "In authorship I hold carelessness to be a mortal sin." "I took unspeakable pains in preparing to write *Romola.*"

For this one book, on which she spent a year and a half, *Cornhill Magazine* paid her the small fortune of thirty-five thousand dollars. She purchased a pleasant home, "The Priory," Regent's Park, where she made her friends welcome, though she never made calls upon any, for lack of time. She had found, like Victor Hugo, that time is a very precious thing for those who wish to succeed in life. Browning, Huxley, and Herbert Spencer often came to dine.

Says Mr. Cross, in his admirable life: "The entertainment was frequently varied by music when any good performer happened to be present. I think, however, that the majority of visitors delighted chiefly to come for the chance of a few words with George Eliot alone. When the drawing-room door of the Priory opened, a first glance revealed her always in the same low arm-chair on the left-hand side of the fire. On entering, a visitor's eye was at once arrested by the massive head. The abundant hair, streaked with gray now, was draped with lace, arranged mantilla fashion, coming to a point at the top of the forehead. If she were engaged in conversation, her body was usually bent forward with eager, anxious desire to get as close as possible to the person with whom she talked. She had a great dislike to raising her voice, and often became so wholly absorbed in conversation that the announcement of an in-coming visitor failed to attract her attention; but the moment the eyes were lifted up, and recognized a friend, they smiled a rare welcome,—sincere, cordial, grave,—a welcome that was felt to come straight from the heart, not graduated according to any social distinction."

After much reading of Fawcett, Mill, and other writers on political economy, *Felix Holt* was written, in 1866, and for this she received from Blackwood twenty-five thousand dollars.

Very much worn with her work, though Mr. Lewes relieved her in every way possible, by writing letters and looking over all criticisms of her books, which she never read, she was obliged to go to Germany for rest.

In 1868 she published her long poem, *The Spanish Gypsy,* reading Spanish literature carefully, and finally passing some time in Spain, that she might be the better able to make a lasting work. Had she given her life to poetry, doubtless she would have been a great poet.

Silas Marner, written before *Romola,* in 1861, had been well received, and *Middlemarch,* in 1872, made a great sensation. It was translated into several languages. George Bancroft wrote her from Berlin that everybody was reading it. For this she received a much larger sum than the thirty-five thousand which she was paid for *Romola.*

A home was now purchased in Surrey with eight or nine acres of pleasure grounds, for George Eliot had always longed for trees and flowers about her house. "Sunlight and sweet air," she said, "make a new creature of me." *Daniel Deronda* followed in 1876, for which, it is said, she read nearly a thousand volumes. Whether this be true or not, the list of books given in her life, of her reading in these later years, is as astonishing as it is helpful for any who desire real knowledge.

At Witley, in Surrey, they lived a quiet life, seeing only a few friends like the Tennysons, the Du Mauriers, and Sir Henry and Lady Holland. Both were growing older, and Mr. Lewes was in very poor health. Finally, after ten days' illness, he died, November 28, 1878.

To George Eliot this loss was immeasurable. She needed his help and his affection. She said, "I like not only to be loved, but also to be told that I am loved," and he had idolized her. He said: "I owe Spencer a debt of gratitude. It was through him that I learned to know Marian,—to know her was to love her, and since then, my life has been a new birth. To her I owe all my prosperity and all my happiness. God bless her!"

Mr. John Walter Cross, for some time a wealthy banker in New York, had long been a friend of the family, and though many years younger than George Eliot, became her helper in these days of need. A George Henry Lewes studentship, of the value of one thousand dollars yearly, was to be given to Cambridge for some worthy student of either sex, in memory of the man she had loved. "I want to live a little time that I may do certain things for his sake," she said. She grew despondent, and the Cross family used every means to win her away from her sorrow.

Mr. Cross' mother, to whom he was devotedly attached, had also died, and the loneliness of both made their companionship more comforting. They read Dante together in the original, and gradually the younger man found that his heart was deeply interested. It was the higher kind of love, the honor of mind for mind and soul for soul.

"I shall be," she said, "a better, more loving creature than I could have been in solitude. To be constantly, lovingly grateful for this gift of a perfect love is the best illumination of one's mind to all the possible good there may be in store for man on this troublous little planet."

Mr. Cross and George Eliot were married, May 6, 1880, a year and a half after Mr. Lewes' death, his son

Charles giving her away, and went at once to Italy. She
wrote: "Marriage has seemed to restore me to my old
self. . . . . To feel daily the loveliness of a nature close
to me, and to feel grateful for it, is the fountain of tenderness and strength to endure." Having passed through
a severe illness, she wrote to a friend: "I have been cared
for by something much better than angelic tenderness. . . . If it is any good for me that my life has
been prolonged till now, I believe it is owing to this mi-
raculous affection that has chosen to watch over me."

She did not forget Mr. Lewes. In looking upon the
Grande Chartreuse, she said, "I would still give up my
own life willingly, if he could have the happiness instead
of me."

On their return to London, they made their winter
home at 4 Cheyne Walk, Chelsea, a plain brick house.
The days were gliding by happily. George Eliot was interested as ever in all great subjects, giving five hundred
dollars for woman's higher education at Girton College,
and helping many a struggling author, or providing for
some poor friend of early times who was proud to be remembered.

She and Mr. Cross began their reading for the day with
the Bible, she especially enjoying Isaiah, Jeremiah, and
St. Paul's Epistles. Then they read Max Muller's works,
Shakespeare, Milton, Scott, and whatever was best in
English, French, and German literature. Milton she
called her demigod. Her husband says she had "a limitless persistency in application." Her health was better,
and she gave promise of doing more great work. When
urged to write her autobiography, she said, half sighing
and half smiling: "The only thing I should care much to
dwell on would be the absolute despair I suffered from,
of ever being able to achieve anything. No one could

ever have felt greater despair, and a knowledge of this might be a help to some other struggler."

Friday afternoon, December 17, she went to see *Agamemnon* performed in Greek by Oxford students, and the next afternoon to a concert at St. James Hall. She took cold, and on Monday was treated for sore throat. On Wednesday evening the doctors came, and she whispered to her husband, "Tell them I have great pain in the left side." This was the last word. She died with every faculty bright, and her heart responsive to all noble things.

She loved knowledge to the end. She said, "My constant groan is that I must leave so much of the greatest writing which the centuries have sifted for me, unread for want of time."

She had the broadest charity for those whose views differed from hers. She said, "The best lesson of tolerance we have to learn, is to tolerate intolerance." She hoped for and "looked forward to the time when the impulse to help our fellows shall be as immediate and irresistible as that which I feel to grasp something firm if I am falling."

Her grave in Highgate Cemetery, London is marked by a gray granite shaft, about twenty-five feet high, with these beautiful words from her great poem :—

"O may I join the choir invisible,
Of these immortal dead who live again
In minds made better by their presence."

FLORENCE NIGHTINGALE

ONE of the most interesting places in the whole of London is St. Thomas' Hospital an immense four-story structure of brick with stone trimmings. Here is the Nightingale Training School for nurses, established through the gift to Miss Nightingale of $250,000 by the government for her wonderful work in the Crimean War. She would not take a cent for herself, but was glad to have this institution opened, that girls through such training might become valuable to the world as nurses, as she had been.

Here is the "Nightingale Home." The dining-room, with its three long tables, is an inviting apartment. The colors of wall and ceiling are in red and light shades. Here is a Swiss clock presented by the Grand Duchess of Baden; here a harpsichord, also a gift. Here is the marble face and figure I had come especially to see, that of lovely Florence Nightingale. It is a face full of sweetness and refinement, having withal an earnest look, as though life were well worth living.

What better work than to direct these girls how to be useful? Some are here from the highest social circles. The "probationers," or nurse pupils, must remain three years before they can become Protestant "sisters." Each ward is in charge of a sister; now it is Leopold, because the ward bears that name; and now Victoria in respect to the Queen, who opened the institution.

The sisters look sunny and healthy, though they work hard. They have regular hours for being off duty, and exercise in the open air. The patients tell me how "home-like it seems to have women in the wards, and what a comfort it is in their agony, to be handled by their careful hands." Here are four hundred persons in all phases of suffering, in neat, cheerful wards, brightened by pots of flowers, and the faces of kind, devoted women.

And who was this woman to whom the government of Great Britain felt that it owed so much, and whom the whole world delighted to honor?

Florence Nightingale, born in 1820, in the beautiful Italian city of that name, was the younger of two daughters of William Shore Nightingale, a wealthy land-owner, who inherited both the name and fortune of his grand-uncle, Peter Nightingale. The mother was the daughter of the eminent philanthropist and member of Parliament, William Smith.

Most of Miss Nightingale's life was spent on their beautiful estate, Lea Hurst, in Derbyshire, a happy home in the midst of picturesque scenery. In her youth her father instructed her carefully in the classics and higher mathematics; a few years later, partly through extensive travel, she became proficient in French, German, and Italian.

Rich, pretty, and well-educated, what was there more that she could wish for? Her heart, however, did not turn toward a fashionable life. Very early she began to visit the poor and the sick near Lea Hurst and her father's other estate at Embly Park, Hampshire. Perhaps the mantle of the mother's father had fallen upon the young girl.

She had also the greatest tenderness toward dumb animals, and never could bear to see them injured. Miss Alldridge, in an interesting sketch of Miss Nightingale, quotes the following story from *Little Folks*:—

"Some years ago, when the celebrated Florence Nightingale was a little girl, living at her father's home, a large old Elizabethan house, with great woods about it, in

Hampshire, there was one thing that struck everybody who knew her. It was that she seemed to be always thinking what she could do to please or help any one who needed either help or comfort. She was very fond, too, of animals, and she was so gentle in her way, that even the shyest of them would come quite close to her, and pick up whatever she flung down for them to eat.

"There was, in the garden behind the house, a long walk with trees on each side, the abode of many squirrels; and when Florence came down the walk, dropping nuts as she went along, the squirrels would run down the trunks of their trees, and, hardly waiting until she passed by, would pick up the prize and dart away, with their little bushy tails curled over their backs, and their black eyes looking about as if terrified at the least noise, though they did not seem to be afraid of Florence.

"Then there was an old gray pony named Peggy, past work, living in a paddock, with nothing to do all day long but to amuse herself. Whenever Florence appeared at the gate, Peggy would come trotting up and put her nose into the dress pocket of her little mistress, and pick it of the apple or the roll of bread that she knew she would always find there, for this was a trick Florence had taught the pony. Florence was fond of riding, and her father's old friend, the clergyman of the parish, used often to come and take her for a ride with him when he went to the farm cottages at a distance. He was a good man and very kind to the poor.

"As he had studied medicine when a young man, he was able to tell the people what would do them good when they were ill, or had met with an accident. Little Florence took great delight in helping to nurse those who were ill; and whenever she went on these long rides, she had a small basket fastened to her saddle, filled with something nice which she saved from her breakfast or dinner, or carried for her mother, who was very good to the poor.

"There lived in one of two or three solitary cottages in the wood an old shepherd of her father's named Roger, who had a favorite sheep-dog called Cap. Roger had neither wife nor child, and Cap lived with him and kept him company at night after he had penned his flock. Cap was a very sensible dog; indeed, people used to say he could do everything but speak. He kept the sheep in wonderfully good order, and thus saved his master a great deal of trouble. One day, as Florence and her old friend were out for a ride, they came to a field where they found the shepherd giving his sheep their night feed; but he was without the dog, and the sheep knew it, for they were scampering in every direction. Florence and her friend noticed that the old shepherd looked very sad, and they stopped to ask what was the matter, and what had become of his dog.

" 'Oh,' said Roger, 'Cap will never be of any more use to me; I'll have to hang him, poor fellow, as soon as I go home to-night.'

" 'Hang him!' said Florence. 'Oh, Roger, how wicked of you! What has dear old Cap done?'

" 'He has done nothing,' replied Roger; 'but he will never be of any more use to me, and I cannot afford to keep him for nothing; one of the mischievous school-boys throwed a stone at him yesterday, and broke one of his legs.' And the old shepherd's eyes filled with tears, which he wiped away with his shirt-sleeve; then he drove his spade deep in the ground to hide what he felt, for he did not like to be seen crying.

" 'Poor Cap!' he sighed; 'he was as knowing almost as a human being.'

" 'But are you sure his leg is broken?' asked Florence.

" 'Oh, yes, miss, it is broken safe enough; he has not put his foot to the ground since.'

"Florence and her friend rode on without saying anything more to Roger.

" 'We will go and see poor Cap,' said the vicar; 'I don't believe the leg is really broken. It would take a big stone and a hard blow to break the leg of a big dog like Cap.'

" 'Oh, if you could but cure him, how glad Roger would be!' replied Florence.

"They soon reached the shepherd's cottage, but the door was fastened; and when they moved the latch, such a furious barking was heard that they drew back, startled. However, a little boy came out of the next cottage, and asked if they wanted to go in, as Roger had left the key with his mother. So the key was got, and the door opened; and there on the bare brick floor lay the dog, his hair dishevelled, and his eyes sparkling with anger at the intruders. But when he saw the little boy he grew peaceful, and when he looked at Florence, and heard her call him 'poor Cap,' he began to wag his tail; and then crept from under the table, and lay down at her feet. She took hold of one of his paws, patted his old rough head, and talked to him, whilst her friend examined the injured leg. It was dreadfully swollen, and hurt very much to have it examined; but the dog knew it was meant kindly, and though he moaned and winced with pain, he licked the hands that were hurting him.

" 'It's only a bad bruise; no bones are broken,' said her old friend; 'rest is all Cap needs; he will soon be well again.'

" 'I am so glad,' said Florence; 'but can we do nothing for him? he seems in such pain.'

" 'There is one thing that would ease the pain and heal the leg all the sooner, and that is plenty of hot water to foment the part.'

"Florence struck a light with the tinder-box, and lighted
the fire, which was already laid. She then set off to the
other cottage to get something to bathe the leg with. She
found an old flannel petticoat hanging up to dry, and
this she carried off, and tore up into slips, which she
wrung out in warm water, and laid them tenderly on
Cap's swollen leg. It was not long before the poor dog
felt the benefit of the application, and he looked grateful,
wagging his little stump of a tail in thanks. On their
way home they met the shepherd coming slowly along,
with a piece of rope in his hand.

" 'Oh, Roger,' cried Florence, 'you are not to hang poor
old Cap; his leg is not broken at all.'

" 'No, he will serve you yet,' said the vicar.

" 'Well, I be main glad to hear it,' said the shepherd,
'and many thanks to you for going to see him.'

"On the next morning Florence was up early and the
first thing she did was to take two flannel petticoats to
give to the poor woman whose skirt she had torn up to
bathe Cap. Then she went to the dog, and was delighted
to find the swelling of his leg much less. She bathed
it again, and Cap was as grateful as before.

"Two or three days afterwards Florence and her friend
were riding together, when they came up to Roger and his
sheep. This time Cap was watching the sheep, though he
was lying quite still, and pretending to be asleep. When
he heard the voice of Florence speaking to his master,
who was portioning out the usual food, his tail wagged
and his eyes sparkled, but he did not get up, for he was
on duty. The shepherd stopped his work, and as he
glanced at the dog with a merry laugh, said, 'Do look at
the dog, Miss; he be so pleased to hear your voice.' Cap's
tail went faster and faster. 'I be glad,' continued the old
man, 'I did not hang him. I be greatly obliged to you,
Miss, and the vicar, for what you did. But for you I

would have hanged the best dog I ever had in my life.' "

A girl who was made so happy in saving the life of an animal would naturally be interested to save human beings. Occasionally her family passed a season in London, and here, instead of giving much time to concerts or parties, she would visit hospitals and benevolent institutions. When the family travelled in Egypt, she attended several sick Arabs, who recovered under her hands. They doubtless thought the English girl was a saint sent down from heaven.

The more she felt drawn toward the sick, the more she felt the need of study, and the more she saw the work that refined women could do in the hospitals. The Sisters of Charity were standing by sick-beds; why could there not be Protestant sisters? When they travelled in Germany, France, and Italy, she visited infirmaries, asylums, and hospitals, carefully noting the treatment given in each.

Finally she determined to spend some months at Kaiserwerth, near Dusseldorf, on the Rhine, in Pastor Fliedner's great Lutheran hospital. He had been a poor clergyman, the leader of a scanty flock, whose church was badly in debt. A man of much enterprise and warm heart, he could not see his work fail for lack of means; so he set out among the provinces, to tell the needs of his little parish. He collected funds, learned much about the poverty and ignorance of cities, preached in some of the prisons, because interested in criminals, and went back to his loyal people.

But so poor were they that they could not meet the yearly expenses, so he determined to raise an endowment fund. He visited Holland and Great Britain, and secured the needed money.

In England, in 1832, he became acquainted with Elizabeth Fry. How one good life influences another to the

FLORENCE NIGHTINGALE

end of time! When he went back to Germany his heart
was aglow with a desire to help humanity.

He at once opened an asylum for discharged prison-
women. He saw how almost impossible it was for those
who had been in prison to obtain situations. Then he
opened a school for the children of such as worked in
factories, for he realized how unfit for citizenship are
those who grow up in ignorance. He did not have much
money, but he seemed able to obtain what he really needed.
Then he opened a hospital; a home for insane women; a
home of rest for his nurses, or for those who needed a
place to live after their work was done. Soon the "Dea-
conesses" at Kaiserwerth became known the country over.
Among the wildest Norwegian mountains we met some of
these Kaiserwerth nurses, refined, educated ladies, getting
in summer a new lease of life for their noble labors.

This Protestant sisterhood grew to some seven
hundred sisters, at about two hundred stations, the annual
expense being about $150,000. What a grand work for
one man, with no money, the pastor of a very humble
church!

Into this work of Pastor Fliedner, Florence Nightingale
heartily entered. Was it strange taste for a pretty and
wealthy young woman, whose life had been one of sunshine and happiness? It was a saintlike taste, and the
world is rendered a little like Paradise by the presence of
such women. Back in London the papers were full of
the great exhibition of 1851, but she was more interested
in her Kaiserwerth work than to be at home. When she
had finished her course of instruction, Pastor Fliedner
said, since he had been director of that institution no one
had ever passed so distinguished an examination, or shown
herself so thoroughly mistress of all she had learned.

On her return to Lea Hurst, she could not rest very

long, while there was so much work to be done in the
world.   In London, a hospital for sick governesses was
about to fail, from lack of means and poor management.
Nobody seemed very deeply interested for these overworked teachers.   But Miss Nightingale was interested,
and leaving her lovely home, she came to the dreary house
in Harley Street, where she gave her time and her fortune
for several years.   Her own frail health sank for a time
from the close confinement, but she had seen the institution placed on a sure foundation, and prosperous.

The Crimean War had begun.   England had sent out
ship-loads of men to the Black Sea, to engage in war with
Russia.   Little thought seemed to have been taken, in the
hurry and enthusiasm of war, to provide proper clothing
or food for the men in that changing climate.   In the desolate country there was almost no means of transporta-
tion, and men and animals suffered from hunger.   After
the first winter cholera broke out, in one camp alone
twenty men died in twenty-four hours.

Matters grew from bad to worse.   William Howard
Russell, the *Times* correspondent, wrote home to England:
"It is now pouring rain,—the skies are black as ink,—
the wind is howling over the staggering tents,—the
trenches are turned into dykes,—in the tents the water is
sometimes a foot deep,—our men have not either warm
or waterproof clothing,—they are out for twelve hours
at a time in the trenches,—they are plunged into the inevitable miseries of a winter campaign,—and not a soul
seems to care for their comfort, or even for their lives.
These are hard truths, but the people of England must
hear them.   They must know that the wretched beggar
who wanders about the streets of London in the rain, leads
the life of a prince, compared with the British soldiers who
are fighting out here for their country.

"The commonest accessories of a hospital are wanting;

there is not the least attention paid to decency or cleanliness; the stench is appalling; the fetid air can barely struggle out to taint the atmosphere, save through the chinks in the walls and roofs; and, for all I can observe, these men die without the least effort being made to save them. There they lie, just as they were let gently down on the ground by the poor fellows, their comrades, who brought them on their backs from the camp with the greatest tenderness, but who are not allowed to remain with them. The sick appear to be tended by the sick, and the dying by the dying."

During the rigorous winter of 1854, with snow three feet thick, many were frozen in their tents. Out of nearly forty-five thousand, over eighteen thousand were reported in the hospitals. The English nation became aroused at this state of things, and in less than two weeks seventy-five thousand dollars poured into the *Times* office for the suffering soldiers. A special commissioner, Mr. Macdonald, was sent to the Crimea with shirts, sheets, flannels, and necessary food.

But one of the greatest of all needs was woman's hand and brain, in the dreadful suffering and the confusion. The testimony of the world thus far has been that men everywhere need the help of women, and women everywhere need the help of men. Right Honorable Sydney Herbert, the Secretary of War, knew of but one woman who could bring order and comfort to those far-away hospitals, and that woman was Miss Nightingale. She had made herself ready at Kaiserwerth for a great work, and now a great work was ready for her.

But she was frail in health, and was it probable that a rich and refined lady would go thousands of miles from her kindred, to live in feverish wards where there were only men? A true woman dares do anything that helps the world.

Mr. Herbert wrote her, October 15: "There is, as far as I know, only one person in England, capable of organizing and directing such a plan, and I have been several times on the point of asking you if you would be disposed to make the attempt. That it will be difficult to form a corps of nurses, no one knows better than yourself. . . . I have this simple question to put to you: Could you go out yourself, and take charge of everything? It is, of course, understood that you will have absolute authority over all the nurses, unlimited power to draw on the government for all you judge necessary to the success of your mission; and I think I may assure you of the cooperation of the medical staff. Your personal qualities, your knowledge, and your authority in administrative affairs, all fit you for this position."

It was a strange coincidence that on that same day, October 15, Miss Nightingale, her heart stirred for the suffering soldiers, had written a letter to Mr. Herbert, offering her services to the government. A few days later the world read, with moistened eyes, this letter from the war office: "Miss Nightingale, accompanied by thirty-four nurses, will leave this evening. Miss Nightingale, who has, I believe, greater practical experience of hospital administration and treatment than any other lady in this country, has, with a self-devotion for which I have no words to express my gratitude, undertaken this noble but arduous work."

The heart of the English nation followed the heroic woman. Mrs. Jameson wrote: "It is an undertaking wholly new to our English customs, much at variance with the usual education given to women in this country. If it succeeds, it will be the true, the lasting glory of Florence Nightingale and her band of devoted assistants, that they have broken down a Chinese wall of prejudices,—religious, social, professional,—and have established a prece-

dent which will, indeed, multiply the good to all time."
She did succeed and the results can scarcely be overesti-
mated.

As the band of nurses passed through France, hotel-
keepers would take no pay for their accommodation; poor
fisherwomen at Boulogne struggled for the honor of carrying their baggage to the railway station. They sailed
in the *Vectis* across the Mediterranean, reaching Scutari,
November 5, the day of the battle of Inkerman.

They found in the great Barrack Hospital which had
been lent to the British by the Turkish government, and
in another large hospital near by, about four thousand
men. The corridors were filled with two rows of mattresses, so close that two persons could scarcely walk between them. There was work to be done at once.

One of the nurses wrote home, "The whole of yesterday one could only forget one's own existence, for it was
spent, first in sewing the men's mattresses together, and
then in washing them, and assisting the surgeons, when
we could, in dressing their ghastly wounds after their
five days' confinement on board ship, during which space
their wounds had not been dressed. Hundreds of men
with fever, dysentery, and cholera (the wounded were the
smaller portion) filled the wards in succession from the
overcrowded transports."

Miss Nightingale, calm and unobtrusive, went quietly
among the men, always with a smile of sympathy for the
suffering. The soldiers often wept, as for the first time
in months, even years, a woman's hand adjusted their
pillows, and a woman's voice soothed their sorrows.

Miss Nightingale's pathway was not an easy one. Her
coming did not meet the general approval of the military
or medical officials. Some thought women would be in
the way; others felt that their coming was an interference.
Possibly some did not like to have persons about who

would be apt to tell the truth on their return to England. But with good sense and much tact she was able to overcome the disaffection, using her almost unlimited power with discretion.

As soon as the wounded were attended to, she established an invalid's kitchen, where appetizing food could be prepared,—one of the essentials in convalescence. Here she overlooked the proper cooking for eight hundred men who could not eat ordinary food. Then she established a laundry. The beds and shirts of the men were in a filthy condition, some wearing the ragged clothing in which they were brought down from the Crimea. It was difficult to obtain either food or clothing, partly from the immense amount of "red tape" in official life.

Miss Nightingale seemed to be everywhere. Dr. Pincoffs said: "I believe that there never was a severe case of any kind that escaped her notice; and sometimes it was wonderful to see her at the bedside of a patient who had been admitted perhaps but an hour before, and of whose arrival one would hardly have supposed it possible she could already be cognizant."

She aided the senior chaplain, in establishing a library and school-room, and in getting up evening lectures for the men. She supplied books and games, wrote letters for the sick, and forwarded their little savings to their home-friends.

For a year and a half, till the close of the war, she did a wonderful work, reducing the death-rate in the Barrack Hospital from sixty per cent. to a little above one per cent. Said the *Times* correspondent: "Wherever there is disease in its most dangerous form, and the hand of the spoiler distressingly nigh, there is that incomparable woman sure to be seen; her benignant presence is an influence for good comfort even amid the struggles of expiring nature. She is a 'ministering angel,' without any exaggeration, in these hospitals, and as her slender form glides quietly along each corridor, every poor fellow's face softens with gratitude at the sight of her. When all the medical officers have retired for the night, and silence and darkness have settled down upon these miles of prostrate sick, she may be observed, alone, with a little lamp in her hand, making her solitary rounds.

"With the heart of a true woman and the manner of a lady, accomplished and refined beyond most of her sex, she combines a surprising calmness of judgment and promptitude and decision of character. The popular instinct was not mistaken, which, when she set out from England on her mission of mercy, hailed her as a heroine; I trust she may not earn her title to a higher, though sadder, appellation. No one who has observed her fragile figure and delicate health can avoid misgivings lest these should fail."

One of the soldiers wrote home: "She would speak to one and another, and nod and smile to many more; but she could not do it to all, you know, for we lay there by hundreds; but we could kiss her shadow as it fell, and lay our heads on our pillows again content." Another wrote home: "Before she came there was such cussin' and swearin', and after that it was as holy as a church." No wonder she was called the "Angel of the Crimea." Once she was prostrated with fever, but recovered after a few weeks.

Finally the war came to an end. London was preparing to give Miss Nightingale a royal welcome, when, lo! she took passage by design on a French steamer, and reached Lea Hurst, August 15, 1856 unbeknown to any one. There was a murmur of disappointment at first but the people could only honor all the more the woman who wished no blare of trumpets for her humane acts.

Queen Victoria sent for her to visit her at Balmoral, and presented her with a valuable jewel; a ruby-red enamel cross on a white field, encircled by a black band, with the words, "Blessed are the merciful." The letters V. R., surmounted by a crown in diamonds, are impressed upon the centre of the cross. Green enamel branches of palm, tipped with gold, form the framework of the shield, while around their stems is a riband of the blue enamel with the single word "Crimea." On the top are three brilliant stars of diamonds. On the back is an inscription written by the Queen. The Sultan sent her a magnificent bracelet, and the government, $250,000, to found the school for nurses at St. Thomas' Hospital.

After her return home, Miss Nightingale was never in strong health, but she wrote several valuable books. Her *Hospital Notes,* published in 1859 furnished plans for scores of new hospitals. Her *Notes on Nursing,* published in 1860, of which over one hundred thousand were sold, deserve to be in every home. She was a most earnest advocate of sunlight and fresh air.

She said: "An extraordinary fallacy is the dread of night air. What air can we breathe at night but night air? The choice is between pure night air from without, and foul night air from within. Most people prefer the latter,—an unaccountable choice. What will they say if it be proved true that fully *one-half of all the disease we suffer from is occasioned by people sleeping with their windows shut?* An open window most nights of the year can never hurt any one. In great cities night air is often the best and purest to be had in the twenty-four hours.

"The five essentials, for healthy houses," she says, are "pure air, pure water, efficient drainage, cleanliness and light. . . . I have known whole houses and hospitals smell of the sink. I have met just as strong a stream of sewer air coming up the back staircase of a grand

London house from the sink, as I have ever met at Scutari;
and I have seen the rooms in that house all ventilated by
the open doors, and the passages all *un*ventilated by the
closed windows, in order that as much of the sewer air as
possible might be conducted into and retained in the bedrooms.   It is wonderful!"

She also wrote *Observations on the Sanitary State of
the Army in India,* 1863; *Life or Death in India,* read before the National Association for the Promotion of Social
Science, 1873, with an appendix on *Life or Death by Ir-
rigation,* 1874.

She was constantly doing deeds of kindness.   With a
subscription sent by her to the Gordon Memorial Fund,
she said: "Might but the example of this great and pure
hero be made to tell, in that self no longer existed to him,
but only God and duty, on the soldiers who have died to
save him, and on boys who should live to follow him."

Florence Nightingale died August 13, 1910, at the age
of ninety.   She had received many distinguished honors:
the freedom of the city of London in 1908, and from
King Edward VII, a year previously, a membership in
the Order of Merit, given only to a select few men.

Her funeral was a quiet one, according to her wishes.
But her memory grows the greener with each passing
year.   The world is a better place to live in, because of
Florence Nightingale.

JEAN INGELOW

THE same friend who had given me Mrs. Browning's five volumes in blue and gold, came one day with a dainty volume just published by Roberts Brothers, of Boston. They had found a new poet, and one possessing a beautiful name. Possibly it was a *non de plume,* for who had heard any real name so musical as that of Jean Ingelow?

I took the volume down by the quiet stream that flows below Amherst College, and day after day, under a grand old tree, read some of the most musical words, wedded to as pure thought as our century has produced.

The world was just beginning to know *The High Tide on the Coast of Lincolnshire.* Eyes were dimming as they read,—

> "I looked without, and lo! my sonne
>   Came riding down with might and main:
> He raised a shout as he drew on,
>   Till all the welkin rang again,
> 'Elizabeth! Elizabeth!'
>   (A sweeter woman ne'er drew breath
>   Than my sonne's wife Elizabeth.)
>
> " 'The olde sea wall (he cried) is downe,
>   The rising tide comes on apace,
> And boats adrift in yonder towne
>   Go sailing uppe the market-place.'
> He shook as one who looks on death:
>   'God save you, mother!' straight he saith;
>   'Where is my wife, Elizabeth?' "

And then the waters laid her body at his very door, and the sweet voice that called, "Cusha! Cusha! Cusha!" was stilled forever.

The *Songs of Seven* soon became as household words, because they were a reflection of real life. Nobody ever pictured a child more exquisitely than the little seven-year-old, who, rich with the little knowledge that seems much to a child, looks down from superior heights upon

> "The lambs that play always, they know no better;
> They are only one times one."

So happy is she that she makes boon companions of the flowers :—

> "O brave marshmary buds, rich and yellow,
> Give me your honey to hold!
>
> "O columbine, open your folded wrapper,
> Where two twin turtle-doves dwell!
> O cuckoopint, toll me the purple clapper
> That hangs in your clear green bell!"

At "seven times two," who of us has not waited for the great heavy curtains of the future to be drawn aside?

> "I wish and I wish that the spring would go faster,
> Nor long summer bide so late;
> And I could grow on, like the fox-glove and aster,
> For some things are ill to wait."

At twenty-one the girl's heart flutters with expectancy :—

> "I leaned out of window, I smelt the white clover,
> Dark, dark was the garden, I saw not the gate;
> Now, if there be footsteps, he comes, my one lover;
> Hush nightingale, hush! O sweet nightingale wait

> Till I listen and hear .
> If a step draweth near,
> For my love he is late!"

At twenty-eight, the happy mother lives in a simple home, made beautiful by her children:—

> "Heigho! daisies and buttercups!
> Mother shall thread them a daisy chain."

At thirty-five a widow; at forty-two giving up her children to brighten other homes; at forty-nine, "Longing for Home."

> "I had a nestful once of my own,
>   Ah, happy, happy I!
> Right dearly I loved them, but when they were grown
>   They spread out their wings to fly.
> O, one after another they flew away,
>   Far up to the heavenly blue,
> To the better country, the upper day,
>   And—I wish I was going too."

The *Songs of Seven* will be read and treasured as long as there are women in the world to be loved, and men in the world to love them.

Years went by, and I was at last to see the author of the poems I had loved in girlhood. I had wondered how she looked, what was her manner, and what were her surroundings.

In Kensington, a suburb of London, in a two-story-and-a-half stone house, cream-colored, then dwelt Jean Ingelow. Tasteful grounds were in front of the home, and in the rear a large lawn bordered with many flowers, and conservatories; a real English garden, soft as velvet, and fragrant as new-mown hay. The house was fit for a poet; roomy, cheerful, and filled with flowers. One end of the large, double parlors seemed a bank of azalias and honeysuckles, while great bunches of yellow primrose and blue forget-me-not were on the tables and in the bay-windows.

But most interesting of all was the poet herself, in middle life, with fine, womanly face, friendly manner, and cultivated mind. For an hour we talked of many things in both countries. Miss Ingelow showed great familiarity with American literature and with our national questions.

While everything about her indicated deep love for poetry, and a keen sense of the beautiful, her conversation, fluent and admirable, showed her to be eminently practical and sensible, without a touch of sentimentality. Her first work in life seemed to be the making of her two brothers happy in the home. She usually spent her forenoons in writing. She went over her literary work thoroughly keeping her productions a long time before they were put into print. As she was never in robust health, she gave little time to society, and passed her winters in the South of France or Italy. A letter from the Alps Maritime, at Cannes, says, "This lovely spot is full of flowers, birds, and butterflies." Who that recalls her *Songs on the Voices of Birds,* the blackbird, and the nightingale, will not appreciate her happiness with such surroundings?

With great fondness for, and pride in, her own country, she had the most kindly feelings toward America and her people. She says in the preface of her novel, *Fated to be Free,* concerning this work and *Off the Skelligs,* "I am told that they are peculiar; and I feel that they must be so, for most stories of human life are, or at least aim at being, works of art—selections of interesting portions of life, and fitting incidents put together and presented as a picture is; and I have not aimed at producing a work of art at all, but a piece of nature." And then she goes on to explain her position to "her American friends," for, she says, "I am sure you more than deserve of me some efforts to please you. I seldom have an opportunity of saying how truly I think so."

Jean Ingelow's life was a quiet but busy and earnest one. She was born in the quaint old city of Boston, England, in 1830. Her father was a well-to-do banker; her mother a cultivated woman of Scotch descent, from Aberdeenshire. Jean grew to womanhood in the midst of eleven brothers and sisters, without the fate of struggle and poverty, so common among the great.

She wrote to a friend concerning her childhood:—

"As a child, I was very happy at times, and generally wondering at something. . . . I was uncommonly like other children. . . . . I remember seeing a star, and that my mother told me of God who lived up there and made the star. This was on a summer evening. It was my first hearing of God, and made a great impression on my mind. I remember better than anything that certain ecstatic sensations of joy used to get hold of me, and that I used to creep into corners to think out my thoughts by myself. I was, however, extremely timid, and easily over-awed by fear. We had a lofty nursery with a bow-window that overlooked the river. My brother and I were constantly wondering at this river. The coming up of the tides, and the ships, and the jolly gangs of towers ragging them on with a monotonous song made a daily delight for us. The washing of the water, the sunshine upon it, and the reflections of the waves on our nursery ceiling supplied hours of talk to us, and days of pleasure. At this time, being three years old, . . . I learned my letters. . . . I used to think a good deal, especially about the origin of things. People said often that they had been in this world, that house, that nursery, before I came. I thought everything must have begun when I did. . . . No doubt other children have such thoughts, but few remember them. Indeed, nothing is more remarkable among intelligent people than the recollections they retain of their early childhood. A few, as I do, remember it all. Many remember nothing whatever which occurred before they were five years old. . . . I have suffered much from a feeling of shyness and reserve, and I have not been able to do things by trying to do them. What comes to me comes of its own accord, and almost in spite of me; and I have hardly any power when verses are once written to make them any better. . . . There were no hardships in my youth, but care was bestowed on me and my brothers and sisters by a father and mother who were both cultivated people."

To another friend she wrote: "I suppose I may take for granted that mine was the poetic temperament, and since there are no thrilling incidents to relate, you may think you should like to have my views as to what that means. I cannot tell you in an hour, or even in a day, for it means so much. I suppose it, of its absence or presence, to make far more difference between one person and another than any contrast of circumstances can do. The possessor does not have it for nothing. It isolates, particularly in childhood; it takes away some common blessings, but then it consoles for them all."

With this poetic temperament, that saw beauty in flower, and sky, and bird, that felt keenly all the sorrow and all the happiness of the world about her that wrote of life rather than art, because to live rightly was the whole problem of human existence, with this poetic temperament, the girl grew to womanhood in the city bordering on the sea.

Boston, at the mouth of the Witham, was once a famous seaport, the rival of London in commercial prosperity, in the thirteenth century. It was the site of the famous monastery of St. Botolph, built by a pious monk in 657. The town which grew up around it was called Botolph's town, contracted finally to Boston. From this town Reverend John Colton came to America, and gave the name to the capital of Massachusetts, in which he settled. The present famous old church of St. Botolph was founded in 1309, having a bell-tower three hundred feet high, which supports a lantern visible at sea for forty miles.

The surrounding country is made up largely of marshes reclaimed from the sea, which are called fens, and slightly elevated tracts of land called moors. Here Jean Ingelow studied the green meadows and the ever-changing ocean.

Her first book, *A Rhyming Chronicle of Incidents and Feelings,* was published in 1850, when she was twenty, and a novel, *Allerton and Dreux,* in 1851; nine years later her *Tales of Orris.* But her fame came at thirty-three, when her first full book of *Poems* was published in 1863.

The London press said: "Miss Ingelow's new volume exhibits abundant evidence that time, study, and devotion to her vocation have both elevated and welcomed the powers of the most gifted poetess we possess, now that Elizabeth Barrett Browning and Adelaide Proctor sing no more on earth. Lincolnshire has claims to be considered the Arcadia of England at present, having given birth to Mr. Tennyson and our present Lady Laureate."

The press of America was not less cordial. "Except Mrs. Browning, Jean Ingelow is first among the women whom the world calls poets," said the *Independent.*

The songs touched the popular heart, and some, set to music, were sung at numberless firesides. Who has not heard the *Sailing beyond Seas?*

Lucretia Mott.

"Methought the stars were blinking bright,
  And the old brig's sails unfurled;
I said, 'I will sail to my love this night
  At the other side of the world.'
I stepped aboard,—we sailed so fast,—
  The sun shot up from the bourne;
But a dove that perched upon the mast
  Did mourn, and mourn, and mourn.

"O fair dove! O fond dove!
  And dove with the white breast,
Let me alone, the dream is my own,
  And my heart is full of rest."

Edmund Clarence Stedman, said: "As the voice of Mrs. Browning grew silent, the songs of Miss Ingelow began, and had instant and merited popularity. They sprang up suddenly and tunefully as skylarks from the daisy-spangled, hawthorn-bordered meadows of old England, with a blitheness long unknown, and in their idyllic underflights moved with the tenderest currents of human life. Miss Ingelow may be termed an idyllic lyrist, her lyrical pieces having always much idyllic beauty. *High Tide, Winstanley, Songs of Seven,* and the *Long White Seam* are lyrical treasures, and the author especially may be said to evince that sincerity which is poetry's most enduring warrant."

In 1864, *Studies for Stories* was published, of which the *Athenœum* said, "They are prose poems, carefully meditated, and exquisitely touched in by a teacher ready to sympathize with every joy and sorrow." The five stories are told in simple and clear language, and without slang, to which she heartily objects. For one so rich in imagination as Miss Ingelow, her prose was singularly free from obscurity and florid language.

Stories told to a Child was published in 1865, and *A*

Story of Doom and *Other Poems* in 1868, the principal poem being drawn from the time of the Deluge. *Mopsa the Fairy,* an exquisite story, followed a year later, with *A Sister's Bye-hours,* and since that time, *Off the Skelligs, Fated to be Free, Sarah de Berenger, Don John,* and *Poems of the Old Days and the New.* Of the latter, the poet Stoddard says: "Beyond all women of the Victorian era, she is the most of an Elizabethan. . . . She has tracked the ocean journeyings of Drake, Raleigh, and Frobisher, and others to whom the Spanish main was a second home, the *El Dorado* of which Columbus and his followers dreamed in their stormy slumbers. . . . The first of her poems in this volume, *Rosamund,* is a masterly battle idyl."

With all her literary work, she did not forget to do good personally. At one time she instituted a "copyright dinner," at her own expense, which she thus described to a friend: "I have set up a dinner-table for the sick poor, or rather, for such persons as are just out of the hospitals, and are hungry, and yet not strong enough to work. We have about twelve to dinner three times a week, and hope to continue the plan. It is such a comfort to see the good it does. I find it one of the great pleasures of writing, that it gives me more command of money for such purposes than falls to the lot of most women." Again, she wrote to an American friend: "I should be much obliged to you if you would give in my name twenty-five dollars to some charity in Boston. I should prefer such a one as does not belong to any party in particular, such as a city infirmary or orphan school. I do not like to draw money from your country, and give none in charity."

Miss Ingelow was very fond of children, and herein lay, perhaps, one secret of her success. In *Off the Skelligs* she says: "Some people appear to feel that they are much wiser, much nearer to the truth and to realities, than they were when they were children.   They think of childhood as immeasurably beneath and behind them.   I have never been able to join in such a notion.   It often seems to me that we lose quite as much as we gain by our lengthened sojourn here.   I should not at all wonder if the thoughts of our childhood, when we look back on it after the rending of this veil of our humanity, should prove less unlike what we were intended to derive from the teaching of life, nature, and revelation, than the thoughts of our more sophisticated days."

Jean Ingelow died at her home in Kensington, London, July 19, 1897, at the age of sixty-seven.   Her long illness ended in simple exhaustion, and she welcomed death gladly.

Best of all, this true woman and true poet as well, like Emerson saw and believed in the progress of the race.

> "Still humanity grows dearer,
>   Being learned the more,"

she says, in that tender poem, *A Mother showing the Portrait of her Child*.   Blessed optimism! that amid all the shortcomings of human nature sees the best, lifts souls upward, and helps to make the world sunny by its singing.

JENNY LIND

JENNY LIND fills a unique place among the world's great artists. She was gifted to a marvellous extent in voice. She was not beautiful in face, though Sir Julius Benedict said that when she was inspired with her theme, "her whole face lighted up and became perfectly beautiful." She was the idol of the public, not simply on account of her talent, for many are talented, but also because she was a veritable prince among givers, and the guardian angel of the poor and the unfortunate.

She was born in Stockholm, Sweden, Oct. 6, 1820. Her father, the son of a lace-maker, was a good-natured but weak man, unable to provide for his wife and child. He had a good voice, and enjoyed music of "a free and convivial kind."

Her mother was a woman of great energy and determination, who, being obliged to care for the child of a former unhappy marriage, and in addition the husband and child of a second marriage, by teaching school, had lost much of her natural sweetness of disposition through stern contact with poverty.

The mother could not care for the child and teach, so Jenny was boarded for three years with a church organist a few miles out of Stockholm. At this early age she showed a love for the country, a passion for the singing of birds, and for trees and wild flowers, which continued through life.

After her return to Stockholm she attended the school kept by her mother, and found much comfort and companionship in her grandmother. The latter first discovered that Jenny had a voice for singing.

Having heard some military bugles in the street, the child crept to the piano one day, thinking that she was alone in the house, and picked out the air which she had heard the soldiers play.

The grandmother, hearing the music, called out the name of the half-sister, Amalia, supposing that it was she. Jenny hid under the piano in terror. When her grandmother found her, she exclaimed, astonished, "Child, was that you?" The girl confessed in tears. When the mother returned, the grandmother said, "Mark my words, that child will bring you help."

Fru Lind's school did not pay—it was the old struggle of the poor to make ends meet—and she determined to become a governess, taking Amalia with her. The grandmother went to the Widow's Home, taking Jenny with her.

The child was not old enough to realize much about privation, and as she said in after life, "sang with every step I took, and with every jump my feet made." She had a pet cat, with a blue ribbon around its neck, to which she sang almost constantly.

Jenny Lind, at Cannes, in 1887, a little before her death, thus spoke of these early days to her eldest son: "Her favorite seat with her cat was in the window of the steward's room, which looked out on the lively street leading up to the Church of St. Jacob's, and there she sat and sang to it; and the people passing in the street used to hear, and wonder; and amongst others the maid of a Mademoiselle Lundberg, a dancer at the Royal Opera House; and the maid told her mistress that she had never heard such beautiful singing as this little girl sang to her cat.

"Mademoiselle Lundberg thereupon found out who she

was, and sent to ask her mother, who seems to have been
in Stockholm at the time, to bring her to sing to her.
And, when she heard her sing, she said, 'The child is a
genius; you must have her educated for the stage.' But
Jenny's mother, as well as her grandmother, had an old-
fashioned prejudice against the stage, and she would not
hear of this.

" 'Then you must, at any rate, have her taught singing,' said Mademoiselle Lundberg; and the mother was
persuaded, in this way, to accept a letter of introduction
to Herr Crœlius, the court secretary and singing-master
at the Royal Theatre.

"Crœlius was moved to tears, and said he must take
her in to Count Puke, the head of the Royal Theatre, and
tell him what a treasure he had found.   And they went at
once, and Count Puke's first question was, 'How old is
she?' and Crœlius answered, 'Nine years old.'   'Nine'
exclaimed the count; 'but this is not a *créche!*   It is the
king's theatre!'   And he would not look at her, she being,
moreover, at that time, what she herself (in her letter
to the 'Biographical Lexicon') calls 'a small, ugly, broad-
nosed, shy, *gauche,* under-grown girl!'

" 'Well,' said Crœlius, 'if the count will not hear her,
then I will teach her gratuitously myself, and she will one
day astonish you!'   Then Count Puke consented to hear
her sing; and, when she sang, he too was moved to tears;
and from that moment she was accepted, and was taken
and taught to sing, and educated, and brought up at the
Government expense."

For ten years Jenny studied and acted at the Royal
Theatre.   The pupils boarded at various homes in the
city, the theatre paying for food and clothes, and as Fru
Lind had given up her position as governess and returned
to Stockholm, she took her own child, among others, to
board.

These early years, full of hard work, were not very happy ones for the young girl. The mother, with her burdens and discouragements, was probably irritable, and Jenny, unable to bear the friction of home life any longer, ran away. After a law-suit between the impecunious Linds, who needed the board-money, and the directors of the theatre, the child was returned to her parents, to whom, unfortunately, she legally belonged.

Jenny began to act almost as soon as she was admitted to the Royal Theatre. At ten she played the part of Angela in "The Polish Mine." The next year she was Johanna in "Testamentet." The press spoke of her acting as showing "fire and feeling far beyond her years."

When about seventeen she began to study the part of Agatha in Weber's "Der Freischütz." One day she thought, to satisfy her teacher, Madame Erikson, of whom she was very fond, she would put her whole soul into her part. She did so, and the teacher met the effort with silence. "Am I, then, so incapable?" thought the girl, till she saw the tears on her teacher's face. "My child, I have nothing to teach you; do as nature tells you," she said.

On the day of her *début,* March 7, 1838, she was extremely nervous and worried, but after the first note on the stage all fear disappeared. The people were surprised and delighted, and she most of all, for she had learned her ability.

She often said afterwards, "I got up that morning one creature; I went to bed another creature. I had found my power." All through life the 7th of March was kept with grateful remembrance; it was a second birthday in her life.

In 1839 her most effective part was Alice in Meyerbeer's "Robert le Diable," which she sang twenty-three times to enthusiastic audiences. So popular was she in this piece that she gave it sixty times in the same theatre during the next four years.

Towards the close of 1839 Jenny removed from her home to the house of the chief of Swedish song-writers, Adolf Fredrik Lindblad. In this family she found companionship and quiet for study. "I have to thank him," said Jenny Lind, forty years later, "for that fine comprehension of art which was implanted by his idealistic, pure, and unsensual nature into me, his ready pupil. Subsequently Christianity stepped in to satisfy the moral needs, and to teach me to look well into my own soul."

Jenny Lind was about five feet and three to four inches in height, with "dove-like blue eyes" and light hair, a face which expressed every emotion, a quick and alert mind which, said N. P. Willis, "comprehended everything by the time it was half expressed," a dislike of the "small talk" of society and of compliments, and a natural, frank, sincere manner. While vivacious, there was an undertone of melancholy in her nature, as perhaps there must always be in those who think deeply, and are conversant with the world's woes.

When she was twenty she was made a member of the Royal Swedish Academy of Music, and was appointed court singer by his Majesty, Carl Johan. She had determined to go to Paris to study, feeling that she had the Eternal Fire of which Geijer had written. The directors of the theatre tried to dissuade her by the offer of a salary of one hundred and fifty pounds, which she declined.

On leaving Sweden, Jenny Lind took a letter of introduction from Queen Desirée (the wife of Maréchal Bernadotte, who became King of Sweden and Norway in 1818, under the title of Carl XIV., Johan) to her relative, Madame la Maréchale Soult. At the house of the latter Jenny sang before Signor Manuel Garcia, the greatest singing-master of the century. Later, Jenny called

JENNY LIND AND SCENE OF HER FIRST AMERICAN
APPEARANCE

upon him, desiring to take lessons. She sang in "Lucia," in which she had appeared thirty-nine times in Stockholm the previous year, and broke down. He said to the frightened girl, who had nearly worn herself out by her hard work, "It would be useless to teach you, Mademoiselle; you have no voice left."

She told Mendelssohn years afterward that the agony of that moment exceeded all she had suffered in her whole life.

She asked Garcia, with tears in her eyes, what she was to do. Evidently moved by her sorrow, he said she must give her voice a complete rest for six weeks, not singing at all, and talking very little. At the end of that time she might come to him again. At once she began diligently to perfect herself in the French language.

On her return to Garcia her voice had so improved that he was willing to give her two lessons a week. She began to practice the scales and exercises four hours or more daily. For ten months she studied almost continuously. Garcia's help was valuable, but she knew that her power came from another source.

In the fall of 1844, she went to Berlin. Through Meyerbeer she was privately presented to the royal family. Before appearing in opera, she was asked to sing at a small party given by Augusta, afterwards empress. The Countess of Westmoreland, whose husband, the earl, was the English ambassador to Prussia, and a noted musician as well, the founder of the Royal Academy of Music in London, was at the party given by Augusta. Lady Westmoreland thus describes the event, as told her by her mother, the countess: "She went in, full of curiosity, and saw sitting by the lamp a thin, pale, plain-featured girl, looking awkward and nervous, and like a very shy country schoolgirl. She could not believe her eyes, and said that she and her neighbors, among whom was Countess Rossi (Henrietta Sontag), whose fame as a singer and a beauty was then still recent, began to speculate whether Meyerbeer was playing a practical joke on them; and when he came up to speak to them, my mother asked him if he was really serious in meaning to bring that frightened child out in his opera. His only answer was, *'Attendez, Miladi.'*

"When the time came for her song, my mother used to say it was the most extraordinary experience she ever remembered. The wonderful notes came ringing out; but over and above that was the wonderful TRANSFIGURATION —no other word could apply—which came over her entire face and figure, lightening them up with the whole fire and dignity of her genius. The effect on the whole audience was simply marvellous.

"When she reached home, my father asked her, 'Well, what do you think of Meyerbeer's wonder?'

"She answered, 'She is simply an angel.'

" 'Is she so very handsome?'

" 'I saw a plain girl when I went in, but when she began to sing her face simply and literally shone like that of an angel. I never *saw* anything, or *heard* anything, the least like it.' "

Every evening was an ovation to the singer. When "La Sonnambula" was given, the prices asked and paid were unprecedented. Meyerbeer wrote her, urging her to overcome her diffidence; but added, "Whether heaven grants you or not this little supplement to your other precious qualities, you will always be, for me, my dear Mademoiselle, one of the most touching and noble characters that I have ever met during my long artistic wanderings, and one to whom I have vowed for my whole life the most profound and sincere admiration and esteem."

Mendelssohn came now and then to Berlin, for while

his devoted family lived there, his duties called him to Leipzig, where he had founded the Conservatorium in 1843, and as leader of the orchestra of the Gewandhaus. Jenny Lind wrote to Judge Munthe, "Felix Mendelssohn comes sometimes to Berlin, and I have often been in his company. He is a *man*, and, at the same time, he has the most supreme talent. Thus should it be."

Mendelssohn took Jenny Lind to Leipzig to assist in his famous Gewandhaus Concerts, the finest in Europe. The rush for tickets was so great that not one-fourth of the applicants could be accommodated. Herr Brockhaus said, "Soul and expression so intimately associated with so beautiful a voice and so perfect a method will never be met with again. . . . One can only wonder, and love her. And this affectionate appreciation is universal,—the same with young and old, with men and with women."

In 1847, she went to London to fill an engagement at Her Majesty's Theatre. She was to receive forty-eight hundred pounds for the season,—April 14 to August 20, —with a furnished house to live in, horses and carriage, and eight hundred pounds extra for a month in Italy, if she wished to study the language more fully, or for rest. This, of course, was more than she had ever received before.

The excitement was intense on the night when Jenny Lind was to make her first appearance. The rush for places was so great that men were thrown down, ladies fainted, and dress-suits were torn in pieces. The Queen and Prince Albert were present, with other distinguished people.

Jenny Lind sang Alice in "Robert le Diable." The Queen, herself an accomplished musician, was delighted, and threw a wreath at the feet of the artist.

Queen Victoria records in her diary, of the air, *"Ah! non credea."* "It was all *piano,* and clear and sweet, and like the sighing of a zephyr, yet all heard. Who could describe those long notes, drawn out till they quite melt away, that shake which becomes softer and softer, those very piano and flute-like notes, and those round fresh tones which are so youthful?"

At Bath, she talked with an aged woman, whom she saw walking backward and forward before the almshouse. "I have lived a long time in the world," said the woman, "and desire nothing before I die but to hear Jenny Lind."

"And would it make you happy?" said the singer.

"Ay, that it would; but such folks as I can't go to the play-house, and so I shall never see her."

"Don't be so sure of that," said the other, as they entered the house. "Sit down and listen."

The old lady heard, and wept at the unusual music. "Now you have heard Jenny Lind," said the stranger, and departed.

The death of Mendelssohn, November 4, 1847, had been a great blow to her. She wrote to a friend in Austria: "For the first two months after it, I could not put a word down on paper, and everything seemed to me to be dead. Never was I so happy, so lifted in spirit, as when I spoke with him! And seldom can there have been in the world two beings who so understood one another, and so sympathized with one another, as we! How glorious and strange are the ways of God! On the one hand, He gives all! On the other, He takes all away! Such is life's outlook!"

For two whole years she could not bear to sing a *Lied* of Mendelssohn's. "As soon as I am obliged to hear or read anything about him," she said, "I get almost incapable of carrying out the great duty which I have taken upon my shoulders."

At the height of her career, Jenny Lind decided to leave

the stage. Her farewell, May 10, 1849, was in Alice in "Robert." At the close three times she came before an enraptured but sorrowing audience, which rose each time she appeared. Tears flowed down her cheeks, while the audience shouted themselves hoarse. For nineteen years, from a child of ten, she had been the idol of the public. She would sing again for a time in concerts, but at twenty-nine she bade adieu to the stage forever.

In eleven years, between her first appearance in opera, in "Der Freischütz," March 7, 1838, and her last in "Robert le Diable," she appeared in thirty operas six hundred and seventy-seven times.

She never regretted her decision to leave the stage. She wrote later to Madame Birch-Pfeiffer: "I cannot tell you in words how happy I feel about it. I shall sing in concerts; . . . in this way I shall be able to work at least five years longer; and that is necessary for me, as, for the last twelve months, I have sung only for institutions and charities. Without a beautiful goal one cannot endure life. At least I cannot. I have begun to sing what has long been the wish of my heart—oratorio. There I can sing the music I love; and the words make me feel a better being."

In the early part of 1850, Jenny Lind sang at Göttingen, where the students made her a "Sister-Associate" of one of their famous guilds, and hung her portrait in their Assembly Room. She sang at Hanover twice for charity; at Brunswick, for pensions for the ducal orchestra; at Lübeck, for the poor; for the widow of the orchestral director, Bach, and for the pianist, Schreinzer, and reached Stockholm May 12, where she gave six concerts for the benefit of the Royal Theatre which had educated her, and sang at two state concerts in honor of the wedding of the crown prince.

The fame of Jenny Lind had, of course, spread to the

New World. The Emperor of Russia, at this time, offered her $56,000 for five months. P. T. Barnum determined to bring the singer before the American public, if possible. He sent his agent to Europe, who made a contract with Jenny Lind for one hundred and fifty concerts, at one thousand dollars a night, with expenses paid for herself, a companion and secretary, a servant, horses and carriage furnished. This contract was afterwards changed by Mr. Barnum in her interest, she to receive half the profits whenever the receipts were above five thousand five hundred dollars a night, and a right to annul the contract after sixty or one hundred concerts, with fixed penalties in either case. Mr. Barnum had faith in his venture, but the American public had not. He had great difficulty in raising the $187,500, which he had pledged Jenny Lind should be in the hands of London bankers for herself and musicians, as her security. When he asked the president of a bank to aid him, the friend laughed and said, "It is generally believed in Wall Street that your engagement with Jenny Lind will ruin you. I do not believe you will ever receive so much as three thousand dollars at a single concert." A clergyman loaned him the last five thousand dollars needed.

When she arrived, thousands were on the dock eager to catch a glimpse of her. Triumphal arches, surmounted by the eagle, bore the inscriptions, "Welcome, Jenny Lind! Welcome to America!" That evening she was serenaded at her hotel, the Irving House, by the New York Musical Fund Society, twenty thousand persons being present.

America seemed even more wild with enthusiasm than Europe had been. Tickets for the first concert, September 11, 1850, in Castle Garden, were sold by auction, some persons paying as high as six hundred and fifty dollars for a single ticket. The "Jenny Lind Mania," as it was called, swept over the country. Jenny Lind's share, from the first concert, was nearly ten thousand dollars. She immediately sent for the mayor of the city, and divided it, according to his advice, among charitable institutions.

From the ninety-three concerts given by Jenny Lind, under Mr. Barnum's management, the proceeds were $712,161. Her portion was $176,675. Sometimes the proceeds from a single concert were over sixteen thousand dollars. In New York City alone she gave away between thirty and forty thousand dollars in charities. When warned against so much liberality, as some unworthy persons were seeking aid, she invariably replied, "Never mind; if I relieve ten, and one is worthy, I am satisfied."

The last sixty nights of the concert series were given under her own management, assisted by Mr. Otto Goldschmidt, of Hamburg, an accomplished musician. At the close of her tour, she was married to Mr. Goldschmidt, at the house of Mr. S. G. Ward, in Boston, by Bishop Wainwright, of New York, February 5, 1852. The Hon. Edward Everett and a few others, were witnesses. Jenny Lind was, at this time, thirty-one and her husband twenty-three, he having been born August 21, 1829.

The marriage proved to be a happy one. She had found, she wrote a friend, "all that her heart ever wanted and loved." Her charities in America were unceasing. "While she habitually declined," says Mr. N. P. Willis, "the calls and attentions of fashionable society, she was in constant dread of driving more humble claimants from her door. She submitted, *every day,* to the visits of strangers, as far as strength and her professional duties would any way endure. To use her own expression, she was 'torn in pieces.' "

In 1852, Jenny Lind-Goldschmidt and her husband returned to Europe, and spent some years in Dresden. During the early half of 1854, she sang in Berlin, Leipzig, Vienna, and Budapest, and in the following year, at Amsterdam, Rotterdam, the Hague, and many other cities, always receiving the same enthusiastic welcome. In 1856, she sang in England, and later, in Ireland and Germany.

After her return to England, Jenny Lind sang on special occasions only. She gave three oratorios for charitable purposes at Exeter Hall during the International Exhibition. In 1865 she appeared in the "Messiah," for the Clergy Fund Corporation; in 1866, at Cannes; in 1867, at the Musical Festival at Hereford; in 1869, in Hamburg and London, in "Ruth" an opera composed by her husband; in Düsseldorf and London, in 1870 and 1871, the latter year, in concert with Madame Schumann; in 1873, at Northumberland House, before it was taken down; in 1877, in behalf of the Turkish Refugee Fund; in 1880, in behalf of the Albert Institute in a royal concert at Windsor; in 1883, her last public appearance in concert, for the Railway Servants' Benevolent Fund, at the Spa, Malvern Hills.

During her last years she gave much time to training the soprano voices in the Bach choir, founded by her husband in 1875, and helping the Royal College of Music, of whose faculty she was a member.

These last years were very happy, as she saw her children and grandchildren grow up around her. In 1887 she was attacked with paralysis, and was ill for several weeks. As she lay on her death-bed, her daughter opened the shutters to let in the morning sun, and she sang the first bars of the song she loved, "An den Sonnenschein," the last notes she ever sang.

She died November 2, 1887, at Wynds Point, her cottage on Malvern Hills. The Queen sent a wreath of white flowers for the woman whom she honored.

In accordance with her oft-expressed desire, the patchwork quilt, which the children of the United States gave her, was buried with her.

Jenny Lind's benevolences have been estimated at a half million dollars, and this is, perhaps, an under estimate.

Though very modest, she knew and appreciated her genius, and spoke to her friends "of the heavenly career" which she had been permitted to have. "If you knew," she wrote in 1847, "what a sensation of the nearness of a higher power one instinctively feels when one is permitted to contribute to the good of mankind, as I have done, and still do! Believe me, it is a great gift of God's mercy!"

MADAME DE STAËL

I⊤ was the twentieth of September, 1881. The sun shone out mild and beautiful upon Lake Geneva, as we sailed up to Coppet. The banks were dotted with lovely homes, half hidden by the foliage, while brilliant flower-beds came close to the water's edge. Snow-covered Mont Blanc looked down upon the restful scene, which seemed as charming as anything in Europe.

We alighted from the boat, and walked up from the landing, between great rows of oaks, horse-chestnuts, and sycamores, to the famous home we had come to look upon,—that of Madame de Staël. It is a French chateau, two stories high, drab, with green blinds, surrounding an open square; vines clamber over the gate and the high walls, and lovely flowers blossom everywhere. As you enter, you stand in a long hall, with green curtains, with many busts, the finest of which is that of Monsieur Necker. The next room is the large library, with furniture of blue and white; and the next, hung with old Gobelin tapestry, is the room where Madame Recamier used to sit with Madame de Staël, and look out upon the exquisite scenery, restful even in their troubled lives. Here is the work-table of her whom Macaulay called "the greatest woman of her times," and of whom Byron said, "She is a woman by herself, and has done more than all the rest of them together, intellectually; she ought to have been a man."

Next we enter the drawing-room, with carpet woven in a single piece; the furniture red and white. We stop to look upon the picture of Monsieur Necker, the father,

74

a strong, noble-looking man; of the mother, in white silk dress, with powdered hair, and very beautiful; and De Staël herself, in a brownish yellow dress, with low neck and short sleeves, holding in her hand the branch of flowers, which she always carried, or a leaf, that thus her hands might be employed while she engaged in the conversation that astonished Europe. Here also are the pictures of the Baron, her husband, in white wig and military dress; here her idolized son and daughter, the latter beautiful, with mild, sad face, and dark hair and eyes.

What brings thousands to this quiet retreat every year? Because here lived and wrote and suffered the only person whom the great Napoleon feared, whom Galiffe, of Geneva, declared "the most remarkable woman that Europe has produced"; learned, rich, the author of *Corinne* and *Allemagne,* whose "talents in conversation," says George Ticknor, "were perhaps the most remarkable of any person that ever lived."

Annie Louise Germaine Necker, born in Paris, April 27, 1766, was the daughter of James Necker, Minister of Finance under Louis XVI., a man of fine intellect, the author of fifteen volumes; and Susanna, daughter of a Swiss pastor, beautiful, educated, and devotedly Christian. Necker had become rich in early life through banking, and had been made, by the republic of Geneva, her resident minister at the Court of Versailles.

When the throne of Louis seemed crumbling, because the people were tired of extravagance and heavy taxation, Necker was called to his aid, with the hope that economy and retrenchment would save the nation. He also loaned the government two million dollars. The home of the Neckers, in Paris, naturally became a social centre, which the mother of the family was well fitted to grace. Gibbon had been deeply in love with her.

He says: "I found her learned without pedantry,

lively in conversation, pure in sentiment, and elegant in manners; and the first sudden emotion was fortified by the habits and knowledge of a more familiar acquaintance. . . . At Crassier and Lausanne I indulged my dream of felicity; but on my return to England I soon discovered that my father would not hear of this strange alliance, and that, without his consent, I was myself destitute and helpless. After a painful struggle, I yielded to my fate; I sighed as a lover; I obeyed as a son." Gibbon never married, but retained his life-long friendship and admiration for Madame Necker.

It was not strange, therefore, that Gibbon liked to be present in her *salon,* where Buffon, Hume, Diderot and D'Alembert were wont to gather. The child of such parents could scarcely be other than intellectual, surrounded by such gifted minds. Her mother, too, was a most systematic teacher, and each day the girl was obliged to sit by her side, erect, on a wooden stool, and learn difficult lessons.

"She stood in great awe of her mother," wrote Simond, the traveller, "but was exceedingly familiar with and extravagantly fond of her father. Madame Necker had no sooner left the room one day, after dinner, than the young girl, till then timidly decorous, suddenly seized her napkin, and threw it across the table at the head of her father, and then flying round to him, hung upon his neck, suffocating all his reproofs by her kisses." Whenever her mother returned to the room, she at once became silent and restrained.

The child early began to show literary talent, writing dramas, and making paper kings and queens to act her tragedies. This the mother thought to be wrong, and it was discontinued. But when she was twelve, the mother having somewhat relented, she wrote a play, which she and her companions acted in the drawing-room.

Grimm was so pleased with her attempts, that he sent extracts to his correspondents throughout Europe. At fifteen she wrote an essay on the *Revocation of the Edict of Nantes,* and another upon Montesquieu's *Spirit of Laws.*

Overtaxing the brain with her continuous study, she became ill, and the physician, greatly to her delight, prescribed fresh air and sunshine. Here often she roamed from morning till night on their estate at St. Ouen. Madame Necker felt deeply the thwarting of her educational plans, and years after, when her daughter had acquired distinction, said, "It is absolutely nothing compared to what I would have made it."

Monsieur Necker's restriction of pensions and taxing of luxuries soon aroused the opposition of the aristocracy, and the weak but good-hearted King asked his minister to resign. Both wife and daughter felt the blow keenly, for both idolized him, so much so that the mother feared lest she be supplanted by her daughter. Madame de Staël says of her father, "From the moment of their marriage to her death, the thought of my mother dominated his life. He was not like other men in power, attentive to her by occasional tokens of regard, but by continual expressions of most tender and most delicate sentiment." Of herself she wrote, "Our destinies would have united us forever, if fate had only made us contemporaries." At his death she said, "If he could be restored to me, I would give all my remaining years for six months." To the last he was her idol.

For the next few years the family travelled most of the time, Necker bringing out a book on the *Finances,* which had a sale at once of a hundred thousand copies. A previous book, the *Compte Rendu au Roi,* showing how for years the moneys of France had been wasted, had also a large sale. For these books, and especially for other correspondence, he was banished forty leagues from

Paris. The daughter's heart seemed well-nigh broken at this intelligence. Loving Paris, saying she would rather live there on "one hundred francs a year, and lodge in the fourth story," than anywhere else in the world, how could she bear for years the isolation of the country? Joseph II., King of Poland, and the King of Naples, offered Necker fine positions, but he declined.

Mademoiselle Necker had come to womanhood, not beautiful, but with wonderful fascination and tact. She could compliment persons without flattery, was cordial and generous, and while the most brilliant talker, could draw to herself the thoughts and confidences of others. She had also written a book on *Rousseau,* which was much talked about. Pitt, of England, Count Fersen, of Sweden, and others, sought her in marriage, but she loved no person as well as her father. Her consent to marriage could be obtained only by the promise that she should never be obliged to leave him.

Baron de Staël a man of learning and fine social position, ambassador from Sweden, and the warm friend of Gustavus, was ready to make any promises for the rich daughter of the Minister Necker. He was thirty-seven, she only a little more than half his age, twenty, but she accepted him because her parents were pleased. Going to Paris, she was, of course, received at Court, Marie Antoinette paying her much attention. Necker was soon recalled from exile to his old position.

The funds rose thirty per cent., and he became the idol of the people. Soon representative government was demanded, and then, though the King granted it, the breach was widened. Necker, unpopular with the bad advisers of the King, was again asked to leave Paris, and make no noise about it; but the people, hearing of it, soon demanded his recall, and he was hastily brought back from Brussels, riding through the streets like "the

sovereign of a nation," said his daughter. The people
were wild with delight.

But matters had gone too far to prevent a bloody Revolution. Soon a mob was marching toward Versailles;
thousands of men, women, and even children armed with
pikes. They reached the palace, killed the guards, and
penetrated to the queen's apartments, while some filled
the court-yard and demanded bread. The brave Marie
Antoinette appeared on the balcony leading her two children, while Lafayette knelt by her side and kissed her
hand. But the people could not be appeased.

Necker finding himself unable to serve his king longer,
fled to his Swiss retreat at Coppet, and there remained till
his death. Madame de Staël, as the wife of the Swedish
ambassador, continued in the turmoil, writing her father
daily, and taking an active interest in politics. "In England," she said, "women are accustomed to be silent before men when political questions are discussed. In
France, they direct all conversation, and their minds readily acquire the facility and talent which this privilege re-
quires." Lafayette, Narbonne, and Talleyrand consulted
with her. She wrote the principal part of Talleyrand's
report on Public Instruction in 1790. She procured the
appointment of Narbonne to the ministry; and later,
when Talleyrand was in exile, obtained his appointment
to the Department of Foreign Affairs.

Matters had gone from bad to worse. In 1792 the
Swedish government suspended its embassy, and Madame
de Staël prepared to fly, but stayed for a time to save
her friends. The seven prisons of Paris were all
crowded under the fearful reign of Danton and Marat.
Great heaps of dead lay before every prison door. During that Reign of Terror it is estimated that eighteen
thousand six hundred persons perished by the guillotine.
Whole squares were shot down. When the police visited

her house, where some of the ministers were hidden, she met them graciously, urging that they must not violate the privacy of an ambassador's house. When her friends were arrested, she went to the barbarous leaders, and with her eloquence begged for their safety, and thus saved the lives of many.

At last she must leave the terror-stricken city. Supposing that her rank as the wife of a foreign ambassador would protect her, she started with a carriage and six horses, her servants in livery. At once a crowd of half-famished and haggard women crowded around, and threw themselves against the horses. The carriage was stopped, and the occupants were taken to the Assembly. She pleaded her case before the noted Robespierre, and then waited for six hours for the decision of the Commune. Meantime she saw the hired assassins pass beneath the windows, their bare arms covered with the blood of the slain. The mob attempted to pillage her carriage, but a strong man mounted the box and defended it. She learned afterward that it was the notorious Santerre, the person who later superintended the execution of Louis XVI., ordering his drummers to drown the last words of the dying King. Santerre had seen Necker distribute corn to the poor of Paris in a time of famine, and now he was befriending the daughter for this noble act. Finally she was allowed to continue her journey, and reached Coppet with her baby, Auguste, well-nigh exhausted after this terrible ordeal.

The Swiss home soon became a place of refuge for those who were flying from the horrors of the Commune. She kept a faithful agent, who knew the mountain passes, busy in this work of mercy.

The following year, 1793, longing for a change from these dreadful times, she visited England, and received much attention from prominent persons, among them

MADAME DE STAËL.
From the painting by Mlle. Godefroy.

Fanny Burny, the author of *Evelina,* who owned "that she had never heard conversation before. The most animated eloquence, the keenest observation, the most sparkling wit, the most courtly grace, were united to charm her."

On January 21 of this year, the unfortunate King had met his death on the scaffold before an immense throng of people. Necker had begged to go before the Convention and plead for his king, but was refused. Madame de Staël wrote a vigorous appeal to the nation in behalf of the beautiful and tender-hearted Marie Antoinette; but on September 16, 1793, at four o'clock in the morning, in an open cart, in the midst of thirty thousand troops and a noisy rabble, she, too, was borne to the scaffold.

The next year, Madame Necker died at Coppet, whispering to her husband, "We shall see each other in Heaven." "She looked heavenward," said Necker in a most affecting manner, "listening while I prayed; then, in dying, raised the finger of her left hand, which wore the ring I had given her, to remind me of the pledge engraved upon it, to love her forever." His devotion to her was beautiful. "No language," says his daughter, "can give any adequate idea of it. Exhausted by wakefulness at night, she slept often in the daytime, resting her head on his arm. I have seen him remain immovable, for hours together, standing in the same position for fear of awakening her by the least movement. Absent from her during a few hours of sleep, he inquired, on his return, of her attendant, if she had asked for him? She could no longer speak, but made an effort to say 'yes, yes.' "

When the Revolution was over, and France had become a republic, Sweden sent back her ambassador, Baron de Staël, and his wife returned to him at Paris. Again her *salon* became the centre for the great men of the time. She loved liberty, and believed in the republican form of government. She had written her book upon the *Influence of the Passions on the Happiness of Individuals and Nations,* prompted by the horrors of the Revolution, and it was considered "irresistible in energy and dazzling in thought."

She was also devoting much time to her child, Auguste, developing him without punishment, thinking that there had been too much rigor in her own childhood. He well repaid her for her gentleness and trust, and was inseparable from her through life, becoming a noble Christian man, and the helper of all good causes. Meantime Madame de Staël saw with alarm the growing influence of the young Corsican officer, Bonaparte. The chief executive power had been placed in the hands of the Directory, and he had control of the army. He had won brilliant victories in Italy, and had been made commander-in-chief of the expedition against Egypt. He now returned to Paris, turned out the Directory, drove out the Council of Five Hundred from the hall of the Assembly at the point of the bayonet, made the government into a consulate with three consuls, of whom he was the first, and lived at the Tuileries in almost royal style.

All this time Madame de Staël felt the egotism and heartlessness of Napoleon. Her *salon* became more crowded than ever with those who had their fears for the future. "The most eloquent of the Republican orators were those who borrowed from her most of their ideas and telling phrases. Most of them went forth from her door with speeches ready for the next day, and with resolution to pronounce them—a courage which was also derived from her." Lucien and Joseph Bonaparte, the brothers of Napoleon, were proud of her friendship, and often were guests at her house, until forbidden by their brother.

When Benjamin Constant made a speech against the "rising tyranny," Napoleon suspected that she had prompted it, and denounced her heartily, all the time declaring that he loved the Republic, and would always defend it! He said persons always came away from De Staël's home "less his friends than when they entered." About this time her book, *Literature Considered in its Relation to Social Institutions,* was published, and made a surprising impression from its wealth of knowledge and power of thought. Its analysis of Greek and Latin literature, and the chief works in Italian, English, German, and French, astonished everybody because written by a woman!

Soon after, Necker published his *Last Views of Politics and Finance* in which he wrote against the tyranny of a single man. At once Napoleon caused a sharp letter to be written to Necker advising him to leave politics to the First Consul, "who was alone able to govern France," and threatening his daughter with exile for her supposed aid in his book. She saw the wisdom of escaping from France, lest she be imprisoned, and immediately hastened to Coppet. A few months later, in the winter of 1802, she returned to Paris to bring home Baron de Staël, who was ill, and from whom she had separated because he was spending all her fortune and that of her three children. He died on the journey. Virtually banished from France, she now wrote her *Delphine,* a brilliant novel which was widely read.

Her home at Coppet became the home of many great people. Sismondi, the author of the *History of the Italian Republics, and Literature of Southern Europe,* encouraged by her, wrote here several of his famous works. Bonstetten made his home here for years. Schlegel, the greatest critic of his age, became the teacher of her children, and a most intimate friend. Benjamin Constant, the author and statesman, was here. All repaired to their rooms for work in the morning, and in the evening enjoyed philosophic, literary, and political discussions.

Bonstetten said: "In seeing her, in hearing her, I feel myself electrified. . . . She daily becomes greater and better; but souls of great talent have great sufferings: they are solitary in the world, like Mont Blanc."

In the autumn of 1803, longing for Paris, she ventured to within ten leagues and hired a quiet home. Word was soon borne to Napoleon that the road to her house was thronged with visitors. He at once sent an officer with a letter signed by himself, exiling her to forty leagues from Paris, and commanding her to leave within twenty-four hours.

At once she fled to Germany. At Frankfort her little daughter was dangerously ill. "I knew no person in the city," she writes. "I did not know the language; and the physician to whom I confided my child could not speak French. But my father shared my trouble; he consulted physicians at Geneva, and sent me their prescriptions. Oh, what would become of a mother trembling for the life of her child, if it were not for prayer!"

Going to Weimar, she met Goethe, Wieland, Schiller, and other noted men. At Berlin, the greatest attention was shown her. The beautiful Louise of Prussia welcomed her heartily. During this exile her father died, with his latest breath saying, "She has loved me dearly! She has loved me dearly!" On his death-bed he wrote a letter to Bonaparte telling him that his daughter was in nowise responsible for his book, but it was never answered. It was enough for Napoleon to know that she did not flatter him; therefore he wished her out of the way.

Madame de Staël was for a time completely overcome by Necker's death. She wore his picture on her person as long as she lived. Only once did she part with it, and then she imagined it might console her daughter in her illness. Giving it to her, she said, "Gaze upon it, gaze upon it, when you are in pain."

She now sought repose in Italy, preparing those beautiful descriptions for her *Corinne,* and finally returning to Coppet, spent a year in writing her book. It was published in Paris, and, says Sainte-Beuve, "its success was instantaneous and universal. As a work of art, as a poem, the romance of *Corinne* is an immortal monument." Jeffrey, in the *Edinburgh Review,* called the author the greatest writer in France since Voltaire and Rousseau, and the greatest woman writer of any age or country. Napoleon, however, in his official paper, caused a scathing criticism on *Corinne* to appear; indeed, it was declared to be from his own pen. She was told by the Minister of Police, that she had but to insert some praise of Napoleon in *Corinne,* and she would be welcomed back to Paris. She could not, however, live a lie, and she feared Napoleon had evil designs upon France.

Again she visited Germany with her children, Schlegel, and Sismondi. So eager was everybody to see her and hear her talk, that Bettina von Arnim says in her correspondence with Goethe: "The gentlemen stood around the table and planted themselves behind us, elbowing one another. They leaned quite over me, and I said in French, 'Your adorers quite suffocate me.' "

While in Germany, her eldest son, then seventeen, had an interview with Bonaparte about the return of his mother. "Your mother," said Napoleon, "could not be six months in Paris before I should be compelled to send her to Bicêtre or the Temple. I should regret this necessity, for it would make a noise and might injure me a little in public opinion. Say, therefore, to her that as long as I live she cannot re-enter Paris. I see what you wish, but it cannot be; she will commit follies; she will have the world about her."

On her return to Coppet, she spent two years in writing her *Allemagne*, for which she had been making researches for four years. She wished it published in Paris, as *Corinne* had been, and submitted it to the censors of the Press. They crossed out whatever sentiments they thought might displease Napoleon, and then ten thousand copies were at once printed, she meantime removing to France, within her proscribed limits, that she might correct the proof-sheets.

What was her astonishment to have Napoleon order the whole ten thousand destroyed, and her to leave France in three days! Her two sons attempted to see Bonaparte, who was at Fontainebleau, but were ordered to turn back, or they would be arrested. The only reason given for destroying the work was the fact that she had been silent about the great but egotistical Emperor.

Broken in spirit, she returned to Geneva. Amid all this darkness a new light was about to beam upon her life. In the social gatherings made for her, she observed a young army officer, Monsieur Rocca, broken in health from his many wounds, but handsome and noble in face, and, as she learned, of irreproachable life. Though only twenty-three and she forty-five, the young officer was fascinated by her conversation, and refreshed in spirit by her presence. She sympathized with his misfortunes in battle; she admired his courage. He was lofty in sentiments, tender in heart, and gave her what she had always needed, an unselfish and devoted love. When discouraged by his friends, he replied, "I will love her so much that I will finish by making her marry me."

They were married in 1811, and the marriage was a

singularly happy one. The reason for it is not difficult
to perceive. A marriage that has not a pretty face or a
passing fancy for its foundation, but appreciation of a
gifted mind and noble heart,—such a marriage stands
the test of time.

The marriage was kept secret from all save a few intimate friends, Madame de Staël fearing that if the news
reached Napoleon, Rocca would be ordered back to
France. Her fears were only too well founded. Schlegel, Madame Recamier, all who had shown any sympathy
for her, began to be exiled. She was forbidden under
any pretext whatever from travelling in Switzerland, or
entering any region annexed to France. She was advised not to go two leagues from Coppet, lest she be imprisoned, and this with Napoleon usually meant death.

The Emperor seemed about to conquer the whole world.
Whither could she fly to escape his persecution? She
longed to reach England, but there was an edict against
any French subject entering that country without special
permit. Truly his heel was upon France. The only way
to reach that country was through Austria, Russia, and
Sweden, two thousand leagues. But she must attempt
it. She passed an hour in prayer by her parent's tomb,
kissed his armchair and table, and took his cloak to wrap
herself in, should death come.

On May 23, 1812, she, with Rocca and two of her children, began their flight by carriage, not telling the servants at the chateau but that they should return for the
next meal.

They reached Vienna, June 6, and were at once put
under surveillance. Everywhere she saw placards admon-
ishing the officers to watch her sharply. Rocca had to
make his way alone, because Bonaparte had ordered his
arrest. They were permitted to remain only a few hours
in any place. Once Madame de Staël was so overcome by

this brutal treatment that she lost consciousness, and was obliged to be taken from her carriage to the roadside till she recovered. Every hour she expected arrest and death.

Finally, worn in body, she reached Russia, and was cordially received by Alexander and Empress Elizabeth. From here she went to Sweden, and had an equally cordial welcome from Bernadotte, the general who became king. Afterward she spent four months in England, bringing out *Allemagne*. Here she received a perfect ovation. At Lord Lansdowne's the first ladies in the kingdom mounted on chairs and tables to catch a glimpse of her. Sir James Mackintosh said: "The whole fashionable and literary world is occupied with Madame de Staël, the most celebrated woman of this, or perhaps of any age." Very rare must be the case where a woman of fine mind does not have many admirers among gentlemen.

Her *Allemagne* was published in 1813, the manuscript having been secretly carried over Germany, Poland, Russia, Sweden, and the Baltic Sea. The first part treated of the manners of Germany; the second, its literature and art; the third, its philosophy and morals; the fourth, its religion. The book had a wonderful sale, and was soon translated into all the principal tongues of Europe. Lamartime said: "Her style, without losing any of its youthful vigor and splendor, seemed now to be illuminated with more lofty and eternal lights as she approached the evening of life, and the diviner mysteries of thought. This style no longer paints, no longer chants; it adores. . . . Her name will live as long as literature, as long as the history of her country."

Meantime, great changes had taken place in France. Napoleon had been defeated at Leipsic, leaving a quarter of a million murdered on his battle-fields; he had abdicated, and was on his way to Elba. She immediately returned to Paris, with much the same feeling as Victor Hugo, when he wept as he came from his long exile under "Napoleon the Little." Again to her *salon* came kings and generals, Alexander of Russia, Wellington, and others.

But soon Napoleon returned, and she fled to Coppet. He sent her an invitation to come to Paris, declaring he would now live for the peace of Europe, but she could not trust him. She saw her daughter, lovely and beautiful, married to the Duc de Broglie, a leading statesman, and was happy in her happiness. Rocca's health was failing, and they repaired to Italy for a time.

In 1816 they returned to Paris, Napoleon having gone from his final defeat to St. Helena. But Madame de Staël was broken with her trials. She seemed to grow more and more frail, till the end came. She said frequently, "My father awaits me on the other shore." To Chateaubriand she said, "I have loved God, my father, and my country." She could not and would not go to sleep the last night, for fear she might never look upon Rocca again. He begged her to sleep and he would awaken her often. "Good night," she said, and it was forever. She never awakened. They buried her beside her father at Coppet, under the grand old trees. Rocca died in seven months, at the age of thirty-one. "I hoped," he said, "to have died in her arms."

Her little son, and Rocca's, five years old, was cared for by Auguste and Albertine, her daughter. After Madame de Staël's death, her *Considerations on the French Revolution* and *Ten Years of Exile* were published. Of the former, Sainte-Beuve says: "Its publication was an event. It was the splendid public obsequies of the authoress. Its politics were destined to long and passionate discussions and a durable influence. She is perfect only from this day; the full influence of her star is only at her tomb."

Chateaubriand said, "Her death made one of those breaches which the fall of a superior intellect produces once in an age, and which can never be closed."

As kind as she was great, loving deeply and receiving love in return, she has left an imperishable name. No wonder that thousands visit that quiet grave beside Lake Geneva.

ROSA BONHEUR

In a simple home in Paris could have been seen, in 1829, Raymond Bonheur and his little family,—Rosa, seven years old, Auguste, Isadore, and Juliette. He was a man of fine talent in painting, but obliged to spend his time in giving drawing-lessons to support his children. His wife, Sophie, gave lessons on the piano, going from house to house all day long, and sometimes sewing half the night, to earn a little more for the necessities of life.

Hard work and poverty soon bore its usual fruit, and the tired young mother died in 1833. The three oldest children were sent to board with a plain woman, "La mère Cathérine," in the Champs Elysées, and the youngest was placed with relatives. For two years this good woman cared for the children, sending them to school, though she was greatly troubled because Rosa persisted in playing in the woods of the Bois de Boulogne, gathering her arms full of daisies and marigolds, rather than to be shut up in a schoolroom. "I never spent an hour of fine weather indoors during the whole of the two years," she has often said since those days.

Finally the father married again and brought the children home. The two boys were placed in school, and M. Bonheur paid their way by giving drawing-lessons three times a week in the institution. If Rosa did not love school, she must be taught something useful, and she was accordingly placed in a sewing establishment to become a seamstress.

The child hated sewing, ran the needle into her fingers at every stitch, cried for the fresh air and sunshine, and finally, becoming pale and sickly, was taken back to the Bonheur home. The anxious painter would try his child once more in school; so he arranged that she should attend, with compensation met in the same way as for his boys. Rosa soon became a favorite with the girls in the Fauborg St. Antoine School, especially because she could draw such witty caricatures of the teachers, which she pasted against the wall, with bread chewed into the consistency of putty. The teachers were not pleased, but so struck were they with the vigor and originality of the drawings, that they carefully preserved the sketches in an album.

The girl was far from happy. Naturally sensitive—as what poet or painter was ever born otherwise?—she could not bear to wear a calico dress and coarse shoes, and eat with an iron spoon from a tin cup, when the other girls wore handsome dresses, and had silver mugs and spoons. She grew melancholy, neglected her books, and finally became so ill that she was obliged to be taken home.

And now Raymond Bonheur very wisely decided not to make plans for his child for a time, but see what was her natural tendency. It was well that he made this decision in time, before she had been spoiled by his well-meant but poor intentions.

Left to herself, she constantly hung about her father's studio, now drawing, now modeling, copying whatever she saw him do. She seemed never to be tired, but sang at her work all the day long.

Monsieur Bonheur suddenly awoke to the fact that his daughter had great talent. He began to teach her carefully, to make her accurate in drawing, and correct in perspective. Then he sent her to the Louvre to copy the works of the old masters. Here she worked with the greatest industry and enthusiasm, not observing anything

that was going on around her. Said the director of the
Louvre, "I have never seen an example of such application and such ardor for work."

One day an elderly English gentleman stopped beside
her easel, and said: "Your copy, my child, is superb,
faultless. Persevere as you have begun, and I prophesy
that you will be a great artist." How glad those few
words made her! She went home thinking over to herself
the determination she had made in the school when she ate
with her iron spoon, that sometime she would be as famous as her schoolmates, and have some of the comforts
of life.

Her copies of the old masters were soon sold, and
though they brought small prices, she gladly gave the
money to her father, who needed it now more than ever.
His second wife had two sons when he married her, and
now they had a third, Germain, and every cent that Rosa
could earn was needed to help support seven children. "La
mamiche," as they called the new mother, was an excellent manager of the meagre finances, and filled her place
well.

Rosa was now seventeen, loving landscape, historical,
and genre painting, perhaps equally; but happening to
paint a goat, she was so pleased in the work, that she determined to make animal painting a specialty. Having
no money to procure models, she must needs make long
walks into the country on foot to the farms. She would
take a piece of bread in her pocket, and generally forget
to eat it. After working all day, she would come home
tired, often drenched with rain, and her shoes covered
with mud.

She took other means to study animals. In the out-
skirts of Paris were great *abattoirs,* or slaughterpens.
Though the girl tenderly loved animals, and shrank
from the sight of suffering, she forced herself to see the

killing, that she might know how to depict the death agony on canvas. Though obliged to mingle more or less with drovers and butchers, no indignity was ever offered her. As she sat on a bundle of hay, with her colors about her, they would crowd around to look at the pictures, and regard her with honest pride. The world soon learns whether a girl is in earnest about her work, and treats her accordingly.

The Bonheur family had moved to the sixth story of a tenement house in the Rue Rumfort, now the Rue Malesherbes. The sons, Auguste and Isadore, had both become artists; the former a painter, the latter a sculptor. Even little Juliette was learning to paint. Rosa was working hard all day at her easel, and at night was illustrating books, or molding little groups of animals for the figure-dealers. All the family were happy despite their poverty, because they had congenial work.

On the roof, Rosa improvised a sort of garden, with honeysuckles, sweet-peas, and nasturtiums, and here they kept a sheep, with long, silky wool, for a model. Very often Isadore would take him on his back and carry him down the six flights of stairs,—the day of elevators had not dawned,—and after he had enjoyed grazing, would bring him back to his garden home. It was a docile creature, and much loved by the whole family. For Rosa's birds, the brothers constructed a net, which they hung outside the window, and then opened the cage into it.

At nineteen Rosa was to test the world, and see what the critics would say. She sent to the Fine Arts Exhibition two pictures, "Goats and Sheep" and "Two Rabbits." The public was pleased, and the press gave kind notices. The next year "Animals in a Pasture" a "Cow Lying in a Meadow," and a "Horse for Sale," attracted still more attention. Two years later she exhibited twelve pictures, some of her father and brother being hung on either side of hers, the first time they had been admitted. More and more the critics praised, and the pathway of the Bonheur family grew less thorny.

Then, in 1849, when she was twenty-seven, came the triumph. Her magnificent picture, "Cantal Oxen," took the gold medal, and was purchased by England. Horace Vernet, the president of the commission of awards, in the midst of a brilliant assembly, proclaimed the new laureate, and gave her, in behalf of the government, a superb Sèvres vase.

Raymond Bonheur seemed to become young again at this fame of his child. It brought honors to him also, for he was at once made director of the government school of design for girls. But the release from poverty and anxiety came too late, and he died the same year, greatly lamented by his family. "He had grand ideas," said his daughter, "and had he not been obliged to give lessons for our support, he would have been more known, and to-day acknowledged with other masters."

Rosa was made director in his place, and Juliette became a professor in the school. This same year appeared her "Plowing Scene in the Nivernais," now in the Luxembourg Gallery, thought to be her most important work after her "Horse Fair." Orders now poured in upon her, so that she could not accede to half the requests for work. A rich Hollander offered her one thousand crowns for a painting which she could have wrought in two hours; but she refused.

Four years later, after eighteen long months of preparatory studies, her "Horse Fair" was painted. This created the greatest enthusiasm both in England and America. It was sold to a gentleman in England for eight thousand dollars, and was finally purchased by A. T. Stewart, of New York, for his famous collection. Later it was presented to the Metropolitan Museum of Art. No one who has seen this picture will ever forget the action and vigor of these Normandy horses. In painting it, a petted horse, it is said, stepped back upon the canvas, putting his hoof through it, thus spoiling the work of months.

So greatly was this picture admired, that Napoleon III. was urged to bestow upon her the Cross of the Legion of Honor, entitled her from French usage. Though she was invited to the state dinner at the Tuileries, always given to artists to whom the Academy of Fine Arts has awarded its highest honors, Napoleon had not the courage to give it to her, lest public opinion might not agree with him in conferring it upon a woman. Possibly he felt, more than the world knew, the insecurity of his throne.

Henry Bacon, in the *Century,* thus describes the way in which Rosa Bonheur finally received the badge of distinction. "The Emperor, leaving Paris for a short summer excursion in 1865, left the Empress as Regent. From the imperial residence at Fontainebleau it was only a short drive to By (the home of Mademoiselle Bonheur). The Empress entered the studio where Mademoiselle Rosa was at work. She arose to receive the visitor, who threw her arms about her neck and kissed her. It was only a short interview. The imperial vision had departed, the rumble of the carriage and the crack of the outriders' whips were lost in the distance. Then, and not till then, did the artist discover that as the Empress had given the kiss, she had pinned upon her blouse the Cross of the Legion of Honor." Since then she has received the Leopold Cross of Honor from the King of Belgium, said to be the first ever conferred upon a woman; also a decoration from the King of Spain. Her brother Auguste, now

ROSA BONHEUR

dead, received the Cross of the Legion of Honor in 1867, two years after Rosa.

In preparing to paint the "Horse Fair" and other similar pictures, which brought her much into the company of men, she found it wise to dress in male costume. A laughable incident is related of this mode of dress. One day when she returned from the country, she found a messenger awaiting to announce to her the sudden illness of one of her young friends. Rosa did not wait to change her male attire, but hastened to the bedside of the young lady. In a few minutes after her arrival, the doctor, who had been sent for, entered, and seeing a young man, as he supposed, seated on the side of the bed, with his arm round the neck of the sick girl, thought he was an intruder, and retreated with all possible speed. "Oh! run after him! He thinks you are my lover, and has gone and left me to die!" cried the sick girl. Rosa flew down stairs, and soon returned with the modest doctor.

She also used this mannish costume for her long journeys over the Pyrenees into Spain or in the Scottish Highlands. She was always accompanied by her most intimate friend, Mademoiselle Micas, herself an artist of repute.

Sometimes in the Pyrenees these two ladies saw no one for six weeks but muleteers with their mules. The people in these lonely mountain passes live entirely upon the curdled milk of sheep. Once Rosa Bonheur and her friend were nearly starving, when Mademoiselle Micas obtained a quantity of frogs, and covering the hind legs with leaves, roasted them over a fire. On these they lived for two days.

In Scotland she painted her exquisite "Denizens of the Mountains," "Morning in the Highlands," and "Crossing a Loch in the Highlands." In England she was treated like a princess. Sir Edwin Landseer, whom some persons thought she would marry, is reported to have said, when he first looked upon her "Horse Fair," "It surpasses me, though it's a little hard to beaten by a woman."

For years she lived in Rue d'Assas, a retired street half made up of gardens. Here she had one of the most beautiful studios of Paris, the room lighted from the ceiling, the walls covered with paintings, with here and there old armor, tapestry, hats, cloaks, sandals, and skins of tigers, leopards, foxes and oxen on the floor. One Friday, the day on which she received guests, one of her friends, coming earlier than usual, found her fast asleep on her favorite skin, that of a magnificent ox, with stuffed head and spreading horns. She had come in tired from the School of Design, and had thrown herself down to rest. Usually after greeting her friends she would say, "Allow me to resume my brush; we can talk just as well together." For those who have any great work to do in this world, there is little time for visiting; interruptions cannot be permitted. No wonder Carlyle groaned when some person had taken two hours of his time. He could better have spared money to the visitor.

For several years Rosa Bonheur lived near Fontainebleau, in the Chateau By. Henry Bacon says: "The chateau dates from the time of Louis XV., and the garden is still laid out in the style of Le Nôtre. Since it has been in the present proprietor's possession, a quaint, picturesque brick building, containing the carriage house and coachman's lodge on the first floor, and the studio on the second, has been added; the roof of the main building has been raised, and the chapel changed into an orangery: beside the main carriage-entrance, which is closed by iron gates and wooden blinds, is a postern gate, with a small grated opening, like those found in convents. The blinds to the gate and the slide to the grating are generally closed, and the only communication with the outside world is by the bell-wire, terminating in a ring beside the gate. Ring, and the jingle of the bell is at once echoed by the barking of numerous dogs,—the hounds and bassets in chorus, the grand Saint Bernard in slow measure, like the bassdrum in an orchestra. After the first excitement among the dogs has begun to abate, a remarkably small house-pet that has been somewhere in the interior arrives upon the scene, and with his sharp, shrill voice again starts and leads the canine chorus. By this time the eagle in his cage has awakened, and the parrot, whose cage is built into the corner of the studio looking upon the street, adds to the racket.

"Behind the house is a large park divided from the forest by a high wall; a lawn and flower-beds are laid out near the buildings; and on the lawn, in pleasant weather, graze a magnificent bull and cow, which are kept as models. In a wire enclosure are two chamois from the Pyrenees, and further removed from the house, in the wooded part of the park, are enclosures for sheep and deer, each of which knows its mistress. Even the stag, bearing its six-branched antlers, receives her caresses like a pet dog. At the end of one of the linden avenues is a splendid bronze, by Isadore Bonheur, of a Gaul attacking a lion.

"The studio is very large, with a huge chimney at one end, the supports of which are life-size dogs, modeled by Isadore Bonheur. Portraits of the father and mother in oval frames hang at each side, and a pair of gigantic horns ornaments the centre. The room is decorated with stuffed heads of animals of various kinds,—boars, bears, wolves, and oxen; and birds perch in every convenient place."

When Prussia conquered France, and swept through this town, orders were given that Rosa Bonheur's home and paintings be carefully preserved. Even her servants went unmolested. The peasants idolized the great woman who lived in the chateau, and were eager to serve her.

The close of her long life found her still quietly and unobtrusively at work. Rosa Bonheur laid down her busy brush at her home on May 25, 1899, but her undying monuments are the marvelous canvases she has given to the world.

HARRIET BEECHER STOWE

In a plain home, in the town of Litchfield, Conn., was born, June 14, 1811, Harriet Beecher Stowe. The house was well-nigh full of little ones before her coming. She was the seventh child, while the oldest was but eleven years old.

Her father, Rev. Lyman Beecher, a man of remarkable mind and sunshiny heart, was preaching earnest sermons in his own and in all the neighboring towns, on the munificent salary of five hundred dollars a year. Her mother, Roxana Beecher, was a woman whose beautiful life has been an inspiration to thousands. With an education superior for those times, she came into the home of the young minister with a strength of mind and heart that made her his companion and reliance.

There were no carpets on the floors till the girl-wife laid down a piece of cotton cloth on the parlor, and painted it in oils, with a border and a bunch of roses and other flowers in the centre. When one of the good deacons came to visit them, the preacher said, "Walk in, deacon, walk in!"

"Why, I can't," said he, " 'thout steppin' on't." Then he exclaimed, in admiration, "D'ye think ye can have all that, *and heaven too?*"

So meagre was the salary for the increasing household, that Roxana urged that a select school be started; and in this she taught French, drawing, painting, and embroidery, besides the higher English branches. With all this work she found time to make herself the idol of her children. While Henry Ward hung round her neck, she

101

made dolls for little Harriet, and read to them from Walter Scott and Washington Irving.

These were enchanting days for the enthusiastic girl with brown curls and blue eyes. She roamed over the meadows, and through the forests, gathering wild flowers in the spring or nuts in the fall, being educated, as she afterwards said, "first and foremost by Nature, wonderful, beautiful, ever-changing as she is in that cloudland, Litchfield. There were the crisp apples of the pink azalea,—honeysuckle-apples, we called them; there were scarlet wintergreen berries; there were pink shell blossoms of trailing arbutus, and feathers of ground pine; there were blue and white and yellow violets, and crowsfoot, and blood root, and wild anemone, and other quaint forest treasures."

A single incident, told by herself in later years, will show the frolic-loving spirit of the girl, and the gentleness of Roxana Beecher. "Mother was an enthusiastic horticulturist in all the small ways that limited means allowed. Her brother John, in New York, had just sent her a small parcel of fine tulip-bulbs. I remember rummaging these out of an obscure corner of the nursery one day when she was gone out, and being strongly seized with the idea that they were good to eat, and using all the little English I then possessed to persuade my brothers that these were onions, such as grown people ate, and would be very nice for us. So we fell to and devoured the whole; and I recollect being somewhat disappointed in the odd, sweetish taste, and thinking that onions were not as nice as I had supposed. Then mother's serene face appeared at the nursery door, and we all ran toward her, and with one voice began to tell our discovery and achievement. We had found this bag of onions and had eaten them all up.

"There was not even a momentary expression of impatience, but she sat down and said, 'My dear children, what you have done makes mamma very sorry; those were not onion roots, but roots of beautiful flowers; and if you had let them alone, ma would have had next summer in the garden, great, beautiful red and yellow flowers, such as you never saw.' I remember how drooping and disappointed we all grew at this picture, and how sadly we regarded the empty paper bag."

When Harriet was five years old, a deep shadow fell upon the happy household. Eight little children were gathered around the bedside of the dying mother. When they cried and sobbed, she told them, with inexpressible sweetness, that "God could do more for them than she had ever done or could do, and that they must trust Him," and urged her six sons to become ministers of the Gospel. When her heart-broken husband repeated to her the verse, "You are now come unto Mount Zion, unto the city of the living God, the heavenly Jerusalem, and to an innumerable company of angels; to the general assembly and church of the first-born, which are written in heaven, and to God the Judge of all, and to the spirits of just men made perfect, and to Jesus the Mediator of the New Covenant," she looked up into his face with a beautiful smile, and closed her eyes forever. That smile Mr. Beecher never forgot to his dying day.

The whole family seemed crushed by the blow. Little Henry (later the great preacher), who had been told that his mother had been buried in the ground, and also that she had gone to heaven, was found one morning digging with all his might under his sister's window, saying, "I'm going to heaven, to find ma."

So much did Mr. Beecher miss her counsel and good judgment, that he sat down and wrote her a long letter, pouring out his whole soul, hoping somehow that she, his guardian angel, though dead, might see it. A year later he wrote a friend: "There is a sensation of loss which nothing alleviates—a solitude which no society interrupts. Amid the smiles and prattle of children, and the kindness of sympathizing friends, I am *alone; Roxana is not here.* She partakes in none of my joys, and bears with me none of my sorrows. I do not murmur; I only feel daily, constantly, and with deepening impression, how much I have had for which to be thankful, and how much I have lost. . . . The whole year after her death was a year of great emptiness, as if there was not motive enough in the world to move me. I used to pray earnestly to God either to take me away, or to restore to me that interest in things and susceptibility to motive I had had before."

Once, when sleeping in the room where she died, he dreamed that Roxana came and stood beside him, and "smiled on me as with a smile from heaven. With that smile," he said, "all my sorrow passed away. I awoke joyful, and I was lighthearted for weeks after."

Harriet went to live for a time with her aunt and grandmother, and then came back to the lonesome home, into which Mr. Beecher had felt the necessity of bringing a new mother. She was a refined and excellent woman, and won the respect and affection of the family. At first Harriet, with a not unnatural feeling of injury, said to her: "Because you have come and married my father, when I am big enough, I mean to go and marry your father"; but she afterwards learned to love her very much.

At seven, with a remarkably retentive memory,—a thing which many of us spoil by trashy reading, or allowing our time and attention to be distracted by the trifles of every-day life,—Harriet had learned twenty-seven hymns and two long chapters of the Bible. She was exceedingly fond of reading, but there was little in a poor minister's library to attract a child. She found

HARRIET BEECHER STOWE

Bell's Sermons, and *Toplady on Predestination.* "Then," she says, "there was a side closet full of documents, a weltering ocean of pamphlets, in which I dug and toiled for hours, to be repaid by disinterring a delicious morsel of a *Don Quixote,* that had once been a book, but was now lying in forty or fifty *dissecta membra,* amid Calls, Appeals, Essays, Reviews, and Rejoinders. The turning up of such a fragment seemed like the rising of an enchanted island out of an ocean of mud." Finally *Ivanhoe* was obtained, and she and her brother George read it through seven times.

At twelve, we find her in the school of Mr. John P. Brace, a well-known teacher, where she developed great fondness for composition. At the exhibition at the close of the year, it was the custom for all the parents to come and listen to the wonderful productions of their children. From the list of subjects given, Harriet had chosen, "Can the Immortality of the Soul be proved by the Light of Nature?"

"When mine was read," she says, "I noticed that father brightened and looked interested. 'Who wrote that composition?' he asked of Mr. Brace. *'Your daughter, sir!'* was the answer. There was no mistaking father's face when he was pleased, and to have interested *him* was past all juvenile triumphs."

A new life was now open to Harriet. Her only sister Catherine a brilliant and noble girl, was engaged to Professor Fisher of Yale College. They were to be married on his return from a European tour, but alas! the *Albion,* on which he sailed, went to pieces on the rocks, and all on board, save one, perished. Her betrothed was never heard from. For months all hope seemed to go out of Catharine's life, and then, with a strong will, she took up a course of mathematical study, *his* favorite study, and Latin under her brother Edward. She was now

twenty-three.   Life was not to be along the pleasant paths
she had hoped, but she must make it tell for the future.

With remarkable energy, she went to Hartford, Conn.,
where her brother was teaching, and thoroughly impressed
with the belief that God had a work for her to do for
girls, she raised several thousand dollars and built the
Hartford Female Seminary.   Her brothers had college
doors opened to them; why, she reasoned, should not
women have equal opportunities?   Society wondered of
what possible use Latin and moral philosophy could be to
girls, but they admired Miss Beecher, and let her do as
she pleased.   Students poured in, and the seminary soon
overflowed.   My own school life in that beloved institution, years afterward, I shall never forget.

And now the little twelve-old Harriet came down from
Litchfield to attend Catharine's school, and soon became
a pupil-teacher, that the burden of support might not
fall too heavily upon the father.   Other children had
come into the Beecher home, and with a salary of eight
hundred dollars, poverty could not be other than a constant attendant.   Once when the family were greatly
straitened for money, while Henry and Charles were in
College, the new mother went to bed weeping, but the
father said, "Well, the Lord always has taken care of
me, and I am sure He always will," and was soon fast
asleep.   The next morning, Sunday, a letter was handed
in at the door, containing a $100 bill, and no name.   It
was a thank-offering for the conversion of a child.

Mr. Beecher, with all his poverty, could not help being
generous.   His wife, by close economy, had saved twenty-
five dollars to buy a new overcoat for him.   Handing him
the roll of bills, he started out to purchase the garment,
but stopped on the way to attend a missionary meeting.
His heart warmed as he stayed, and when the contribu-
tion-box was passed, he put in the roll of bills for the

Sandwich Islanders, and went home with his threadbare coat!

Three years later, Mr. Beecher, who had now become widely known as a revivalist and brilliant preacher, was called to Boston, where he remained for six years. His six sermons on intemperance had stirred the whole country.

Though he loved Boston, his heart often turned toward the great West, and he longed to help save her young men. When, therefore, he was asked to go to Ohio and become the president of Lane Theological Seminary at Cincinnati, he accepted. Singularly dependent upon his family, Catharine and Harriet must needs go with him to the new home. The journey was a toilsome one, over the corduroy roads and across the mountains by stagecoach. Finally they were settled in a pleasant house on Walnut Hills, one of the suburbs of the city, and the sisters opened another school.

Four years later, in 1836, Harriet, now twenty-five, married the professor of biblical criticism and Oriental literature in the seminary, Calvin E. Stowe, a learned and able man.

Meantime the question of slavery had been agitating the minds of Christian people. Cincinnati being near the border-line of Kentucky, was naturally the battle-ground of ideas. Slaves fled into the free State and were helped into Canada by means of the "Underground Railroad," which was in reality only a friendly house about every ten miles, where the colored people could be secreted during the day, and then carried in wagons to the next "station" in the night.

Lane Seminary became a hot-bed of discussion. Many of the Southern students freed their slaves, or helped to establish schools for colored children in Cincinnati, and were disinherited by their fathers in consequence. Dr.

Bailey, a Christian man who attempted to carry on a fair discussion of the question in his paper, had his presses broken twice and thrown into the river. The feeling became so intense, that the houses of free colored people were burned, some killed, and the seminary was in danger from the mob. The members of Professor Stowe's family slept with firearms, ready to defend their lives. Finally the trustees of the college forbade all slavery discussion by the students, and as a result, nearly the whole body left the institution.

Dr. Beecher, meantime, was absent at the East, having raised a large sum of money for the seminary, and came back only to find his labor almost hopeless. For several years, however, he and his children stayed and worked on. Mrs. Stowe opened her house to colored children, whom she taught with her own. One bright boy in her school was claimed by an estate in Kentucky, arrested, and was to be sold at auction. The half-crazed mother appealed to Mrs. Stowe, who raised the needed money among her friends, and thus saved the lad.

Finally, worn out with the "irrepressible conflict," the Beecher family, with the Stowes, came North in 1850, Mr. Stowe accepted a professorship at Bowdoin College, Brunswick, Maine. A few boarders were taken into the family to eke out the limited salary, and Mrs. Stowe earned a little from a sketch written now and then for the newspapers. She had even obtained a prize of fifty dollars for a New England story. Her six brothers had fulfilled their mother's dying wish, and were all in the ministry. She was now forty years old, a devoted mother, with an infant; a hard-working teacher, with her hands full to overflowing. It seemed improbable that she would ever do other than this quiet, unceasing labor. Most women would have said, "I can do no more than I am doing. My way is hedged up to any outside work."

But Mrs. Stowe's heart burned for those in bondage. The Fugitive Slave Law was hunting colored people and sending them back into servitude and death. The people of the North seemed indifferent. Could she not arouse them by something she could write?

One Sunday, as she sat at the communion table in the little Brunswick church, the pattern of Uncle Tom formed itself in her mind, and, almost overcome by her feelings, she hastened home and wrote out the chapter on his death. When she had finished, she read it to her two sons, ten and twelve, who burst out sobbing, "Oh! mamma, slavery is the most cursed thing in the world."

After two or three more chapters were ready, she wrote to Dr. Bailey, who had moved his paper from Cincinnati to Washington, offering the manuscript for the columns of the *National Era,* and it was accepted. Now the matter must be prepared each week. She visited Boston, and at the Anti-Slavery rooms borrowed several books to aid in furnishing facts. And then the story wrote itself out of her full heart and brain. When it neared completion, Mr. Jewett of Boston, through the influence of his wife, offered to become the publisher, but feared if the serial were much longer, it would be a failure. She wrote him that she could not stop till it was done. *Uncle Tom's Cabin* was published March 20, 1852. Then came the reaction in her own mind. Would anybody read this book? The subject was unpopular. It would indeed be a failure, she feared, but she would help the story make its way if possible. She sent a copy of the book to Prince Albert, knowing that both he and Queen Victoria were deeply interested in the subject; another copy to Macaulay, whose father was a friend of Wilberforce; one to Charles Dickens; and another to

Charles Kingsley. And then the busy mother, wife, teacher, housekeeper, and author waited in her quiet Maine home to see what the busy world would say.

In ten days, ten thousand copies had been sold. Eight presses were run day and night to supply the demand. Thirty different editions appeared in London in six months. Six theatres in that great city were playing it at one time. Over three hundred thousand copies were sold in less than a year.

Letters poured in upon Mrs. Stowe from all parts of the world. Prince Albert sent his hearty thanks. Dickens said, "Your book is worthy of any head and any heart that ever inspired a book." Kingsley wrote, "It is perfect." The noble Earl of Shaftesbury wrote, "None but a Christian believer could have produced such a book as yours, which has absolutely startled the whole world. . . . I live in hope—God grant it may rise to faith!— that this system is drawing to a close. It seems as though our Lord had sent out this book as the messenger before His face to prepare His way before Him." He wrote out an address of sympathy "From the women of England to the women of America," to which were appended the signatures of 562,448 women. These were in twenty-six folio volumes, bound in morocco, with the American eagle on the back of each, the whole in a solid oak case, sent to the care of Mrs. Stowe.

The learned reviews gave long notices of *Uncle Tom's Cabin*. *Blackwood's* said, "There are scenes and touches in this book which no living writer that we know can surpass, and perhaps none can equal." George Eliot wrote her beautiful letters.

How the heart of Lyman Beecher must have been gladdened by this wonderful success of his daughter! How Roxana Beecher must have looked down from heaven, and smiled that never-to-be-forgotten smile! How Har-

riet Beecher Stowe herself must have thanked God for this
unexpected fulness of blessing! Thousands of dollars
were soon paid to her as her share of the profits from
the sale of the book. How restful it must have seemed
to the tired, overworked woman, to have more than
enough for daily needs!

The following year, 1853, Professor Stowe and his
now famous wife decided to cross the ocean for needed
rest. What was their astonishment, to be welcomed by
immense public meetings in Liverpool, Glasgow, Edinburgh, Aberdeen, Dundee; indeed, in every city which they
visited. People in the towns stopped her carriage, to fill
it with flowers. Boys ran along the streets, shouting,
"That's her—see the *courls!*" A penny offering was
made her, given by people of all ranks, consisting of one
thousand golden sovereigns on a beautiful silver salver.
When the committee having the matter in charge visited
one little cottage, they found only a blind woman, and
said, "She will feel no interest, as she cannot read the
book."

"Indeed," said the old lady, "if I cannot read, my son
has read it to me, and I've got my penny saved to give."

The beautiful Duchess of Sutherland entertained Mrs.
Stowe at her house, where she met Lord Palmerston, the
Duke of Argyle, Macaulay, Gladstone, and others. The
duchess gave her a solid gold bracelet in the form of a
slave's shackle, with the words, "We trust it is a memorial
of a chain that is soon to be broken." On one link was
the date of the abolition of the slave trade, March 25,
1807, and of slavery in the English territories, August 1,
1834. On the other links are now engraved the dates of
Emancipation in the District of Columbia; President Lincoln's proclamation abolishing slavery in the States in re-
bellion, January 1, 1863; and finally, on the clasp, the date
of the Constitutional amendment, abolishing slavery for-

ever in the United States. Only a decade after *Uncle Tom's Cabin* was written, and nearly all this accomplished! Who could have believed it possible?

On Mrs. Stowe's return from Europe, she wrote *Sunny Memories of Foreign Lands,* which had a large sale. Her husband was now appointed to the professorship of sacred literature in the Theological Seminary at Andover, Mass., and here they made their home. The students found in her a warm-hearted friend, and an inspiration to intellectual work. Other books followed from her pen: *Dred,* a powerful anti-slavery story; *The Minister's Wooing,* with lovely Mary Scudder as its heroine; *Agnes of Sorrento,* an Italian story; the *Pearl of Orr's Island,* a tale of the New England coast; *Old Town Folks; House and Home Papers; My Wife and I; Pink and White Tyranny;* and some others, all of which have been widely read.

The sale of *Uncle Tom's Cabin* has not ceased. It is estimated that over one and a half million copies have been sold in Great Britain and her colonies, and probably an equal or greater number in this country. There have been twelve French editions, eleven German, and six Spanish. It has been published in nineteen different languages,— Russian, Hungarian, Armenian, Modern Greek, Finnish, Welsh, Polish, and others. In Bengal the book is very popular. A lady of high rank in the court of Siam, liberated her slaves, one hundred and thirty in number, after reading this book, and said, "I am wishful to be good like Harriet Beecher Stowe, and never again to buy human bodies, but only to let them go free once more." In France the sale of the Bible was increased because the people wished to read the book Uncle Tom loved so much.

Uncle Tom's Cabin, like *Les Miserables,* and a few other novels, will live, because written with a purpose.

No work of fiction is permanent without some great underlying principle or object.

Soon after the Civil War, Mrs. Stowe bought a home among the orange groves of Florida. With the proceeds of public readings she built a church, in which her husband preached as long as his health permitted.

On Mrs. Stowe's seventy-first birthday, her publishers, gave a garden party in her honor, at the hospitable home of Governor Claflin and his wife, at Newton, Mass. Poets and artists, statesmen and reformers, were invited to meet the famous author. On a stage, under a great tent, she sat, while poems were read and speeches made. The brown curls had become snowy white, and the bright eyes of girlhood had grown deeper and more earnest. The manner was the same as ever, unostentatious, courteous, kindly.

Mrs. Stowe died July 1, 1896 of paralysis in her home at Hartford, Conn., at the age of eighty-five. She passed away as if to sleep, her son, the Rev. Charles Edward Stowe, and her daughters, Eliza and Harriet, standing by her bedside. After the death of her husband, in 1886, Mrs. Stowe had gradually failed physically and mentally. She was buried July 3 in the cemetery connected with the Theological Seminary at Andover, Mass., between the graves of her husband and her son, Henry.

HELEN HUNT JACKSON

THOUSANDS were saddened when, August 12, 1885, it was flashed across the wires that Helen Hunt Jackson was dead. The *Nation* said, "The news will probably carry a pang of regret into more American homes than similar intelligence in regard to any other woman, with the possible exception of Mrs. Harriet Beecher Stowe."

How, with the simple initials, "H. H.," had she won this place in the hearts of the people? Was it because she was a poet? Oh no! many persons of genius have few friends. It was because an earnest life was back of her gifted writings. A great book needs a great man or woman behind it to make it a perfect work. Mrs. Jackson's literary work will be abiding, but her life, with its dark shadows and bright sunlight, its deep affections and sympathy with the oppressed, will furnish a rich setting for the gems of thought which she gave to the world.

Born in the cultured town of Amherst, Mass., October 18, 1831, she inherited from her mother a sunny, buoyant nature, and from her father, Nathan W. Fiske, professor of languages and philosophy in the college, a strong and vigorous mind. Her own vivid description of the "naughtiest day of my life," in *St. Nicholas,* September and October, 1880, shows the ardent, wilful child who was one day to stand out fearlessly before the nation and tell its statesmen the wrong they had done to "her Indians."

She and her younger sister Annie were allowed, by their mother, one April day, to go into the woods just before school hours, to gather checkerberries. Helen, finding the woods very pleasant, determined to spend the day in them, even though sure she would receive a whipping on her return home. The sister could not be coaxed to do wrong, but a neighbor's child, with the promise of seeing live snails with horns, was induced to accompany the truant. They wandered from one forest to another, till hunger compelled them to seek food at a stranger's home. The kind farmer and his wife were going to a funeral, and wished to lock their house; but they took pity on the little ones, and gave them some bread and milk.

"There," said the woman, "now, you just make yourselves comfortable, and eat all you can; and when you're done, you push the bowls in among them lilac-bushes, and nobody'll get 'em."

Urged on by Helen, she and her companion wandered into the village, to ascertain where the funeral was to be held. It was in the meeting-house, and thither they went, and seated themselves on the bier outside the door. Becoming tired of this, they trudged on. One of them lost her shoe in the mud, and stopping at a house to dry their stockings, they were captured by two Amherst professors, who had come over to Hadley to attend the funeral. The children had walked four miles, and nearly the whole town, with the frightened mother, were in search of the runaways. Helen, greatly displeased at being caught, jumped out of the carriage, but was soon retaken. At ten o'clock at night they reached home, and the child walked in as rosy and smiling as possible, saying, "Oh, mother! I've had a perfectly splendid time!"

A few days passed, and then her father sent for her to come into his study, and told her because she had not said she was sorry for running away, she must go into the garret, and wait till he came to see her. Sullen at this punishment, she took a nail and began to bore holes in the plastering. This so angered the professor, that he gave her a severe whipping, and kept her in the garret for a week. It is questionable whether she was more penitent at the end of the week than she was at the beginning.

When Helen was twelve, both father and mother died, leaving her to the care of a grandfather. She was soon placed in the school of the author, Rev. J. S. C. Abbott, of New York, and here some of her happiest days were passed. She grew to womanhood, frank, merry, impulsive, brilliant in conversation, and fond of society.

At twenty-one she was married to a young army officer, Captain, afterward Major, Edward B. Hunt, whom his friends called "Cupid" Hunt from his beauty and his curling hair. He was a brother of Governor Hunt of New York, an engineer of high rank, and a man of fine scientific attainments. They lived much of their time at West Point and Newport, and the young wife moved in a fashionable social circle, and won hosts of admiring friends. Now and then, when he read a paper before some learned society, he was proud to take his vivacious and attractive wife with him.

Their first baby died when he was eleven months old, but another beautiful boy came to take his place, named after two friends, Warren Horsford, but familiarly called "Rennie." He was an uncommonly bright child, and Mrs. Hunt was passionately fond and proud of him. Life seemed full of pleasures. She dressed handsomely, and no wish of her heart seemed ungratified.

Suddenly, like a thunder-bolt from a clear sky, the happy life was shattered. Major Hunt was killed, October 2, 1863, while experimenting in Brooklyn, with a submarine gun of his own invention. The young widow still had her eight-year-old boy, and to him she clung more tenderly than ever, but in less than two years she stood by his dying bed. Seeing the agony of his mother, and forgetting his own fight with that dread destroyer, diphtheria, he said, almost at the last moment, "Promise me, mamma, that you will not kill yourself."

She promised, and exacted from him also a pledge that if it were possible, he would come back from the other world to talk with his mother. He never came, and Mrs. Hunt could have no faith in spiritualism, because what Rennie could not do, she believed to be impossible.

For months she shut herself into her own room, refusing to see her nearest friends. "Any one who really loves me ought to pray that I may die, too, like Rennie," she said. Her physician thought she would die of grief; but when her strong, earnest nature had wrestled with itself and come off conqueror, she came out of her seclusion, cheerful as of old. The pictures of her husband and boy were ever beside her, and these doubtless spurred her on to the work she was to accomplish.

Three months after Rennie's death, her first poem, *Lifted Over*, appeared in the *Nation:*—

"As tender mothers, guiding baby steps,
When places come at which the tiny feet
Would trip, lift up the little ones in arms
Of love, and set them down beyond the harm,
So did our Father watch the precious boy,
Led o'er the stones by me, who stumbled oft
Myself, but strove to help my darling on:
He saw the sweet limbs faltering, and saw
Rough ways before us, where my arms would fail;
So reached from heaven, and lifting the dear child,
Who smiled in leaving me, He put him down
Beyond all hurt, beyond my sight, and bade
Him wait for me! Shall I not then be glad,
And, thanking God, press on to overtake?"

The poem was widely copied, and many mothers were comforted by it. The kind letters she received in consequence were the first gleam of sunshine in the darkened life. If she were doing even a little good, she could live and be strong.

And then began, at thirty-four, absorbing, painstaking literary work. She studied the best models of composition. She said to a friend, years after, "Have you ever tested the advantages of an analytical reading of some writer of finished style? There is a little book called *Out-Door Papers,* by Wentworth Higginson, that is one of the most perfect specimens of literary composition in the English language. It has been my model for years. I go to it as a text-book, and have actually spent hours at a time, taking one sentence after another, and experimenting upon them, trying to see if I could take out a word or transpose a clause, and not destroy their perfection." And again, "I shall never write a sentence, so long as I live, without studying it over from the standpoint of whether you would think it could be bettered."

Her first prose sketch, on a walk up Mt. Washington from the Glen House, appeared in the *Independent,* September 13, 1866; and from this time she wrote for that able journal three hundred and seventy-one articles. She worked rapidly, writing usually with a lead-pencil, on large sheets of yellow paper, but she pruned carefully. Her first poem in the *Atlantic Monthly,* entitled *Coronation,* delicate and full of meaning, appeared in 1869, being taken to Mr. Fields, the editor, by a friend.

At this time she spent a year abroad, principally in Germany and Italy, writing home several sketches. In Rome she became so ill that her life was despaired of. When she was partially recovered, and went away to regain her strength, her friends insisted that a professional nurse should go with her; but she took a hard-working young Italian girl of sixteen, to whom this vacation would be a blessing.

On her return, in 1870, a little book of *Verses* was published. Like most beginners, she was obliged to pay for the stereotyped plates. The book was well received. Emerson liked especially her sonnet, *Thought.* He ranked her poetry above that of all American women, and most American men. Some persons praised the "exquisite musical structure" of the *Gondoliers,* and others read and reread her beautiful *Down to Sleep.* But the world's favorite was *Spinning:*—

> "Like a blind spinner in the sun,
>   I tread my days;
> I know that all the threads will run
>   Appointed ways;
> I know each day will bring its task,
> And, being blind, no more I ask.
>
> .   .   .   .   .   .
>
> "But listen, listen, day by day,
>   To hear their tread
> Who bear the finished web away,
>   And cut the thread,
> And bring God's message in the sun,
> 'Thou poor blind spinner, work is done.'"

After this came two other small books, *Bits of Travel* and *Bits of Talk about Home Matters.* She paid for the plates of the former. Fame did not burst upon Helen Hunt; it came after years of work, after it had been fully earned. The road to authorship is a hard one, and only those should attempt it who have courage and perseverance.

Again her health failed, but not her cheerful spirits. She travelled to Colorado, and wrote a book in praise of it. Everywhere she made lasting friends. Her German landlady in Munich thought her the kindest person in the world. The newsboy, the little urchin on the street with a basketful of wares, the guides over the mountain passes, all remembered her cheery voice and helpful words. She used to say, "She is only half mother who does not see her own child in every child. Oh, if the world could only stop long enough for one generation of mothers to be made all right, what a Millennium could be begun in thirty years!" Some one, in her childhood, called her a "stupid child" before strangers, and she never forgot the sting of it.

In Colorado, in 1876, eleven years after the death of Major Hunt, she married Mr. William Sharpless Jackson, a Quaker and a cultured banker. Her home, at Colorado Springs, became an ideal one, sheltered under the great Manitou, and looking toward the Garden of the Gods, full of books and magazines, of dainty rugs and dainty china gathered from many countries, and richly colored Colorado flowers. Once when Eastern guests were invited to luncheon, twenty-three varieties of wild-flowers, each massed in its own color, adorned the home. A friend of hers says: "There is not an artificial flower in the house, on embroidered table-cover or sofa cushion or tidy; indeed, Mrs. Jackson holds that the manufacture of silken poppies and crewel sun-flowers is a 'respectable industry,' intended only to keep idle hands out of mischief."

Mrs. Jackson loved flowers almost as though they were children. She writes. "I bore on this June day a sheaf of the white columbine,—one single sheaf, one single root; but it was almost more than I could carry. In the open spaces, I carried it on my shoulder; in the thickets, I bore it carefully in my arms, like a baby. . . . There is a part of Cheyenne Mountain which I and one other have come to call 'our garden.' When we drive down from 'our garden,' there is seldom room for another flower in our carriage. The top thrown back is filled, the space in front

HELEN HUNT JACKSON

of the driver is filled, and our laps and baskets are filled with the more delicate blossoms. We look as if we were on our way to the ceremonies of Decoration Day. So we are. All June days are decoration days in Colorado Springs, but it is the sacred joy of life that we decorate, —not the sacred sadness of death." But Mrs. Jackson, with her pleasant home, could not rest from her work. Two novels came from her pen, *Mercy Philbrick's Choice* and *Hetty's Strange History*. It is probable also that she helped to write the beautiful and tender *Saxe Holm Stories*. It is said that *Draxy Miller's Dowry* and *Esther Wynn's Love Letters* were written by another, while Mrs. Jackson added the lovely poems; and when a request was made by the publishers for more stories from the same author, Mrs. Jackson was prevailed upon to write them.

The time had now come for her to do her last and perhaps her best work. She could not write without a definite purpose, and now the purpose that settled down upon her heart was to help the defrauded Indians. She believed they needed education and Christianization rather than extermination. She left her home and spent three months in the Astor Library of New York, writing her *Century of Dishonor,* showing how we have despoiled the Indians and broken our treaties with them. She wrote to a friend, "I cannot think of anything else from night to morning and from morning to night." So untiringly did she work that she made herself ill, and was obliged to go to Norway, leaving a literary ally to correct the proofs of her book.

At her own expense, she sent a copy to each member of Congress. Its plain facts were not relished in some quarters, and she began to taste the cup that all reformers have to drink; but the brave woman never flinched in her duty. So much was the Government impressed by her earnest-

ness and good judgment, that she was appointed a Special
Commissioner with her friend, Abbott Kinney, to exam-
ine and report on the condition of the Mission Indians in
California.

Could an accomplished, tenderly reared woman go
into their *adobe* villages and listen to their wrongs?
What would the world say of its poet? Mrs. Jackson
did not ask; she had a mission to perform, and the more
culture, the more responsibility. She brought cheer and
hope to the red men and their wives, and they called her
"the Queen." She wrote able articles about them in the
Century.

The report made by Mr. Kinney and herself, which she
prepared largely, was clear and convincing. How different all this from her early life! Mrs. Jackson had become more than poet and novelist; even the leader of an
oppressed people. At once, in the winter of 1883, she began to write her wonderfully graphic and tender *Ramona,*
and into this, she said, "I put my heart and soul." The
book was immediately reprinted in England, and has had
great popularity. She meant to do for the Indian what
Mrs. Stowe did for the slave, and she lived long enough
to see the great work well in progress.

This true missionary work had greatly deepened the
earnestness of the brilliant woman. Not always tender to
other people's "hobbies," as she said, she now had one
of her own, into which she was putting her life. Her
horizon, with her great intellectual gifts, had now become
as wide as the universe. Had she lived, how many more
great questions she would have touched.

In June, 1884, falling on the staircase of her Colorado
home, she severely fractured her leg, and was confined to
the house for several months. Then she was taken to
Los Angeles, for the winter months. The broken limb

mended rapidly, but malarial fever set in, and she was carried to San Francisco. Her first remark was, as she entered the house looking out upon the broad and lovely bay, "I did not imagine it was so pleasant! What a beautiful place to die in!"

To the last her letters to her friends were full of cheer. "You must not think because I speak of not getting well that I am sad over it," she wrote. "On the contrary, I am more and more relieved in mind, as it seems to grow more and more sure that I shall die. You see that I am growing old" (she was but fifty-four), "and I do believe that my work is done. You have never realized how, for the past five years, my whole soul has been centered on the Indian question. *Ramona* was the outcome of those five years. The Indian cause is on its feet now; powerful friends are at work."

To another she wrote. "I am heartily, honestly, and cheerfully ready to go. In fact, I am glad to go. My *Century of Dishonor* and *Ramona* are the only things I have done of which I am glad now. The rest is of no moment. They will live, and they will bear fruit. They already have. The change in public feeling on the Indian question in the last three years is marvellous; an Indian Rights Association in every large city in the land."

She had no fear of death. She said, "It is only just passing from one country to another. . . . My only regret is that I have not accomplished more work; especially that it was so late in the day when I began to work in real earnest. But I do not doubt we shall keep on working. . . . There isn't so much difference, I fancy, between this life and the next as we think, nor so much barrier. . . . I shall look in upon you in the new rooms some day; but you will not see me. Good-bye."

Four days before her death she wrote to President Cleveland :—

"From my death-bed I send you a message of heart-felt thanks for what you have already done for the Indians. I ask you to read my *Century of Dishonor*. I am dying happier for the belief I have that it is your hand that is destined to strike the first steady blow toward lifting this burden of infamy from our country, and righting the wrongs of the Indian race."

Thus to the last she forgot self and devoted her strength to the cause of others. That is why the name of Helen Hunt Jackson will live.

LUCRETIA MOTT

Years ago I attended, at some inconvenience, a large public meeting, because I heard that Lucretia Mott was to speak. After several addresses, a slight lady, with white cap and drab Quaker dress, came forward. Though well in years, her eyes were bright; her smile was winsome, and I thought her face one of the loveliest I had ever looked upon. The voice was singularly sweet and clear, and the manner had such naturalness and grace as a queen might envy. I have forgotten the words, forgotten even the subject, but the benign presence and gracious smile I shall never forget.

Born among the quiet scenes of Nantucket, January 3, 1793, Lucretia grew to girlhood with habits of economy, neatness, and helpfulness in the home. Her father, Thomas Coffin, was a sea-captain of staunch principle; her mother, a woman of great energy, wit, and good sense. The children's pleasures were such as a plain country home afforded. When Mrs. Coffin went to visit her neighbors, she would say to her daughters, "Now after you have finished knitting twenty bouts, you may go down cellar and pick out as many as you want of the smallest potatoes,—the very smallest,—and roast them in the ashes." Then the six little folks gathered about the big fireplace and enjoyed a frolic.

When Lucretia was twelve years old, the family moved to Boston. At first all the children attended a private school; but Captain Coffin, fearing this would make them proud, removed them to a public school, where they could "mingle with all classes without distinction." Years after Lucretia said, "I am glad, because it gave me a feeling of sympathy for the patient and struggling poor, which, but for this experience, I might never have known."

A year later, she was sent to a Friends' boarding-school at Nine Partners, N. Y. Both boys and girls attended this school, but were not permitted to speak to each other unless they were near relatives; if so, they could talk a little on certain days over a certain corner of the fence, between the playgrounds! Such grave precautions did not entirely prevent the acquaintance of the young people; for when a lad was shut up in a closet, on bread and water, Lucretia and her sister supplied him with bread and butter under the door. This boy was a cousin of the teacher, James Mott, who was fond of the quick-witted school-girl, so that it is probable that no harm came to her from breaking the rules.

At fifteen, Lucretia was appointed an assistant teacher, and she and Mr. Mott, with a desire to know more of literature, and quite possibly more of each other, began to study French together. He was tall, with light hair and blue eyes, and shy in manner; she, petite, with dark hair and eyes, quick in thought and action, and fond of mirth. When she was eighteen and James twenty-one, the young teachers were married, and both went to her father's home in Philadelphia to reside, he assisting in Mr. Coffin's business.

The war of 1812 brought financial failure to many, and young Mott soon found himself with a wife and infant daughter to support, and no work. Hoping that he could obtain a situation with an uncle in New York State, he took his family thither, but came back disappointed. Finally he found work in a plow store at a salary of six hundred dollars a year.

Captain Coffin meantime had died, leaving his family poor. James could do so little for them all with his limited salary, that he determined to open a small store; but the experiment proved a failure. His health began to be affected by this ill success, when Lucretia, with her brave heart, said, "My cousin and I will open a school; thee must not get discouraged, James."

The school was opened with four pupils, each paying seven dollars a quarter. The young wife put so much good cheer and earnestness into her work, that soon there were forty pupils in the school. Mr. Mott's prospects now brightened, for he was earning one thousand dollars a year. The young couple were happy in their hard work, for they loved each other, and love lightens all care and labor.

But soon a sorrow worse than poverty came. Their only son, Thomas, a most affectionate child, died, saying with his last breath, "I love thee, mother." It was a crushing blow; but it proved a blessing in the end, leading her thoughts heavenward.

A few months afterwards her voice was heard for the first time in public, in prayer, in one of the Friends' meetings. The words were simple, earnest, eloquent. The good Quakers marvelled, and encouraged the "gift." They did not ask whether man or woman brought the message, so it came from heaven.

And now, at twenty-five, having resigned her position as teacher, she began close study of the Bible and theological books. She had four children to care for, did all her sewing, even cutting and making her own dresses; but she learned what every one can learn,—to economize time. Her house was kept scrupulously clean. She says: "I omitted much unnecessary stitching and ornamental work in the sewing for my family, so that I might have more time for the improvement of my mind. For novels and light reading I never had much taste; the ladies' department in the periodicals of the day had no attraction for me." She would lay a copy of William Penn's ponderous volumes open at the foot of her bed, and drawing her chair close to it, with her baby on her lap, would study the book diligently. A woman of less energy and less will-power than young Mrs. Mott would have given up all hope of being a scholar. She read the best books in philosophy and science. John Stuart Mill and Dean Stanley, though widely different, were among her favorite authors.

James Mott was now prospering in the cotton business, so that they could spare time to go in their carriage and speak at the Quaker meetings in the surrounding country. Lucretia would be so absorbed in thought as not to notice the beauties of the landscape, which her husband always greatly enjoyed. Pointing out a fine view to her, she replied, "Yes, it is beautiful, now that thou points it out, but I should not have noticed it. I have always taken more interest in *human* nature." From a child she was deeply interested for the slave. She had read in her school-books Clarkson's description of the slave ships, and these left an impression never to be effaced. When, December 4, 1833, a convention met in Philadelphia for the purpose of forming the American Anti-Slavery Society, Lucretia Mott was one of the four women who braved the social obloquy, as friends of the despised abolitionists. She spoke, and was listened to with attention. Immediately the Philadelphia Female Anti-Slavery Society was formed, and Mrs. Mott became its president and its inspiration. So unheard-of a thing was an association of women, and so unaccustomed were they to the methods of organization, that they were obliged to call a colored man to the chair to assist them.

The years of martyrdom which followed, we at this day can scarcely realize. Anti-slavery lecturers were tarred and feathered. Mobs in New York and Philadelphia swarmed the streets, burning houses and breaking church windows. In the latter city they surrounded the hall of the Abolitionists, where the women were holding a large convention, and Mrs. Mott was addressing them. All day long they cursed and threw stones, and as soon as the women left the building, they burned it to ashes. Then, wrought up to fury, the mob started for the house of James and Lucretia Mott. Knowing that they were coming, the calm woman sent her little children away, and then in the parlor, with a few friends, peacefully awaited a probable death.

In the turbulent throng was a young man who, while he was no friend of the colored man, could not see Lucretia Mott harmed. With skilful ruse, as they neared the house, he rushed up another street, shouting at the top of his voice, "On to Motts!" and the wild crowd blindly followed, wreaking their vengeance in another quarter.

A year later, in Delaware, where Mrs. Mott, was speaking, one of her party, a defenceless old man, was dragged from the house, and tarred and feathered. She followed, begging the men to desist, and saying that she was the real offender, but no violent hands were laid upon her.

At another time, when the annual meeting of the Anti-Slavery Society in New York was broken up by the mob, some of the speakers were roughly handled. Perceiving that several ladies were timid, Mrs. Mott, said to the gentleman who was accompanying her, "Won't thee look after some of the others?"

"But who will take care of you?" he said.

With great tact and a sweet smile, she answered, "This man," laying her hand on the arm of one of the roughest of the mob; "he will see me safe through."

The astonished man had, like others, a tender heart beneath the roughness, and with respectful manner took her to a place of safety. The next day, going into a restaurant, she saw the leader of the mob, and immediately sat down by him, and began to converse. Her kindness and her sweet voice left a deep impression. As he went out of the room, he asked at the door, "Who is that lady?"

"Why, that is Lucretia Mott!"

For a second he was dumbfounded; but he added, "Well, she's a good, sensible woman."

In 1839 a World's Convention was called at London to debate the slavery question. Among the delegates chosen were James and Lucretia Mott, Wendell Phillips and his wife, and others. Mrs. Mott was jubilant at the thought of the world's interest in this great question, and glad for an opportunity to cross the ocean and enjoy a little rest, and the pleasure of meeting friends who had worked in the same cause.

When the party arrived, they were told, to their astonishment, that no women were to be admitted to the Convention as delegates. They had faced mobs and ostracism; they had given money and earnest labor, but they were to be ignored. William Lloyd Garrison, hurt at such injustice, refused to take part in the Convention, and sat in the gallery with the women. Although Mrs. Mott did not speak in the assembly, the *Dublin Herald* said, "Nobody doubts that she was the lioness of the Convention." She was entertained at public breakfasts, and at these spoke with the greatest acceptance to both men and women. The Duchess of Sutherland and Lady Byron showed her great attention. Carlyle was "much pleased with the Quaker lady, whose quiet manner had a soothing effect on him," wrote Mrs. Carlyle to a friend. At Glasgow "she held a delighted audience for nearly two hours in breathless attention," said the press.

After some months of devoted Christian work, along

with sight-seeing, Mr. and Mrs. Mott started homeward. He had spoken less frequently than his wife, but always had been listened to with deep interest. Her heart was moved toward a large number of Irish emigrants in the steerage, and she desired to hold a religious meeting among them. When asked about it, they said they would not hear a woman preacher, for women priests were not allowed in their church. Then she asked that they would come together and consider whether they would have a meeting. This seemed fair, and they came. She explained to them that she did not intend to hold a church service; that, as they were leaving their old homes and seeking new ones in her country, she wanted to talk with them in such a way as would help them in the land of strangers. And then, if they would listen,—they were all at the time listening very eagerly,—she would give an outline of what she had intended to say, if the meeting had been held. At the close, when all had departed, it dawned upon some of the quicker-witted ones that they "had got the preachment from the woman preacher, after all."

The steamer arrived at the close of a twenty-nine days' voyage, and, after a brief rest, Mrs. Mott began again her public work. She spoke before the legislatures of New Jersey, Delaware, and Pennsylvania. She called on President Tyler, and he talked with her cordially and freely about the slave. In Kentucky, says one of the leading papers, "For an hour and a half she enchained an ordinarily restless audience—many were standing—to a degree never surpassed here by the most popular orators. She said some things that were far from palatable, but said them with an air of sincerity that commanded respect and attention."

Mrs. Mott was deeply interested in other questions besides slavery,—suffrage for women, total abstinence, and national differences settled by arbitration instead of war. Years before, when she began to teach school, and found that while girls paid the same tuition as the boys, "when they became teachers, women received only half as much as men for their services," she says: "The injustice of this distinction was so apparent, that I early resolved to claim for myself all that an impartial Creator had bestowed."

In 1848, Mrs. Mott, with Elizabeth Cady Stanton and some others, called the first Woman's Suffrage Convention in this country, at Seneca Falls, N. Y. There was much ridicule,—we had not learned, forty-years ago, to treat with courtesy those whose opinions are different from our own,—but the sweet Quaker preacher went serenely forward, as though all the world were on her side. When she conversed with those who differed, she listened so courteously to objections, and stated her own views so delicately and kindly, and often so wittily, that none could help liking her, even though they did not agree with her. She realized that few can be driven, while many can be won with gentleness and tact.

In all these years of public speaking, her home was not only a refuge for the oppressed, but a delightful social center, where prominent people gathered from both Europe and America. At the table black and white were treated with equal courtesy. One young man, a frequent visitor, finding himself seated at dinner next a colored man, resolved to keep away from the house in future; but as he was in love with one of Mrs. Mott's pretty daughters, he found that his "principles" gave way to his affections. He renewed his visits, became a son-in-law, and, later, was himself an ardent advocate of equality for the colored people.

Now the guests at the hospitable home were a mother

and seven children, from England, who, meeting with disappointments, had become reduced to poverty. Now it was an escaped slave, who had come from Richmond, Virginia, in a dry-goods box, by express. This poor man, whose wife and three children had been sold from him, determined to seek his freedom, even if he died in the effort. Weighing nearly two hundred pounds, he was encased in a box two feet long, twenty-three inches wide, and three feet high, in a sitting posture. He was provided with a few crackers, and a bladder filled with water. With a small gimlet he bored holes in the box to let in fresh air, and fanned himself with his hat, to keep the air in motion. The box was covered with canvas, that no one might suspect its contents. His sufferings were almost unbearable. As the box was tossed from one place to another, he was badly bruised, and sometimes he rested for miles on his head and shoulders, when it seemed as though his veins would burst. Finally he reached the Mott home, and found shelter and comfort.

Their large house was always full. Mr. Mott had given up a prosperous cotton business, because the cotton was the product of slave labor; but he had been equally successful in the wool trade, so that the days of privation had passed by long ago. Two of their six children, with their families, lived at home, and the harmony was remarked by everybody. Mrs. Mott rose early, and did much housework herself. She wrote to a friend: "I prepared mince for forty pies, doing every part myself, even to meat-chopping; picked over lots of apples, stewed a quantity, chopped some more, and made apple pudding; all of which kept me on my feet till almost two o'clock, having to come into the parlor every now and then to receive guests." As a rule, those women are the best house-keepers whose lives are varied by some outside interests.

In the broad hall of the house stood two armchairs, which the children called "beggars' chairs," because they were in constant use for all sorts of people, "waiting to see the missus." She never refused to see anybody.

When letters came from all over the country, asking for all sorts of favors, bedding, silver spoons, a silk umbrella, or begging her to invest some money in the manufacture of an article, warranted "to take the kink out of the hair of the negro," she would always check the merriment of her family by saying, "Don't laugh too much; the poor souls meant well."

Mrs. Mott was now sixty-three years of age. For forty years she had been seen and loved by thousands. Strangers would stop her on the street and say, "God bless you, Lucretia Mott!" Once, when a slave was being tried for running away, Mrs. Mott sat near him in the court, her son-in-law, Mr. Edward Hopper, defending his case. The opposing counsel asked that her chair might be moved, as her face would influence the jury against him! Benjamin H. Brewster, afterwards United States Attorney-General, also counsel for the Southern master, said: "I have heard a great deal of your mother-in-law, Hopper; but I never saw her before to-day. She is an angel." Years after, when Mr. Brewster was asked how he dared to change his political opinions, he replied, "Do you think there is anything I dare not do, after facing Lucretia Mott in that court-room?"

It seemed best at this time, in 1856, as Mrs. Mott was much worn with care, to sell the large house in town and move eight miles into the country, to a quaint, roomy house which they called Roadside. Before they went, however, at the last family gathering a long poem was read, ending with:—

"Who constantly will ring the bell,
And ask if they will please to tell
Where Mrs. Mott has gone to dwell?
    The beggars.

"And who persistently will say,
'We cannot, cannot go away;
Here in the entry let us stay?'
    Colored beggars.

"Who never, never, nevermore
Will see the 'lions' at the door
That they've so often seen before?
    The neighbors.

"And who will miss, for months at least,
That place of rest for man and beast,
From North, and South, and West, and East?
    Everybody."

Much of the shrubbery was cut down at Roadside, that Mrs. Mott might have the full sunlight. So cheery a nature must have sunshine. Here life went on quietly and happily. Many papers and books were on her table, and she read carefully and widely. She loved especially Milton and Cowper. Arnold's *Light of Asia* was a great favorite in her later years. The papers were sent to hospitals and infirmaries, that no good reading might be lost. She liked to read aloud; and if others were busy, she would copy extracts to read them when they were at leisure. Who can measure the power of an educated, intellectual mother in a home?

The golden wedding of Mr. and Mrs. Mott was celebrated in 1861, and a joyous season it was. James, the prosperous merchant, was proud of his gifted wife, and aided her in every way possible; while Lucretia loved and honored the true-hearted husband. Though Mrs.

Mott was now seventy, she did not cease her benevolent work. Her carriage was always full of fruits, vegetables, and gifts for the poor. In buying goods she traded usually with the small stores, where things were dearer, but she knew that for many of the proprietors it was a struggle to make ends meet. A woman so considerate of others would of course be loved.

Once when riding on the street-cars in Philadelphia, when no black person was allowed to ride inside, every fifth car being reserved for their use, she saw a frail-looking and scantily-dressed colored woman, standing on the platform in the rain. The day was bitter cold, and Mrs. Mott begged the conductor to allow her to come inside. "The company's orders must be obeyed," was the reply. Whereupon the slight Quaker lady of seventy walked out and stood beside the colored woman. It would never do to have the famous Mrs. Mott seen in the rain on his car; so the conductor, in his turn, went out and begged her to come in.

"I cannot go in without this woman," said Mrs. Mott quietly. Nonplussed for a moment, he looked at the kindly face, and said, "Oh, well, bring her in then!" Soon the "company's orders" were changed in the interests of humanity, and colored people as well as white enjoyed their civil rights, as becomes a great nation.

With all this beauty of character, Lucretia Mott had her trials. Somewhat early in life she and her husband had joined the so-called Unitarian branch of Quakers, and for this they were persecuted. So deep was the sectarian feeling, that once, when suffering from acute neuralgia, a physician who knew her well, when called to attend her, said, "Lucretia, I am so deeply afflicted by thy rebellious spirit, that I do not feel that I can prescribe for thee," and he left her to her sufferings. Such lack of toleration reads very strangely at this day.

In 1868, Mr. Mott and his wife, the one eighty, and the other seventy-five, went to Brooklyn, N. Y., to visit their grandchildren. He was taken ill of pneumonia, and expressed a wish to go home, but added, "I suppose I shall die here, and then I shall be at home; it is just as well." Mrs. Mott watched with him through the night, and at last, becoming weary, laid her head upon his pillow and went to sleep. In the morning, the daughter coming in, found the one resting from weariness, the other resting forever.

At the request of several colored men, who respected their benefactor, Mr. Mott was borne to his grave by their hands. Thus ended, for this world, what one who knew them well called "the most perfect wedded life to be found on earth."

Mrs. Mott said, "James and I loved each other more than ever since we worked together for a great cause." She carried out the old couplet:—

> "And be this thy pride, what but few have done,
> To hold fast the love thou hast early won."

After his death, she wrote to a friend, "I do not mourn, but rather remember my blessings, and the blessing of his long life with me."

For twelve years she lived and did her various duties. She had seen the slave freed, and was thankful. The other reforms for which she labored were progressing. At eighty-five she still spoke in the great meetings. Each Christmas she carried turkeys, pies, and a gift for each man and woman to the "Aged Colored Home," in Philadelphia, driving twenty miles, there and back. Each year she sent a box of candy to each conductor and brakeman on the North Pennsylvania Railroad, "Because," she said, "they never let me lift out my bundles, but catch them up so quickly, and they all seem to know me."

Finally the time came for her to go to meet James. As the end drew near, she seemed to think that she was conducting her own funeral, and said, as though addressing an audience, "If you resolve to follow the Lamb wherever you may be led, you will find all the ways pleasant and the paths peace. Let me go! Do take me!"

There was a large and almost silent funeral at the house, and at the cemetery several thousand persons were gathered. When friends were standing by the open grave, a low voice said, "Will no one say anything?" and another responded, "Who can speak? the preacher is dead!"

Memorial services were held in various cities. For such a woman as Lucretia Mott, with cultured mind, noble heart, and holy purpose, there are no sex limitations. Her field is the world.

MARY A. LIVERMORE

When a nation passes through a great struggle like our Civil War, great leaders are developed. Had it not been for this, probably Mrs. Livermore, like many other noble women, would have spent her years in some pleasant home, doing the common duties of every-day life, instead of becoming the famous lecturer, the gifted writer, the leader of the Sanitary Commission in the West; a brilliant illustration of the work a woman may do in the world, and still retain the truest womanliness.

She was born in Boston, descended from ancestors who for six generations had been Welsh preachers, and reared by parents of the strictest Calvinistic faith. Mr. Rice, her father, was a man of honesty and integrity, while the mother was a woman of remarkable judgment and common sense.

Mary was an eager scholar, and a great favorite in school, because she took the part of all the poor children. If a little boy or girl was a cripple, or wore shabby clothes, or had scanty dinners, or was ridiculed, he or she found an earnest friend and defender in the courageous girl.

So fond was she of the five children in the home younger than herself, and so much did she take upon herself the responsibility of their conversion, that when but ten years old, unable to sleep, she would rise from her bed and waken her father and mother that they might pray for the sisters, "It's no matter about me," she would say; "if they are saved, I can bear anything."

Mature in thought and care-taking beyond her years, she was still fond of out-of-door sport and merry times.

Sliding on the ice was her especial delight. One day, after a full hour's fun in the bracing air, she rushed into the house, the blood tingling in every vein, exclaiming, "It's splendid sliding!" "Yes," replied the father, "it's good fun, but wretched for shoes."

All at once the young girl saw how hard it was for her parents to buy shoes, with their limited means; and from that day she never again slid upon the ice.

There were few playthings in the simple home, but her chief pastime was in holding meetings in her father's woodshed, with the other children. Great logs were laid out for benches, and split sticks were set upon them for people. Mary was always the leader, both in praying and preaching, and the others were good listeners. Mrs. Rice would be so much amused at the queer scene, that a smile would creep over her face; but Mr. Rice would look on reverently, and say, "I wish you had been a boy; you could have been trained for the ministry."

When she was twelve years old she began to be eager to earn something. She could not bear to see her father work so hard for her. Alas! how often young women, twice twelve, allow their father's hair to grow white from overwork, because they think society will look down upon them if they labor. Is work more a disgrace to a girl than a boy? Not at all. Unfortunate is the young man who marries a girl who is either afraid or ashamed to work.

Though not fond of sewing, Mary decided to learn dressmaking, because this would give her self-support. For three months she worked in a shop, that she might learn the trade, and then she stayed three months longer and earned thirty-seven cents a day. As this seemed meagre, she looked about her for more work. Going to a clothing establishment, she asked for a dozen red flannel shirts to make. The proprietor might have wondered

who the child was, but he trusted her honest face, and
gave her the bundle. She was to receive six and a quarter
cents apiece, and to return them on a certain day. Working night after night, sometimes till the early morning
hours, she was able to finish only half at the time speci-
fied.

On that day a man came to the door and asked, "Does
Mary Rice live here?"

The mother had gone to the door, and answered in the
affirmative.

"Well, she took a dozen red flannel shirts from my shop
to make, and she hain't returned 'em!"

"It can't be my daughter," said Mrs. Rice.

The man was sure he had the right number, but he
looked perplexed. Just then Mary, who was in the sitting-room, appeared on the scene.

"Yes, mother, I got these shirts of the man."

"You promised to get 'em done, Miss," he said, "and
we are in a great hurry."

"You shall have the shirts to-morrow night," said Mrs.
Rice.

After the man left the house, the mother burst into
tears, saying, "We are not so poor as that. My dear
child, what is to become of you if you take all the cares
of the world upon your shoulders?"

When the work was done, and the seventy-five cents received, Mary would take only half of it, because she had
earned but half.

A brighter day was dawning for Mary Rice. A little
later, longing for an education, Dr. Meale, their good minister, encouraged and assisted her to go to the Charles-
town Female Seminary. Before the term closed one of
the teachers died, and the bright, earnest pupil was asked
to fill the vacancy. She accepted, reciting out of school
to fit herself for her classes, earning enough by her teach-

ing to pay her way, and taking the four years' course in two years. Before she was twenty she taught two years on a Virginia plantation as a governess, and came North with six hundred dollars and a good supply of clothes. She had never felt so rich in her life.

She was now asked to take charge of the Duxbury High School, where she became an inspiration to her scholars. Even the dullest learned under her enthusiasm. She took long walks to keep up her health and spirits, thus making her body as vigorous as her heart was sympathetic.

It was not to be wondered at that the bright young teacher had many admirers. Who ever knew an educated, genial girl who was not a favorite with young men? It is a libel on the sex to think that they prefer ignorant or idle girls.

Among those who saw the beauty of character and the mental power of Miss Rice was a young minister, whose church was near her schoolhouse. The first time she attended his services, he preached from the text, "And thou shalt call his name Jesus; for he shall save his people from their sins." Her sister had died, and the family were in sorrow; but this gospel of love, which he preached with no allusion of eternal punishment, was full of comfort. What was the minister's surprise to have the young lady ask to take home the sermon and read it, and afterwards, some of his theological books. What was the teacher's surprise, a little later, to find that while she was interested in his sermons and books, he had become interested in her. The sequel can be guessed easily; she became the wife of Rev. D. P. Livermore at twenty-three.

He had idolized his mother; very naturally, with deep reverence for women, he would make a devoted husband. For fifteen years the intelligent wife aided him in editing *The New Covenant*, a religious paper published in Chicago, in which city they had made their home. Her writings were always clear, strong, and helpful. Three children had been born into their home, and life, with its cares and its work, was a very happy one.

But the time came for the quiet life to be entirely changed. In 1861 the nation found itself plunged into war. The slave question was to be settled once for all at the point of the bayonet. Like every other true-hearted woman, Mrs. Livermore had been deeply stirred by passing events. When Abraham Lincoln's call for seventy-five thousand men was eagerly responded to, she was in Boston, and saw the troops, all unused to hardships, start for the battle-fields. The streets were crowded with tens of thousands. Bells rang, bands played, and women smiled and said good-bye, when their hearts were breaking. After the train moved out of the station, four women fainted; nature could no longer bear the terrible strain. Mrs. Livermore helped restore the women to consciousness. She had no sons to send; but when such partings were seen, and such sorrows were in the future, she could not rest.

What could women do to help in the dreadful struggle? A meeting of New York ladies was called, which resulted in the formation of an Aid Society, pledging loyalty to the Government, and promising assistance to soldiers and their families. Two gentlemen were sent to Washington to ask what work could be done, but word came back that there was no place for women at the front, nor no need for them in the hospitals. Such words were worse than wasted on American women. Since the day when men and women together breasted the storms of New England in the Mayflower, and together planted a new civilization, together they have worked side by side in all great matters. They were untiring in the Revolutionary War; they worked faithfully in the dark days of anti-slavery agitation, taking their very lives in their hands. And now their husbands and sons and brothers had gone from their homes. They would die on battle-fields, and in lonely camps untended, and the women simply said, "Some of us must follow our best-beloved."

The United States Sanitary Commission was soon organized, for working in hospitals, looking after camps, and providing comforts for the soldiers. Branch associations were formed in ten large cities. The great Northwestern Branch was put under the leadership of Mrs. Livermore and Mrs. A. H. Hoge. Useful things began to pour in from all over the country—fruits, clothing, bedding, and all needed comforts for the army. Then Mrs. Livermore, now a woman of forty, with great executive ability, warm heart, courage, and perseverance, with a few others, went to Washington to talk with President Lincoln.

"Can no women go to the front?" they asked.

"No civilian, either man or woman, is permitted by *law*," said Mr. Lincoln. But the great heart of the greatest man in America was superior to the law, and he placed not a straw in their way. He was in favor of anything which helped the men who fought and bled for their country.

Mrs. Livermore's first broad experience in the war was after the battle of Fort Donelson. There were no hospitals for the men, and the wounded were hauled down the hillside in rough-board Tennessee wagons, most of them dying before they reached St. Louis. Some poor fellows lay with the frozen earth around them, chopped out after lying in the mud from Saturday morning until Sunday evening.

One blue-eyed lad of nineteen, with both legs and both arms shattered, when asked, "How did it happen that you were left so long?" said, "Why, you see, they couldn't

MARY A. LIVERMORE

stop to bother with us, *because they had to take the fort.*
When they took it, we forgot our sufferings, and all over
the battle-field cheers went up from the wounded, and
even from the dying."

At the rear of the battle-fields the Sanitary Commission now began to keep its wagons with hot soup and hot
coffee, women, fitly chosen, always joining in this work,
in the midst of danger. After the first repulse at Vicks-
burg, there was great sickness and suffering. The Commission sent Mrs. Hoge, two gentlemen accompanying
her, with a boat-load of supplies for the sick. One emaci-
ated soldier, to whom she gave a little package of white
sugar, with a lemon, some green tea, two herrings, two
onions, and some pepper, said, "Is that *all* for me?" She
bowed assent. She says: "He covered his pinched face
with his thin hands and burst into a low, sobbing cry.
I laid my hand upon his shoulder, and said, 'Why do you
weep?' 'God bless the women!' he sobbed out. 'What
should we do but for them? I came from father's farm,
where all knew plenty; I've lain sick these three months;
I've seen no woman's face, nor heard her voice, nor felt
her warm hand till to-day, and it unmans me; but don't
think I rue my bargain, for I don't. I've suffered much
and long, but don't let them know at home. Maybe I'll
never have a chance to tell them how much; but I'd go
through it all for the old flag.' "

Shortly after, accompanied by an officer, she went into
the rifle-pits. The heat was stifling, and the minie-balls
were whizzing. "Why, madam, where did you come
from? Did you drop from heaven into these rifle-pits?
You are the first lady we have seen here"; and then the
voice was choked with tears.

"I have come from your friends at home, and bring
messages of love and honor. I have come to bring you
the comforts we owe you, and love to give. I've come

to see if you receive what they send you," she replied.

"Do you think as much of us as that? Why, boys, we can fight another year on that, can't we?"

"Yes, yes!" they cried, and almost every hand was raised to brush away the tears.

She made them a kindly talk, shook the hard, honest hands, and said good-bye. "Madam," said the officer, "promise me that you'll visit my regiment to-morrow; 'twould be worth a victory to them. You don't know what good a lady's visit to the army does. These men whom you have seen to-day will talk of your visit for six months to come. Around the fires, in the rifle-pits, in the dark night, or on the march, they will repeat your words, describe your looks, voice, size, and dress; and all agree in one respect,—that you look like an angel, and exactly like each man's wife or mother." Ah! was there no work for women to do?

The Sanitary and Christian Commissions expended about fifty million dollars during the war, and of this, the women raised a generous portion. Each battle cost the Sanitary Commission about seventy-five thousand dollars, and the Battle of Gettysburg, a half million dollars. Mrs. Livermore was one of the most efficient helpers in raising this money. She went among the people, and solicited funds and supplies of every kind.

One night it was arranged that she should speak in Dubuque, Iowa, that the people of that State might hear directly from their soldiers at the front. When she arrived, instead of finding a few women as she had expected, a large church was packed with both men and women eager to listen. The governor of the State and other officials were present. She had never spoken in a mixed assembly. Her conservative training made her shrink from it, and, unfortunately, made her feel incapable of doing it.

"'I cannot speak!' she said to the women who had asked her to come.

Disappointed and disheartened, they finally arranged with a prominent statesman to jot down the facts from her lips; and then, as best he could, tell to the audience the experiences of the woman who had been on battle-fields, amid the wounded and dying. Just as they were about to go upon the platform, the gentleman said, "Mrs. Livermore, I have heard you say at the front, that you would give your all for the soldiers,—a foot, a hand, or a voice. Now is the time to give your voice, if you wish to do good."

She meditated a moment, and then she said, "I will try."

When she arose to speak, the sea of faces before her seemed blurred. She was talking into blank darkness. She could not even hear her own voice. But as she went on, and the needs of the soldiers crowded upon her mind, she forgot all fear, and for two hours held the audience spell-bound. Men and women wept, and patriotism filled every heart. At eleven o'clock eight thousand dollars were pledged, and then, at the suggestion of the presiding officer, they remained until one o'clock to perfect plans for a fair, from which they cleared sixty thousand dollars. After this, Mrs. Livermore spoke in hundreds of towns, helping to organize many of the more than twelve thousand aid societies formed during eighteen months.

As money became more and more needed, Mrs. Livermore decided to try a sanitary commission fair in Chicago. The women said, "We will raise twenty-five thousand dollars," but the men laughed at such an impossibility. The farmers were visited, and solicited to give vegetables and grain, while the cities were not forgotten. Fourteen of Chicago's largest halls were hired. The women had gone into debt ten thousand dollars, and the men of the city began to think they were crazy. The Board of Trade called upon them and advised that the fair be given up; the debts should be paid, and the men would give the twenty-five thousand, when, in their judgment, it was needed! The women thanked them courteously, but pushed forward in the work.

It had been arranged that the farmers should come on the opening day, in a procession, with their gifts of vegetables. Of this plan the newspapers made great sport, calling it the "potato procession." The day came. The school children had a holiday, the bells were rung, one hundred guns were fired, and the whole city gathered to see the "potato procession." Finally it arrived,—great loads of cabbages, onions, and over four thousand bushels of potatoes. The wagons each bore a motto, draped in black, with the words, "We buried a son at Donelson," "Our father lies at Stone River," and other similar ones. The flags on the horses' heads were bound with black; the women who rode beside a husband or son, were dressed in deep mourning. When the procession stopped before Mrs. Livermore's house, the jeers were over, and the dense crowd wept like children.

Six of the public halls were filled with beautiful things for sale, while eight were closed so that no other attractions might compete with the fair. Instead of twenty-five thousand, the women cleared one hundred thousand dollars.

Then Cincinnati followed with a fair, making two hundred and twenty-five thousand; Boston, three hundred and eighty thousand; New York, one million; and Philadelphia, two hundred thousand more than New York. The women had found that there was work enough for them to do.

Mrs. Livermore was finally ordered to make a tour of the hospitals and military posts on the Mississippi River, and here her aid was invaluable. It required a remarkable woman to undertake such a work. At one point she found twenty-three men, sick and wounded, whose regiments had left them, and who could not be discharged because they had no descriptive lists. She went at once to General Grant, and said, "General, if you will give me authority to do so, I will agree to take these twenty-three wounded men home."

The officials respected the noble woman, and the red tape of army life was broken for her sake. When the desolate company arrived in Chicago, on Saturday, the last train had left which could have taken a Wisconsin soldier home. She took him to the hotel, had a fire made for him, and called a doctor.

"Pull him through till Monday, Doctor," she said, "and I'll get him home." Then, to the lad, "You shall have a nurse, and Monday morning I will go with you to your mother."

"Oh, don't go away," he pleaded; "I never shall see you again."

"Well, then, I'll go home and see my family, and come back in two hours. The door shall be left open, and I'll put this bell beside you, so that the chambermaid will come when you ring."

He consented, and Mrs. Livermore came back in two hours. The soldier's face was turned toward the door, as though waiting for her, but he was dead. He had gone home, but not to Wisconsin.

After the close of the war, so eager were the people to hear her, that she entered the lecture field and for years held the foremost place among women as a public speaker. She lectured five nights a week, for five months, travelling twenty-five thousand miles each year. Her fine voice, womanly, dignified manner, and able thought brought crowded houses before her, year after year.

Mrs. Livermore spent ten years in the temperance reform. While she showed the dreadful results of the liquor traffic, she was kind both in word and deed. Passing along a Boston street, she saw a man in the ditch, and a poor woman bending over him.

"Who is he?" she asked of the woman.

"He's my husband, ma'am. He's a good man when he's sober, and earns four dollars a day in the foundry. I keep a saloon."

Mrs. Livermore called a hack. "Will you carry this man to number——?"

"No, madam, he's too dirty. I won't soil my carriage."

"Oh!" pleaded the wife, "I'll clean it all up for ye, if ye'll take him," and pulling off her dress-skirt, she tried to wrap it around her husband. Stepping to a saloon near by, Mrs. Livermore asked the men to come out and help lift him. At first they laughed, but were soon made ashamed, when they saw that a lady was assisting. The drunken man was gotten upon his feet, wrapped in his wife's clothing, put into the hack, and then Mrs. Livermore and the wife got in beside him, and he was taken home. The next day the good Samaritan called, and brought the priest, from whom the man took the pledge. A changed family was the result.

Her life was filled with thousands of acts of kindness, on the cars, in the poor homes, and in various charitable institutions. She was the author of two books, *What Shall We Do with Our Daughters?* and *Reminiscences of the War;* but her especial power was her eloquent words, spoken all over the country, in pulpits, before colleges, in city and country, from the Atlantic to the Pacific Coast.

Like Abraham Lincoln, who said, "I go for all sharing the privileges of the government, who assist in bearing its burdens,—by no means excluding women," she advocated the enfranchisement of her sex, along with her other work.

Mrs. Livermore died at her home, at Melrose, Mass. May 23, 1905, of bronchitis. She was in her eighty-fourth year, and had survived her husband six years. When her funeral services were held, the schools of Melrose closed, business was suspended, bells were tolled, and flags floated at half-mast. Her death came as a summons to well-earned rest, after a singularly useful life.

MARGARET FULLER OSSOLI

MARGARET FULLER, in some respects the most remarkable of American women, lived a pathetic life and died a tragic death. Without money and without beauty, she became the idol of an immense circle of friends; men and women were alike her devotees. It is the old story: that the woman of brain makes lasting conquests of hearts, while the pretty face holds its sway only for a month or a year.

Margaret, born in Cambridgeport, Mass., May 23, 1810, was the oldest child of a scholarly lawyer, Mr. Timothy Fuller, and a sweet-tempered, devoted mother. The father, with small means, had one absorbing purpose in life,—to see that each of his children was finely educated. To do this, and to make ends meet, was a struggle. His daughter said, years after, in writing of him: "His love for my mother was the green spot on which he stood apart from the commonplaces of a mere bread-winning existence. She was one of those fair and flower-like natures, which sometimes spring up even beside the most dusty highways of life. Of all persons whom I have known, she had in her most of the angelic,—of that spontaneous love for every living thing, for man and beast and tree, which restores the Golden Age."

Very fond of his oldest child, Margaret, the father determined that she should be as well educated as his boys. In those days there were no colleges for girls, and none where they might enter with their brothers, so that Mr. Fuller was obliged to teach his daughter after the wearing work of the day.   The bright child began to read Latin at six, but was necessarily kept up late for the recitation. When a little later she was walking in her sleep, and dreaming strange dreams, he did not see that he was over-taxing both body and brain.   When the lessons had been learned, she would go into the library, and read eagerly. One Sunday afternoon, when she was eight years old, she took down Shakespeare from the shelves, opened at *Romeo and Juliet,* and soon became fascinated with the story.

"What are you reading?" asked her father.

"Shakespeare," was the answer, not lifting her eyes from the page.

"That won't do—that's no book for Sunday; go put it away, and take another."

Margaret did as she was bidden; but the temptation was too strong, and the book was soon in her hands again.

"What is that child about, that she doesn't hear a word we say?" said an aunt.

Seeing what she was reading, the father said, angrily, "Give me the book, and go directly to bed."

There could have been a wiser and gentler way of control, but he had not learned that it is better to lead children than to drive them.

When not reading, Margaret enjoyed her mother's little garden of flowers.   "I loved," she says, "to gaze on the roses, the violets, the lilies, the pinks; my mother's hand had planted them, and they bloomed for me.   I kissed them, and pressed them to my bosom with passionate emotions.   An ambition swelled my heart to be as beautiful, as perfect as they."

Margaret grew to fifteen with an exuberance of life and affection, which the chilling atmosphere of that New England home somewhat suppressed, and with an increasing love for books and cultured people.   "I rise a little

before five," she writes, "walk an hour, and then practise
on the piano till seven, when we breakfast. Next, I read
French—Sismondi's *Literature of the South of Europe*—
till eight; then two or three lectures in Brown's *Philosophy*. About half past nine I go to Mr. Perkin's school,
and study Greek till twelve, when, the school being dismissed, I recite, go home, and practise again till dinner,
at two. Then, when I can, I read two hours in Italian."

And why all this hard work for a girl of fifteen? The
"all-powerful motive of ambition," she says. "I am determined on distinction, which formerly I thought to win
at an easy rate; but now I see that long years of labor
must be given."

She had learned the secret of most prominent lives.
The majority in this world will always be mediocre, because they lack high-minded ambition and the willingness
to work.

Two years after, at seventeen, she writes: "I am
studying Madame de Staël, Epictetus, Milton, Racine,
and the Castilian ballads, with great delight. . . . I am
engrossed in reading the elder Italian poets, beginning
with Berni, from whom I shall proceed to Pulci and Poli-
tan." How almost infinitely above "beaus and dresses"
was such intellectual work as this!

It was impossible for such a girl not to influence the
mind of every person she met. At nineteen she became
the warm friend of Rev. James Freeman Clarke, "whose
friendship," he says, "was to me a gift of the gods. . . .
With what eagerness did she seek for knowledge! What
fire, what exuberance, what reach, grasp, overflow of
thought, shone in her conversation! . . . And what she
thus was to me, she was to many others. Inexhaustible
in power of insight, and with a good will 'broad as ether,'
she could enter into the needs, and sympathize with the
various excellences, of the greatest variety of characters.

One thing only she demanded of all her friends, that they should not be satisfied with the common routine of life, —that they should aspire to something higher, better, holier, than they had now attained."

Witty, learned, imaginative, she was conceded to be the best conversationalist in any circle. She possessed the charm that every woman may possess,—appreciation of others, and interest in their welfare. This sympathy unlocked every heart to her. She was made the confidante of thousands. All classes loved her. Now it was a serving girl who told Margaret her troubles and her cares; now it was a distinguished man of letters. She was always an inspiration. Men never talked idle, commonplace talk with her; she could appreciate the best of their minds and hearts, and they gave it. She was fond of social life, and no party seemed complete without her.

At twenty-two she began to study German, and in three months was reading with ease Goethe's *Faust, Tasso and Iphigenia,* Körner, Richter, and Schiller. She greatly admired Goethe, desiring, like him, "always to have some engrossing object of pursuit." Besides all this study she was teaching six little children, to help bear the expenses of the household.

The family at this time moved to Gorton, a great privation for Margaret, who enjoyed and needed the culture of Boston society. But she says, "As, sad or merry, I must always be learning, I laid down a course of study at the beginning of the winter." This consisted of the history and geography of modern Europe, and of America, architecture, and the works of Alfieri, Goethe, and Schiller. The teaching was continued because her brothers must be sent to Harvard College, and this required money; not the first nor the last time that sisters have worked to give brothers an education superior to their own.

At last the constitution, never robust, broke down, and for nine days Margaret lay hovering between this world and the next. The tender mother called her "dear lamb," and watched her constantly, while the stern father, who never praised his children, lest it might harm them, said, "My dear, I have been thinking of you in the night, and I cannot remember that you have any *faults*. You have defects, of course, as all mortals have, but I do not know that you have a single fault."

While Margaret recovered, the father was taken suddenly with cholera, and died after a two days' illness. He was sadly missed, for at heart he was devoted to his family. When the estate was settled, there was little left for each; so for Margaret life would be more laborious than ever. She had expected to visit Europe with Harriet Martineau, who was just returning home from a visit to this country, but the father's death crushed this long-cherished and ardently-prayed-for journey. She must stay at home and work for others.

Books were read now more eagerly than ever,—*Sartor Resartus,* Coleridge, Wordsworth, and Heine. But money must be earned. Ah! if genius could only develop in ease and prosperity. It rarely has the chance. The tree grows best when the dirt is oftenest stirred about the roots; perhaps the best in us comes only from such stirring.

Margaret now obtained a situation as teacher of French and Latin in Bronson Alcott's school. Here she was appreciated by both master and pupils. Mr. Alcott said, "I think her the most brilliant talker of the day. She has a quick and comprehensive wit, a firm command of her thoughts, and a speech to win the ear of the most cultivated." She taught advanced classes in German and Italian, besides having several private pupils.

Before this time she had become a valued friend of the

Emerson famiy. Mr. Emerson says, "Sometimes she stayed a few days, often a week, more seldom a month, and all tasks that could be suspended were put aside to catch the favorable hour in walking, riding, or boating, to talk with this joyful guest, who brought wit, anecdotes, love-stories, tragedies, oracles with her. . . . The day was never long enough to exhaust her opulent memory and I, who knew her intimately for ten years, never saw her without surprise at her new powers."

She was passionately fond of music and of art, saying, "I have been very happy with four hundred and seventy designs of Raphael in my possession for a week." She loved nature like a friend, paying homage to rocks and woods and flowers. She said, "I hate not to be beautiful when all around is so."

After teaching with Mr. Alcott, she became the principal teacher in a school at Providence, R. I. Here, as ever, she showed great wisdom both with children and adults. The little folks in the house were allowed to look at the gifts of many friends in her room, on condition that they should not touch them. One day a young visitor came, and insisted on taking down a microscope, and broke it. The child who belonged in the house was well-nigh heart-broken over the affair, and, though protesting her innocence, was suspected both of the deed and of falsehood. Miss Fuller took the weeping child upon her knee, saying, "Now, my dear little girl, tell me all about it; only remember that you must be careful, for I shall believe every word you say." Investigation showed that the child thus confided in told the whole truth.

After two years in Providence she returned to Boston, and in 1839 began a series of parlor lectures, or "conversations," as they were called. This seemed a strange thing for a woman, when public speaking by her sex was almost unknown. These talks were given weekly, from eleven o'clock till one, to twenty-five or thirty of the most cultivated women of the city.   Now the subject of discussion was Grecian mythology; now it was fine arts, education, or the relations of woman to the family, the church, society, and literature.   These meetings were continued through five winters, supplemented by evening "conversations," attended by both men and women.   In these gatherings Margaret was at her best,—brilliant, eloquent, charming.

During this time a few gifted men, Emerson, Channing, and others decided to start a literary and philosophical magazine called the *Dial*.   Probably no woman in the country would have been chosen as the editor, save Margaret Fuller.   She accepted the position, and for four years managed the journal ably, writing for it some valuable essays.   Some of these were published later in her book on *Literature and Art*.   Her *Woman in the Nineteenth Century,* a learned and vigorous essay on woman's place in the world, first appeared in part in the *Dial*. Of this work, she said, in closing it, "After taking a long walk, early one most exhilarating morning, I sat down to work, and did not give it the last stroke till near nine in the evening.   Then I felt a delightful glow, as if I had put a good deal of my true life in it, and as if, should I go away now, the measure of my footprint would be left on the earth."

Miss Fuller had published, besides these works, two books of translations from the German, and a sketch of travel called *Summer on the Lakes*.   Her experience was like that of most authors who are beginning,—some fame, but no money realized.   All this time she was frail in health, overworked, struggling against odds to make a living for herself and those she loved.   But there were some compensations in this life of toil.   One person wrote her, "What I am I owe in large measure to the stimulus you imparted. You roused my heart with high hopes; you raised my aims from paltry and vain pursuits to those which lasted and fed the soul; you inspired me with a great ambition, and made me see the worth and the meaning of life."

William Hunt, the renowned artist, was looking in a book that lay on the table of a friend. It was Mrs. Jameson's *Italian Painters.* In describing Correggio, she said he was "one of those superior beings of whom there are so few." Margaret had written on the margin, "And yet all might be such." Mr. Hunt said, "These words struck out a new strength in me. They revived resolutions long fallen away, and made me set my face like a flint."

Margaret was now thirty-four. The sister was married, the brothers had finished their college course, and she was about to accept an offer from the *New York Tribune* to become one of its constant contributors, an honor that few women had ever received. Early in December, 1844, Margaret moved to New York and became a member of Mr. Greeley's family. Her literary work here was that of, says Mr. Higginson, "the best literary critic whom America has yet seen."

Sometimes her reviews, like those on the poetry of Longfellow and Lowell, were censured, but she was impartial and able. Society opened wide its doors to her, as it had in Boston. Mrs. Greeley became her devoted friend, and their little son "Pickie," five years old, the idol of Mr. Greeley, her restful playmate.

A year and a half later an opportunity came for Margaret to go to Europe. Now, at last, she would see the art-galleries of the old world, and places rich in history, like Rome. Still there was the trouble of scanty means, and poor health from overwork. She said, "A noble career is yet before me, if I can be unimpeded by cares.

If our family affairs could now be so arranged that I
might be tolerably tranquil for the next six or eight years,
I should go out of life better satisfied with the page I
have turned in it than I shall if I must still toil on."

After two weeks on the ocean, the party of friends arrived in London, and Miss Fuller received a cordial welcome. Wordsworth, now seventy-six, showed her the
lovely scenery of Rydal Mount, pointing out as his especial pride, his avenue of hollyhocks—crimson, straw-
color, and white. De Quincey showed her many courtesies. Dr. Chalmers talked eloquently, while William and
Mary Howitt seemed like old friends. Carlyle invited
her to his home. "To interrupt him," she said, "is a
physical impossibility. If you get a chance to remons-
trate for a moment, he raises his voice and bears you
down."

In Paris, Margaret attended the Academy lectures, saw
much of George Sand, waded through melting snow at
Avignon to see Laura's tomb, and at last was in Italy, the
country she had longed to see. Here Mrs. Jameson, Powers, and Greenough, and the Brownings and Storys, were
her warm friends. Here she settled down to systematic
work, trying to keep her expenses for six months within
four hundred dollars. Still, when most cramped for
means herself, she was always generous. Once, when
living on a mere pittance, she loaned fifty dollars to a
needy artist. In New York she gave an impecunious
author five hundred dollars to publish his book, and, of
course, never received a dollar in return. Yet the race for
life was wearing her out. So tired was she that she
said, "I should like to go to sleep, and be born again into
a state where my young life should not be prematurely
taxed."

Meantime the struggle for Italian unity was coming
to its climax. Mazzini and his followers were eager for

a republic. Pius IX, had given promises to the Liberal party, but afterwards abandoned it, and fled to Gaeta. Then Mazzini turned for help to the President of the French Republic, Louis Napoleon, who, in his heart, had no love for republics, but sent an army to reinstate the Pope. Rome, when she found herself betrayed, fought like a tiger. Men issued from the workshops with their tools for weapons, while women from the housetops urged them on. One night over one hundred and fifty bombs were thrown into the heart of the city.

Margaret was the friend of Mazzini, and enthusiastic for Roman liberty. All those dreadful months she administered to the wounded and dying in the hospitals, and was their "saint," as they called her. But there was another reason why Margaret Fuller loved Italy.

Soon after her arrival in Rome, as she was attending vespers at St. Peter's with a party of friends, she became separated from them. Failing to find them, seeing her anxious face, a young Italian came up to her, and politely offered to assist her. Unable to regain her friends, Angelo Ossoli walked with her to her home, though he could speak no English, and she almost no Italian. She learned afterward that he was of a noble and refined family; that his brothers were in the Papal army, and that he was highly respected.

After this he saw Margaret once or twice, before she left Rome for some months. On her return, he renewed the acquaintance, shy and quiet though he was for her influence seemed great over him. His father, the Marquis Ossoli, had just died, and Margaret, with her large heart, sympathized with him, as she alone knew how to sympathize. He joined the Liberals, thus separating himself from his family, and was made a captain of the Civic Guard.

Finally he confessed to Margaret that he loved her,

and that he "must marry her or be miserable." She refused to listen to him as a lover, said he must marry a younger woman,—she was thirty-seven, and he but thirty,—but she would be his friend. For weeks he was dejected and unhappy. She debated the matter with her own heart. Should she, who had had many admirers, now marry a man her junior, and not of surpassing intellect, like her own? If she married him, it must be kept a secret till his father's estate was settled, for marriage with a Protestant would spoil all prospect of an equitable division.

Love conquered, and she married the young Marquis Ossoli in December, 1847. He gave to Margaret the kind of love which lasts after marriage, veneration of her ability and her goodness. "Such tender, unselfish love," writes Mrs. Story, "I have rarely before seen; it made green her days, and gave her an expression of peace and serenity which before was a stranger to her. When she was ill, he nursed and watched over her with the tenderness of a woman. No service was too trivial, no sacrifice too great for him. 'How sweet it is to do little things for you,' he would say."

To her mother Margaret wrote, though she did not tell her secret, "I have not been so happy since I was a child, as during the last six weeks."

But days of anxiety soon came, with all the horrors of war. Ossoli was constantly exposed to death, in that dreadful siege of Rome. Then Rome fell, and with it the hopes of Ossoli and his wife. There would be neither fortune nor home for a Liberal now—only exile. Very sadly Margaret said good-bye to the soldiers in the hospitals, brave fellows whom she honored, who in the midst of death itself, would cry "Viva l' Italia!"

But before leaving Rome, a day's journey must be made to Rieta, at the foot of the Umbrian Apennines.

And for what? The most precious thing of Margaret's life was there,—her baby. The fair child, with blue eyes and light hair like her own, had already been named by the people in the house, Angelino, from his beauty. She had always been fond of children. Emerson's Waldo, for whom *Threnody* was written was an especial favorite; then "Pickie," Mr. Greeley's beautiful boy, and now a new joy had come into her heart, a child of her own. She wrote to her mother: "In him I find satisfaction, for the first time, to deep wants of my heart. Nothing but a child can take the worst bitterness out of life, and break the spell of loneliness. I shall not be alone in other worlds whenever Eternity may call me. . . . I wake in the night,—I look at him. He is so beautiful and good, I could die for him!"

When Ossoli and Margaret reached Rieta, what was their horror to find their child worn to a skeleton, half starved through the falsity of a nurse. For four weeks the distressed parents coaxed him back to life, till the sweet beauty of the rounded face came again, and then they carried him to Florence, where, despite poverty and exile, they were happy.

"In the morning," she says, "as soon as dressed, he signs to come into our room; then draws our curtain with his little dimpled hand, kisses me rather violently, and pats my face. . . . I feel so refreshed by his young life, and Ossoli diffuses such a power and sweetness over every day, that I cannot endure to think yet of our future. . . . It is very sad we have no money, we could be so quietly happy a while. I rejoice in all Ossoli did; but the results, in this our earthly state, are disastrous, especially as my strength is now so impaired. This much I hope, —in life or death, to be no more separated from Angelino."

Margaret's friends now urged her return to America.

She had nearly finished a history of Rome in this trying time, 1848, and could better attend to its publication in this country. Ossoli, though coming to a land of strangers, could find something to help support the family.

To save expense, they started from Leghorn, May 17, 1850, in the *Elizabeth,* a sailing vessel, though Margaret dreaded the two months' voyage, and had premonitions of disaster. She wrote: "I have a vague expectation of some crisis,—I know not what. But it has long seemed that, in the year 1850, I should stand on a plateau in the ascent of life, when I should be allowed to pause for a while, and take more clear and commanding views than ever before. Yet my life proceeds as regularly as the fates of a Greek tragedy, and I can but accept the pages as they turn. . . . I shall embark, praying fervently that it may not be my lot to lose my boy at sea, either by unsolaced illness, or amid the howling waves; or, if so, that Ossoli, Angelo, and I may go together, and that the anguish may be brief."

For a few days all went well on shipboard; and then the noble Captain Hasty died of small-pox, and was buried at sea. Angelino took this dread disease, and for a time his life was despaired of, but he finally recovered, and became a great pet with the sailors. Margaret was putting the last touches to her book. Ossoli and young Sumner, brother of Charles, gave each other lessons in Italian and English, and thus the weeks went by.

On Thursday, July 18, after two months, the *Elizabeth* stood off the Jersey Coast, between Cape May and Barnegat. Trunks were packed, good-nights were spoken, and all were happy, for they would be in New York on the morrow. At nine that night a gale arose; at midnight it was a hurricane; at four o'clock, Friday morning, the ship struck Fire Island beach. The passengers sprang from their berths. "We must die!" said Sumner to Mrs. Hasty. "Let us die calmly, then!" was the response of the widow of the captain.

At first, as the billows swept over the vessel, Angelino, wet and afraid, began to cry; but his mother held him closely in her arms and sang him to sleep. Noble courage on a sinking ship! The Italian girl who had come with them was in terror; but after Ossoli prayed with her, she became calm. For hours they waited anxiously for help from the shore. They could see the life-boat, and the people collecting the spoils, which had floated thither from the ship, but no relief came. One sailor and another sprang into the waves and saved themselves. Then Sumner jumped overboard, but sank.

One of the sailors suggested that if each passenger sat on a plank, holding on by ropes, they would attempt to push him or her to land. Mrs. Hasty was the first to venture, and after being twice washed off, half-drowned, reached the shore. Then Margaret was urged, but she hesitated, unless all three could be saved. Every moment the danger increased. The crew were finally ordered "to save themselves," but four remained with the passengers. It was useless to look longer to the people on shore for help, though it was now past three o'clock,—twelve hours since the vessel struck.

Margaret had finally been induced to try the plank. The steward had taken Angelino in his arms, promising to save him or die with him, when a strong sea swept the forecastle, and all went down together. Ossoli caught the rigging for a moment, but Margaret sank at once. When last seen, she was seated at the foot of the foremast, still clad in her white nightdress, with her hair fallen loose upon her shoulders. Angelino and the steward were washed upon the beach twenty minutes later, both dead, though warm.   Margaret's prayer was answered,—that they "might go together, and that the anguish might be brief."

The pretty boy of two years was dressed in a child's frock taken from his mother's trunk, which had come to shore, laid in a seaman's chest, and buried in the sand, while the sailors, who loved him, stood around, weeping. His body was finally removed to Mt. Auburn, and buried in the family lot.   The bodies of Ossoli and Margaret were never recovered.   The only papers of value which came to shore were their love letters, now deeply prized. The book ready for publication was never found.

When those on shore were asked why they did not launch the life-boat, they replied, "Oh! if we had known there were any such persons of importance on board, we should have tried to do our best!"

Thus, at forty, died one of the most gifted women in America, when her work seemed just begun.   To us, who see how the world needed her, her death is a mystery; to Him who "worketh all things after the counsel of His own will" there is no mystery.   She filled her life with charities and her mind with knowledge, and such are ready for the progress of Eternity.

MARIA MITCHELL

In the quiet, picturesque island of Nantucket, in a simple home, lived William and Lydia Mitchell with their family of ten children. William had been a school-teacher, beginning when he was eighteen years of age, and receiving two dollars a week in winter, while in summer he kept soul and body together by working on a small farm, and fishing.

In this impecunious condition he had fallen in love with and married Lydia Coleman, a true-hearted Quaker girl, a descendant of Benjamin Franklin, one singularly fitted to help him make his way in life. She was quick, intelligent, and attractive in her usual dress of white, and was a clerk of the Friends' meeting where he attended. She was enthusiastic in reading, becoming librarian successively of two circulating libraries, till she had read every book upon the shelves, and then in the evenings repeating what she had read to her associates, her young lover among them.

When they were married, they had nothing but warm hearts and willing hands to work together. After a time William joined his father in converting a ship-load of whale oil into soap, and then a little money was made; but at the end of seven years he went back to school-teaching because he loved the work. At first he had charge of a fine grammar school established at Nantucket, and later, of a school of his own.

Into this school came his third child, Maria, shy and retiring, with all her mother's love of reading. Faithful at home, with, as she says, "an endless washing of dishes," not to be wondered at where there were ten little folks, she was not less faithful at school. The teacher could not help seeing that his little daughter had a mind which would well repay all the time he could spend upon it.

While he was a good school-teacher, he was an equally good student of nature, born with a love of the heavens above him. When eight years old, his father called him to the door to look at the planet Saturn, and from that time the boy calculated his age from the position of the planet, year by year. Always striving to improve himself, when he became a man, he built a small observatory upon his own land, that he might study the stars. He was thus enabled to earn one hundred dollars a year in the work of the United States Coast Survey. Teaching at two dollars a week, and fishing, could not always cramp a man of such aspiring mind.

Brought up beside the sea, he was as broad as the sea in his thought and true nobility of character. He could see no reason why his daughters should not be just as well educated as his sons. He therefore taught Maria the same as his boys, giving her especial drill in navigation. Perhaps it is not strange that, after such teaching, his daughter could have no taste for making worsted work or Kensington stitches. She often says to this day, "A woman might be learning seven languages while she is learning fancy work," and there is little doubt that the seven languages would make her seven times more valuable as a wife and mother. If teaching navigation to girls would give us a thousand Maria Mitchells in this country, by all means let it be taught.

Maria left the public school at sixteen, and for a year attended a private school; then, loving mathematics, and being deeply interested in her father's studies, she became at seventeen his helper in the work of the Coast Survey. This astronomical labor brought Professors Agassiz,

Bache, and other noted men to the quiet Mitchell home, and thus the girl heard the stimulating conversation of superior minds.

But the family needed more money. Though Mr. Mitchell wrote articles for *Silliman's Journal,* and delivered an able course of lectures before a Boston society of which Daniel Webster was president, scientific study did not put many dollars in a man's pocket. An elder sister was earning three hundred dollars yearly by teaching and Maria felt that she too must help more largely to share the family burdens. She was offered the position of librarian at the Nantucket library, with a salary of sixty dollars the first year, and seventy-five the second. While a dollar and twenty cents a week seemed very little, there would be much time for study, for the small island did not afford a continuous stream of readers. She accepted the position, and for twenty years, till youth had been lost in middle life, Maria Mitchell worked for one hundred dollars a year, studying on, that she might do her noble work in the world.

Did not she who loved nature, long for the open air and the blue sky, and for some days of leisure which so many girls thoughtlessly waste? Yes, doubtless. However, the laws of life are as rigid as mathematics. A person cannot idle away the hours and come to prominence. No great singer, no great artist, no great scientist, comes to honor without continuous labor. Society devotees are heard of only for a day or a year, while those who develop minds and ennoble hearts have lasting remembrance.

Miss Mitchell says, "I was born of only ordinary capacity, but of extraordinary persistency," and herein is the secret of a great life. She did not dabble in French or music or painting and give it up; she went steadily on to success. Did she neglect home duties? Never. She knit stockings a yard long for her aged father till his death, usually studying while she knit. To those who learn to be industrious early in life, idleness is never enjoyable.

There was another secret of Miss Mitchell's success. She read good books early in life. She says: "We always had books, and were bookish people. There was a public library in Nantucket before I was born. It was not a free library; but we always read and studied from it. I remember among its volumes Hannah More's books and Rollin's *Ancient History.* I remember, too, that Charles Folger, the present Secretary of the Treasury, and I had both read this latter work through before we were ten years old, though neither of us spoke of it to the other until a later period."

All this study had made Miss Mitchell a superior woman. It was not strange, therefore, that fame should come to her. One autumn night, October, 1847, she was gazing through the telescope, as usual, when, lo! she was startled to perceive an unknown comet. She at once told her father, who thus wrote to Professor William C. Bond, director of the Observatory at Cambridge:—

My DEAR FRIEND,—I write now merely to say that Maria discovered a telescopic comet at half-past ten on the evening of the first instant, at that hour nearly above Polaris five degrees. Last evening it had advanced westerly; this evening still further, and nearing the pole. It does not bear illumination. Maria has obtained its right ascension and declination, and will not suffer me to announce it. Pray tell me whether it is one of Georgi's, and whether it has been seen by anybody. Maria supposes it may be an old story. If quite convenient, just drop a line to her; it will oblige me much. I expect to leave home in a day or two, and shall be in Boston next week, and I would like to have her hear from you before I can meet you. I hope it will not give thee much trouble amidst thy close engagements. Our regards are to all of you most truly.

WILLIAM MITCHELL.

The answer showed that Miss Mitchell had indeed made a new discovery. Frederick VI., King of Denmark, had, sixteen years before, offered a gold medal of the value of twenty ducats to whomever should discover a telescopic comet. That no mistake might be made as to the real discoverer, the condition was made that word be sent at once to the Astronomer Royal of England. This the Mitchells had not done, on account of their isolated position. Hon. Edward Everett, then President of Harvard College, wrote to the American Minister at the Danish Court, who in turn presented the evidence to the King. "It would gratify me," said Mr. Mitchell, "that this generous monarch should know that there is a love of science even in this, to him, remote corner of the earth."

The medal was at last awarded, and the woman astronomer of Nantucket found herself in the scientific journals and in the press as the discoverer of "Miss Mitchell's Comet." Another had been added to the list of Mary Somervilles and Caroline Herschels. Perhaps there was additional zest now in the mathematical work in the Coast Survey. She also assisted in compiling the *American Nautical Almanac,* and wrote for the scientific periodicals. Did she break down from her unusual brain work! Oh, no! Probably astronomical work was not nearly so hard as her mother's,—care of a house and ten children!

For ten years more Miss Mitchell worked in the library, and in studying the heavens. But she had longed to see the observatories of Europe, and the great minds outside their quiet island. Therefore, in 1857, she visited England, and was at once welcomed to the most learned circles. Brains always find open doors. Had she been rich or beautiful simply, Sir John Herschel, and Lady Herschel as well, would not have reached out both hands, and said, "You are always welcome at this house," and given her some of his own calculations and some of his Aunt Caroline's writing. Had she been rich or handsome simply, Alexander Von Humboldt would not have taken her to his home, and, seating himself beside her on the sofa, talked as she says, "on all manner of subjects, and on all varieties of people. He spoke of Kansas, India, China, observatories; of Bache, Maury, Gould, Ticknor, Buchanan, Jefferson, Hamilton, Brunow, Peters, Encke, Airy, Leverrier, Mrs. Somerville, and a host of others."

What if he had said these things to some women who go abroad! It is prudent for women who travel to read widely, for ignorance is quickly detected.

Miss Mitchell said of Humboldt: "He is handsome— his hair is thin and white, his eyes very blue. He is a little deaf, and so is Mrs. Somerville. He asked me what instruments I had, and what I was doing; and when I told him that I was interested in the variable stars, he said I must go to Bonn and see Agelander."

There was no end of courtesies to the scholarly woman. Professor Adams, of Cambridge, who, with his charming wife, years afterward helped to make our own visit to the University a delight, showed her the spot on which he made his computations for Neptune, which he discovered at the same time as Leverrier. Sir George Airy, the Astronomer Royal of England, wrote to Leverrier in Paris to announce her coming. When they met, she said, "His English was worse than my French."

Later she visited Florence, where she met, several times, Mrs. Somerville, who, she says, "talks with all the readiness and clearness of a man," and is still "very gentle and womanly, without the least pretence or the least coldness." She gave Miss Mitchell two of her books, and desired a photographed star sent to Florence. "She had never heard of its being done, and saw at once the importance of such a step." She said with her Scotch accent, "Miss Mitchell, ye have done yeself great credit."

In Rome she saw much of the Hawthornes, of Miss Bremer, who was visiting there, and of the artists. From here she went to Venice, Vienna, and Berlin, where she met Encke, the astronomer, who took her to see the wedding presents of the Princess Royal.

Mrs. Julia Ward Howe, in an admirable sketch of Miss Mitchell, tells how the practical woman, with her love of republican institutions, was impressed. "The presents were in two rooms," says Miss Mitchell, "ticketed and numbered, and a catalogue of them sold. All the manufacturing companies availed themselves of the opportunity to advertise their commodities, I suppose, as she had presents of all kinds. What she will do with sixty albums I can't see, but I can understand the use of two clothes-lines, because she can lend one to her mother, who must have a large Monday's wash."

After a year, Miss Mitchell returned to her simple Nantucket home, as devoted to her parents and her scientific work as ever. Two years afterward, in 1860, her good mother died, and a year later, desiring to be near Boston, the family removed to Lynn. Here Miss Mitchell purchased a small house for sixteen hundred and fifty dollars. From her yearly salary of one hundred dollars, and what she could earn in her government work, she had saved enough to buy a home for her father! The rule is that the fathers wear themselves out for daughters; the rule was reversed in this case.

Miss Mitchell now earned five hundred dollars yearly for her government computations, while her father received a pension of three hundred more for his efficient services. Five years thus passed quietly and comfortably.

Meanwhile another life was carrying out its cherished plan, and Miss Mitchell, unknowingly, was to have an important part in it. Soon after the Revolutionary War there came to this country an English wool-grower and his family, who settled on a little farm near the Hudson River. The mother, a hard-working and intelligent woman, was eager in her help toward earning a living, and would drive her farm-wagon to market, with butter and eggs, and fowls, while her seven-year-old boy sat beside her. To increase the income some English ale was brewed. The lad grew up with an aversion to making beer, and when fourteen, his father insisting that he should enter the business, his mother helped him to run away. Tying all his worldly possessions, a shirt and a pair of stockings, in a cotton handkerchief, the mother and her boy walked eight miles below Poughkeepsie when, giving him all the money she had, seventy-five cents, she kissed him, and with tears in her eyes saw him cross the ferry and land safely on the other side. He trudged on till a place was found in a country store, and here, for five years, he worked honestly and industriously, coming home to his now reconciled father with one hundred and fifty dollars in his pocket.

Changes had taken place. The father's brewery had burned, the oldest son had been killed in attempting to save something from the wreck, all were poorer than ever, and there seemed nothing before the boy of nineteen but to help support the parents, his two unmarried sisters, and two younger brothers. Whether he had the old dislike for the ale business or not, he saw therein a means of support, and adopted it. The world had not then thought so much about the misery which intoxicants cause, and had not learned that we are better off without stimulants than with them.

Every day the young man worked in his brewery, and

in the evening till midnight tended a small oyster house, which he had opened. Two years later, an Englishman who had seen Matthew Vassar's untiring industry and honesty, offered to furnish all the capital which he needed. The long, hard road, of poverty had opened at last into a field of plenty. Henceforward, while there was to be work and economy, there was to be continued prosperity, and finally, great wealth.

Realizing his lack of early education, he began to improve himself by reading science, art, history, poetry, and the Bible. He travelled in Europe, and being a close observer, was a constant learner.

One day, standing by the great London hospital, built by Thomas Guy, a relative, and endowed by him with over a million dollars, Mr. Vassar read these words on the pedestal of the bronze statue:—

SOLE FOUNDER OF THE HOSPITAL IN HIS LIFETIME

The last three words left a deep impression on his mind. He had no children. He desired to leave his money where it would be of permanent value to the world. He debated many plans in his own mind. It is said that his niece, a hard-working teacher, Lydia Booth, finally influenced him to his grand decision.

There was no real college for women in the land. He talked the matter over with his friends, but they were full of discouragements. "Women will never desire college training," said some. "They will be ruined in health, if they attempt it," said others. "Science is not needed by women; classical education is not needed; they must have something appropriate to their sphere," was constantly reiterated. Some wise heads thought they knew just what that education should be, and just what were the limits of woman's sphere; but Matthew Vassar had his own thoughts.

Calling together, February 26, 1861, some twenty or thirty of the men in the State most conversant with educational matters, the white-haired man, now nearly seventy, laid his hand upon a round tin box, labelled "Vassar College Papers," containing four hundred thousand dollars in bonds and securities, and said: "It has long been my desire, after suitably providing for those of my kindred who have claims upon me, to make such a disposition of my means as should best honor God and benefit my fellowmen. It is my hope to be the instrument in the hands of Providence, of founding and perpetuating an institution which shall accomplish for young women what our colleges are accomplishing for young men."

For four years Matthew Vassar watched the great buildings take form and shape in the midst of two hundred acres of lake and river and green sward, near Poughkeepsie; the main building, five hundred feet long, two hundred broad, and five stories high; the museum of natural history, with school of art and library; the great observatory, three stories high, furnished with the then third largest telescope in the country.

In 1865 Vassar College was opened, and three hundred and fifty students came pouring in from all parts of the land. Girls, after all, did desire an education equal to that of young men. Matthew Vassar was right. His joy seemed complete. He visited the college daily, and always received the heartiest welcome. Each year his birthday was celebrated as "Founder's Day." On one of these occasions he said: "This is almost more happiness than I can bear. This one day more than repays me for all I have done."

After the observatory was completed, there was but one wish as to who should occupy it; of course, the person desired was Maria Mitchell. She hesitated to accept the position. Her father was seventy and needed her care, but he said, "Go, and I will go with you." So she left her Lynn home for the arduous position of a teacher. For four years Mr. Mitchell lived to enjoy the enthusiastic work of his gifted daughter. He said, "Among the teachers and pupils I have made acquaintances that a prince might covet."

Miss Mitchell made the observatory her home. Here were her books, her pictures, her great astronomical clock, and a bust of Mrs. Somerville, the gift of Frances Power Cobbe. Here for twenty years she helped to make Vassar College known and honored both at home and abroad. Hundreds were drawn thither by her name and fame. A friend of mine who went, intending to stay two years, remained five, for her admiration of and enjoyment in Miss Mitchell. She testified: "She is one of the few genuine persons I have ever known. There is not one particle of deceit about her. For girls who accomplish something she has great respect; for idlers, none. She has no sentimentality, but much wit and common sense. No one can be long under her teaching without learning dignity of manner and self-reliance."

In the succeeding years the astronomer's fame steadily increased. In 1868, in the great meteoric shower, she and her pupils recorded the paths of four thousand meteors, and gave valuable data of their height above the earth. In the summer of 1869 she joined the astronomers who went to Burlington, Iowa, to observe the total eclipse of the sun, August 7. Her observations on the transit of Venus were also valuable. She wrote on the *Satellites of Saturn,* and also prepared a work on the *Satellites of Jupiter.*

In 1873 she again visited Europe, spending some time with the family of the Russian astronomer, Professor Sturve, at the Imperial Observatory at Pultowa.

Miss Mitchell resigned her position at Vassar in 1888

on account of failing health. She died on the morning of June 28, 1889 at Lynn, Mass., at the age of seventy-one. She was an honor to her sex, a striking example of what a quiet country girl could accomplish, without financial or other aid than her indomitable will.

LOUISA M. ALCOTT

A DOZEN of us sat about the dinner-table at the Hotel Bellevue, Boston. One was the gifted wife of a gifted clergyman; one had written two or three novels; one was a journalist; one was on the eve of a long journey abroad; and one, whom we were all glad to honor, was the brilliant author of *Little Women*. She had a womanly face, bright, gray eyes, that looked full of merriment, and would not see the hard side of life, and an air of common sense that made all defer to her judgment. She told witty stories of the many who wrote her for advice or favors, and good-naturedly gave bits of her own personal experience. Nearly twenty years before, I had seen her, just after her *Hospital Sketches* were published, over which I, and thousands of others, had shed tears. Though but thirty years old then, Miss Alcott looked frail and tired. That was the day of her struggle with life. Now, at fifty, she looked happy and comfortable. The desire of her heart had been realized,—to do good to tens of thousands, and earn enough money to care for those whom she loved.

Louisa Alcott's life, like that of so many famous women, had been full of obstacles. She was born in Germantown, Pa., November 29, 1832, in the home of an extremely lovely mother and cultivated father, Amos Bronson Alcott. Beginning life poor, his desire for knowledge led him to obtain an education and become a teacher. In 1830 he married Miss May, a descendant of the well-known Sewells and Quincys, of Boston. Louise Chandler Moulton says, in her excellent sketch of Miss

Alcott, "I have heard that the May family were strongly opposed to the union of their beautiful daughter with the penniless teacher and philosopher"; but he made a devoted husband, though poverty was long their guest.

For eleven years, mostly in Boston, he was the earnest and successful teacher. Margaret Fuller was one of his assistants. Everybody respected his purity of life and his scholarship. His kindness of heart made him opposed to corporal punishment, and in favor of self-government. The world had not come then to his high ideal, but has been creeping toward it ever since, until whipping, both in schools and homes, is fortunately becoming one of the lost arts.

He believed in making studies interesting to pupils; not the dull, old-fashioned method of learning by rote, whereby, when a hymn was taught, such as, "A Charge to Keep I Have," the children went home to repeat to their astonished mothers, "Eight yards to keep I have," having learned by ear, with no knowledge of the meaning of the words. He had friendly talks with his pupils on all great subjects; and some of these Miss Elizabeth Peabody, the sister of Mrs. Hawthorne, so greatly enjoyed, that she took notes, and compiled them in a book.

New England, always alive to any theological discussion, at once pronounced the book unorthodox. Emerson had been through the same kind of a storm, and bravely came to the defence of his friend. Another charge was laid at Mr. Alcott's door: he was willing to admit colored children to his school, and such a thing was not countenanced, except by a few fanatics (so-called) like Whittier, and Phillips, and Garrison. The heated newspaper discussion lessened the attendance at the school; and finally, in 1839, it was discontinued, and the Alcott family moved to Concord.

Here were gifted men and women with whom the philosopher could feel at home, and rest. Here lived Emerson, in the two-story drab house, with horsechestnut-trees in front of it. Here lived Thoreau, near his beautiful Walden Lake, a restful place, with no sound save, perchance, the dipping of an oar or the note of a bird, which the lonely man loved so well. Here he built his house, twelve feet square, and lived for two years and a half, giving to the world what he desired others to give, —his inner self. Here was his bean-field, where he "used to hoe from five o'clock in the morning till noon," and made, as he said, an intimate acquaintance with weeds, and a pecuniary profit of eight dollars seventy-one and one-half cents! Here, too, was Hawthorne, "who," as Oliver Wendell Holmes says, "brooded himself into a dream-peopled solitude."

Here Mr. Alcott could live with little expense and teach his four daughters. Louisa, the eldest, was an active, enthusiastic child, getting into little troubles from her frankness and lack of policy, but making friends with her generous heart. Who can ever forget Jo in *Little Women,* who was really Louisa, the girl who, when reproved for whistling by Amy, the art-loving sister, says: "I hate affected, niminy-piminy chits! I'm not a young lady; and if turning up my hair makes me one, I'll wear it in two tails till I'm twenty. I hate to think I've got to grow up, and be Miss March, and wear long gowns, and look as prim as a china-aster! It's bad enough to be a girl, anyway, when I like boy's games and work and manners!"

At fifteen, "Jo was very tall, thin, and brown, and reminded one of a colt; for she never seemed to know what to do with her long limbs, which were very much in her way. She had a decided mouth, a comical nose, and sharp, gray eyes, which appeared to see everything, and were by turns fierce or funny or thoughtful. Her long,

thick hair was her one beauty, but it was usually bundled
into a net to be out of her way.   Round shoulders had
Jo, and big hands and feet, a fly-away look to her clothes,
and the uncomfortable appearance of a girl who was
rapidly shooting up into a woman and didn't like it."

The four sisters lived a merry life in the Concord
haunts, notwithstanding their scanty means.   Now, at the
dear mother's suggestion, they ate bread and milk for
breakfast, that they might carry their nicely prepared meal
to a poor woman, with six children, who called them
Engel-kinder, much to Louisa's delight.   Now they improvised a stage, and produced real plays, while the
neighbors looked in and enjoyed the fun.

Louisa was especially fond of reading Shakespeare,
Goethe, Emerson, Margaret Fuller, Miss Edgeworth, and
George Sand.   As early as eight years of age she wrote
a poem of eight lines, *To a Robin,* which her mother
carefully preserved, telling her that "if she kept on in
this hopeful way, she might be a second Shakespeare in
time."   Blessings on those people who have a kind smile
or a word of encouragement as we struggle up the hard
hills of life!

At thirteen she wrote *My Kingdom.*   When, years afterward, Mrs. Eva Munson Smith wrote to her, asking
for some poems for *Woman in Sacred Song,* Miss Alcott sent her this one, saying, "It is the only hymn I
ever wrote.   It was composed at thirteen, and as I still
find the same difficulty in governing my kingdom, it still
expresses my soul's desire, and I have nothing better to
offer."

> "A little kingdom I possess
>   Where thoughts and feelings dwell,
> And very hard the task I find
>   Of governing it well;
> For passion tempts and troubles me,

A wayward will misleads,
And selfishness its shadow casts
On all my words and deeds."

Louisa was very imaginative, telling stories to her sisters and her mates, and at sixteen wrote a book for Miss Ellen Emerson, entitled *Flower Fables*. It was not published till six years later, and then, being florid in style, did not bring her any fame. She was now anxious to earn her support. She was not the person to sit down idly and wait for marriage, or for some rich relation to care for her; but she determined to make a place in the world for herself. She says in *Little Women,* "Jo's ambition was to do something very splendid; what it was she had no idea, as yet, but left it for time to tell her," and at sixteen the time had come to make the attempt.

She began to teach school with twenty pupils. Instead of the theological talks which her father gave his scholars, she told them stories, which she says made the one pleasant hour in her school-day. Now the long years of work had begun—fifteen of them—which should give the girl such rich yet sometimes bitter experiences, that she could write the most fascinating books from her own history. Into her volume called *Work,* published when she had become famous, she put many of her own early sorrows in those of "Christie."

Much of this time was spent in Boston. Sometimes she cared for an invalid child; sometimes she was a governess; sometimes she did sewing, adding to her slender means by writing late at night. Occasionally she went to the house of Rev. Theodore Parker, where she met Emerson, Sumner, Garrison, and Julia Ward Howe. Emerson always had a kind word for the girl whom he had known in Concord, and Mr. Parker would take her by the hand and say, "How goes it, my child? God bless you; keep your heart up, Louisa," and then she would go home to her lonely room, brave and encouraged.

At nineteen, one of her early stories was published in *Gleason's Pictorial,* and for this she received five dollars. How welcome was this brain-money! Some months later she sent a story to the *Boston Saturday Gazette,* entitled *The Rival Prima Donnas,* and, to her great delight, received ten dollars; and what was almost better still, a request from the editor for another story. Miss Alcott made *The Rival Prima Donnas* into a drama, and it was accepted by a theatre, and would have been put upon the stage but for some disagreement among the actors. However, the young teacher received for her work a pass to the theatre for forty nights. She even meditated going upon the stage, but the manager quite opportunely broke his leg, and the contract was annulled. What would the boys and girls of America have lost, had their favorite turned actress.

A second story was, of course, written for the *Saturday Evening Gazette.* And now Louisa was catching a glimpse of fame. She says, "One of the memorable moments of my life is that in which, as I trudged to school on a wintry day, my eye fell upon a large poster with these delicious words, *'Bertha,* a new tale by the author of *The Rival Prima Donnas,* will appear in the *Saturday Evening Gazette.'* I was late; it was bitter cold; people jostled me; I was mortally afraid I should be recognized; but there I stood, feasting my eyes on the fascinating poster, and saying proudly to myself, in the words of the great Vincent Crummles, 'This, this is fame!' That day my pupils had an indulgent teacher; for, while they struggled with their pot-hooks, I was writing immortal works; and when they droned out the multiplication table, I was counting up the noble fortune my pen was to earn for me in the dim, delightful future. That after-

LOUISA M. ALCOTT

noon my sisters made a pilgrimage to behold this famous placard, and finding it torn by the wind, boldly stole it, and came home to wave it like a triumphal banner in the bosom of the excited family. The tattered paper still exists, folded away with other relics of those early days, so hard and yet so sweet, when the first small victories were won, and the enthusiasm of youth lent romance to life's drudgery."

Finding that there was money in sensational stories, she set herself eagerly to work, and soon could write ten or twelve a month. She says in *Little Women*: "As long as *The Spread Eagle* paid her a dollar a column for her 'rubbish,' as she called it, Jo felt herself a woman of means, and spun her little romances diligently. But great plans fermented in her busy brain and ambitious mind, and the old tin kitchen in the garret held a slowly increasing pile of blotted manuscript, which was one day to place the name of March upon the roll of fame."

But sensational stories did not bring much fame, and the conscientious Louisa tired of them. A novel, *Moods,* written at eighteen, shared nearly the same fate as *Flower Fables.* Some critics praised, some condemned, but the great world was indifferent. After this, she offered a story to Mr. James T. Fields, at that time editor of the *Atlantic Monthly,* but it was declined, with the kindly advice that she stick to her teaching. But Louisa Alcott had a strong will and a brave heart, and would not be overcome by obstacles.

The Civil War had begun, and the school-teacher's heart was deeply moved. She was now thirty, having had such experience as makes us very tender toward suffering. The perfume of natures does not usually come forth without bruising. She determined to go to Washington and offer herself as a nurse at the hospital for soldiers. After much official red tape, she found herself in the midst of scores of maimed and dying, just brought from the defeat at Fredericksburg. She says: "Round the great stove was gathered the dreariest group I ever saw,—ragged, gaunt, and pale, mud to the knees, with bloody bandages untouched since put on days before; many bundled up in blankets, coats being lost or useless, and all wearing that disheartened look which proclaimed defeat more plainly than any telegram, of the Burnside blunder. I pitied them so much, I dared not speak to them. I yearned to serve the dreariest of them all.

"Presently there came an order, 'Tell them to take off socks, coats, and shirts; scrub them well, put on clean shirts, and the attendants will finish them off, and lay them in bed.'

"I chanced to light on a withered old Irishman," she says, "wounded in the head, which caused that portion of his frame to be tastefully laid out like a garden, the bandages being the walks, and his hair the shrubbery. He was so overpowered by the honor of having a lady wash him, as he expressed it, that he did nothing but roll up his eyes and bless me, in an irresistible style which was too much for my sense of the ludicrous, so we laughed together; and when I knelt down to take off his shoes, he wouldn't hear of my touching 'them dirty craters.' Some of them took the performance like sleepy children, leaning their tired heads against me as I worked; others looked grimly scandalized, and several of the roughest colored like bashful girls."

When food was brought, she fed one of the badly wounded men, and offered the same help to his neighbor. "Thank you, ma'am," he said, "I don't think I'll ever eat again, for I'm shot in the stomach. But I'd like a drink of water, if you ain't too busy."

"I rushed away," she says; "but the water pails were

gone to be refilled, and it was some time before they re-appeared. I did not forget my patient, meanwhile, and, with the first mugful, hurried back to him. He seemed asleep; but something in the tired white face caused me to listen at his lips for a breath. None came. I touched his forehead; it was cold; and then I knew that, while he waited, a better nurse than I had given him a cooler draught, and healed him with a touch. I laid the sheet over the quiet sleeper, whom no noise could now disturb; and, half an hour later, the bed was empty."

With cheerful face and warm heart she went among the soldiers, now writing letters, now washing faces, and now singing lullabies. One day a tall, manly fellow was brought in. He seldom spoke, and uttered no complaint. After a little, when his wounds were being dressed, Miss Alcott observed the big tears roll down his cheeks and drop on the floor.

She says: "My heart opened wide and took him in, as, gathering the bent head in my arms, as freely as if he had been a child, I said, 'Let me help you bear it, John!' Never on any human countenance have I ever seen so swift and beautiful a look of gratitude, surprise, and comfort as that which answered me more eloquently than the whispered—

" 'Thank you ma'am; this is right good! this is what I wanted.'

" 'Then why not ask for it before?'

" 'I didn't like to be a trouble, you seemed so busy, and I could manage to get on alone.' "

Two days later Miss Alcott was sent for. John stretched out both hands as he said, "I knew you'd come. I guess I'm moving on, ma'am." Then clasping her hand so close that the death marks remained long upon it, he slept the final sleep. An hour later John's letter came, and putting it in his hand, Miss Alcott kissed the dead brow of the Virginia blacksmith, for his aged mother's sake, and buried him in the government lot.

The noble teacher after a while became ill from overwork, and was obliged to return home, soon writing her book, *Hospital Sketches*, published in 1865. This year, needing rest and change, she went to Europe as companion to an invalid lady, spending a year in Germany, Switzerland, Paris, and London. In the latter city she met Jean Ingelow, Frances Power Cobbe, John Stuart Mill, George Lewes, and others, who had known of the brilliant Concord coterie. Such persons did not ask if Miss Alcott were rich, nor did they care.

In 1868 her father took several of her more recent stories to Roberts Brothers to see about their publication in book form. Mr. Thomas Niles, a member of the firm, a man of refinement and good judgment, said: "We do not care just now for volumes of collected stories. Will not your daughter write us a new book consisting of a single story for girls?"

Miss Alcott feared she could not do it, and set herself to write *Little Women*, to show the publishers that she could *not* write a story for girls. But she did not succeed in convincing them or the world of her inability. In two months the first part was finished, and published October, 1868. It was a natural, graphic story of her three sisters and herself in that Concord home. How we, who are grown-up children, read with interest about the "Lawrence boy," especially if we had boys of our own, and sympathized with the little girl who wrote Miss Alcott, "I have cried quarts over Beth's sickness. If you don't have her marry Laurie in the second part, I shall never forgive you, and none of the girls in our school will ever read any more of your books. Do! do! have her, please."

The second part appeared in April, 1869, and Miss

Alcott found herself famous. The "pile of blotted manuscript" had "placed the name of March upon the roll of fame." Some of us could not be reconciled to dear Jo's marriage with the German professor, and their school at Plumfield, when Laurie loved her so tenderly. We cried over Beth, and felt how strangely like most young housekeepers was Meg. How the tired teacher, and tender-hearted nurse for the soldiers must have rejoiced at her success! "This year," she wrote her publishers, "after toiling so many years along the uphill road, always a hard one to women writers, it is peculiarly grateful to me to find the way growing easier at last, with pleasant little surprises blossoming on either side, and the rough places made smooth."

When *Little Men* was announced, fifty thousand copies were ordered in advance of its publication! About this time Miss Alcott visited Rome with her artist sister May, the "Amy" of *Little Women,* and on her return, wrote *Shawl-straps*, a bright sketch of their journey, followed by an *Old-Fashioned Girl*; that charming book *Under the Lilacs,* where your heart goes out to Ben and his dog Sancho; six volumes of *Aunt Jo's Scrap-bag; Jack and Jill;* and others. From these books Miss Alcott received over one hundred thousand dollars.

She was ever the most devoted of daughters. Till the mother went out of life, in 1877, she provided for her every want. May, the gifted youngest sister, who was married in Paris in 1878 to Ernest Nieriker, died a year and a half later, leaving her infant daughter, Louisa May Nieriker, to Miss Alcott's loving care. The father, who became paralyzed in 1882, had her constant ministries. How proud he was of his Louisa! I heard him say, years ago, "I am riding in her golden chariot."

Miss Alcott, like Elizabeth Stuart Phelps, was an earnest advocate of women's suffrage, and temperance.

When Meg in *Little Women* prevails upon Laurie to take the pledge on her wedding-day, the delighted Jo beams her approval. In 1883 she wrote of the suffrage reform, "Every year gives me greater faith in it, greater hope of its success, a larger charity for those who cannot see its wisdom, and a more earnest wish to use what influence I possess for its advancement."

Miss Alcott died March 6, 1888, at the age of fifty-five, three days after the death of her distinguished father, Bronson Alcott. She had been ill for some months, from care and overwork. On the Saturday morning before she died, she wrote to a friend: "I am told that I must spend another year in this 'Saint's Rest,' and then I am promised twenty years of health. I don't want so many, and I have no idea I shall see them. But as I don't live for myself, I will live on for others."

MARY LYON

THERE are two women whose memory the girls in this country should especially revere,—Mary Lyon and Catharine Beecher. When it was unfashionable for women to know more than to read, write, and cipher (the "three R's," as reading, writing, and arithmetic were called), these two had the courage to ask that women have an education equal to men, a thing which was laughed at as impracticable and impossible. To these two pioneers we are greatly indebted for the grand educational advantages for women to-day in America.

Amid the mountains of Western Massachusetts, at Buckland, February 28, 1797, the fifth of seven children, Mary Lyon came into the world, in obscurity. The little farm-house was but one story high, in the midst of rocks and sturdy trees. The father, Aaron Lyon, was a godly man, beloved by all his neighbors,—"the peacemaker," he was called,—who died at forty-five, leaving his little family well-nigh helpless—no, not helpless, because the mother was of the same material of which Eliza Garfields are made.

Such women are above circumstances. She saw to it that the farm yielded its best. She worked early and late, always cheerful, always observing the Sabbath most devotedly, always keeping the children clean and tidy. In her little garden the May pinks were the sweetest and the peonies the reddest of any in the neighborhood. One person begged to set a plant in the corner of her garden, sure that if Mrs. Lyon tended it, it could never die. "How is it," said the hard-working wife of a farmer, "that the widow can do more for me than any one else?"

She had her trials, but she saw no use in telling them to others, so with a brave heart she took up her daily tasks and performed them.

Little Mary was an energetic, frank, warm-hearted child, full of desire to help others. Her mind was eager in grasping new things, and curious in its investigations. Once, when her mother had given her some work to do, she studied the hour-glass, and turning it upside down at the end of the hour, she said, "I know I have found a way to *make more time.*"

At the village school she showed a remarkable memory and the power of committing lessons easily. She was especially good in mathematics and grammar. In four days she learned all of Alexander's Grammar, which scholars were accustomed to commit, and recited it accurately to the astonished teacher.

When Mary was thirteen, the mother married a second time, and soon after removed to Ohio. The girl remained at the old homestead, keeping house for the only brother, and so well did she do the work, that he gave her a dollar a week for her services. This she used in buying books and clothes for school. Besides, she found opportunities to spin and weave for some of the neighbors, and thus added a little more to her purse.

After five years, the brother married and sought a home in New York State. Mary, thus thrown upon herself, began to teach school for seventy-five cents a week and her board. This amount would not buy many silks or embroideries, but Mary did not care much for these. "She is all intellect," said a friend who knew her well; "she does not know that she has a body to care for."

She had now saved enough money to enable her to spend one term at the Sanderson Academy at Ashfield. What an important event in life that seemed to the struggling country girl! The scholars watched her bright, intellectual face, and when she began to recite, laid aside their books to hear her. The teacher said, "I should like to see what she would make if she could be sent to college." When the term ended, her little savings were all spent, and now she must teach again. If she could only go forward with her classmates! but the laws of poverty are inexorable. Just as she was leaving the school, the trustees came and offered the advantages of the academy free, for another term. Did ever such a gleam of sunshine come into a cloudy day?

But how could she pay her board? She owned a bed and some table linen, and taking these to a boarding house, a bargain was made whereby she could have a room and board in exchange for her household articles.

Her red-letter days had indeed come. She might never have a chance for schooling again; so, without regard to health, she slept only four hours out of the twenty-four, ate her meals hurriedly, and gave all her time to her lessons. Not a scholar in the school could keep up with her. When the teacher gave her Adam's *Latin Grammar*, telling her to commit such portions as were usual in going over the book the first time, she learned them all in three days!

When the term closed, she had no difficulty in finding a place to teach. All the towns around had heard of the surprising scholar, Mary Lyon, and probably hoped she could inspire the same scholarship in her pupils, a matter in which she was most successful.

As soon as her schools were finished, she would spend the money in obtaining instruction in some particular study, in which she thought herself deficient. Now she would go into the family of Rev. Edward Hitchcock, afterward president of Amherst College, and study natural science of him, meantime taking lessons of his wife in drawing and painting. Now she would study penmanship, following the copy as closely as a child. Once when a teacher, in deference to her reputation, wrote the copy in Latin, she handed it back and asked him to write it in English, lest when the books were examined, she might be thought wiser than she really was. Thus conscientious was the young school-teacher.

She was now twenty-four, and had laid up enough money to attend the school of Rev. Joseph Emerson, at Byfield. He was an unusual man in his gifts of teaching and broad views of life. He had been blest with a wife of splendid talents, and as Miss Lyon was wont to say, "Men judge of the whole sex by their own wives," so Mr. Emerson believed women could understand metaphysics and theology as well as men. He discussed science and religion with his pupils, and the result was a class of self-respecting, self-reliant, thinking women.

Miss Lyon's friends discouraged her going to Byfield, because they thought she knew enough already. "Why," said they, "you will never be a minister, and what is the need of going to school?" She improved her time here. One of her classmates wrote home, "Mary sends love to all; but time with her is too precious to spend in writing letters. She is gaining knowledge by handfuls."

The next year, an assistant was wanted in the Sanderson Academy. The principal thought a man must be engaged. "Try Mary Lyon," said one of her friends, "and see if she is not sufficient," and he employed her, and found her a host. But she could not long be retained, for she was wanted in a larger field, at Derry, N. H. Miss Grant, one of the teachers at Mr. Emerson's school, had sent for her former bright pupil. Mary was glad to be associated with Miss Grant, for she was very fond of her; but before going, she must attend some lectures in chemistry and natural history by Professor

Eaton at Amherst. Had she been a young man, how easily could she have secured a scholarship, and thus worked her way through college; but for a young woman, neither Amherst, nor Dartmouth, nor Williams, nor Harvard, nor Yale, with all their wealth, had an open door. Very fond of chemistry, she could only learn in the spare time which a busy professor could give.

Was the cheerful girl never despondent in these hard working years? Yes; because naturally she was easily discouraged, and would have long fits of weeping; but she came to the conclusion that such seasons of depression were wrong, and that "there was too much to be done, for her to spend her time in that manner." She used to tell her pupils that "if they were unhappy, it was probably because they had so many thoughts about themselves, and so few about the happiness of others." The friend who had recommended her for the Sanderson Academy now became surety for her for forty dollars' worth of clothing, and the earnest young woman started for Derry. The school there numbered ninety pupils, and Mary Lyons was happy. She wrote her mother, "I do not number it among the least of my blessings that I am permitted to *do something*. Surely I ought to be thankful for an active life."

But the Derry school was held only in the summers, so Miss Lyon came back to teach at Ashfield and Buckland, her birthplace, for the winters. The first season she had twenty-five scholars; the last, one hundred. The families in the neighborhood took the students into their homes to board, charging them one dollar or one dollar and twenty-five cents per week, while the tuition was twenty-five cents a week. No one would grow very rich on such an income. So popular was Miss Lyon's teaching that a suitable building was erected for her school, and the Ministerial Association passed a resolution of praise, urging her to remain permanently in the western part of Massachusetts.

However, Miss Grant had removed to Ipswich, and had urged Miss Lyon to join her, which she did. For six years they taught a large and most successful school. Miss Lyon was singularly happy in her intercourse with the young ladies. She won them to her views, while they scarcely knew that they were being controlled. She would say to them: "Now, young ladies, you are here at great expense. Your board and tuition cost a great deal, and your time ought to be worth more than both; but, in order to get an equivalent for the money and time you are spending, you must be systematic, and that is impossible, unless you have a regular hour for rising. . . . Persons who run round all day after the half-hour they lost in the morning never accomplish much. You may know them by a rip in the glove, a string pinned to the bonnet, a shawl left on the balustrade, which they had no time to hang up, they were in such a hurry to catch their lost thirty minutes. You will see them opening their books and trying to study at the time of general exercises in school; but it is a fruitless race; they never will overtake their lost half-hour. Good men, from Abraham to Washington, have been early risers." Again, she would say, "Mind, wherever it is found, will secure respect. . . . Educate the women, and the men will be educated. Let the ladies understand the great doctrine of seeking the greatest good, of loving their neighbors as themselves; let them indoctrinate their children in this fundamental truth, and we shall have wise legislators."

"You won't do so again, will you, dear?" was almost always sure to win a tender response from a pupil.

She would never allow a scholar to be laughed at.

If a teacher spoke jestingly of a scholar's capacity, Miss Lyon would say, "Yes, I know she has a small mind, but we must do the best we can for her."

For nearly sixteen years she had been giving her life to the education of girls. She had saved no money for herself, giving it to her relatives or aiding poor girls in going to school. She was simple in her tastes, the blue cloth dress she generally wore having been spun and woven by herself. A friend tells how, standing before the mirror to tie her bonnet, she said, "Well, I *may* fail of Heaven, but I shall be very much disappointed if I do —very much disappointed"; and there was no thought of what she was doing with the ribbons.

Miss Lyon was now thirty-three years old. It would be strange indeed if a woman with her bright mind and sunshiny face should not have offers of marriage. One of her best opportunities came, as is often the case, when about thirty, and Miss Lyon could have been made supremely happy by it, but she had in her mind one great purpose, and she felt that she must sacrifice home and love for it. This was the building of a high-grade school or college for women. Had she decided otherwise, there probably would have been no Mount Holyoke College.

She had the tenderest sympathy for poor girls; they were the ones usually most desirous of an education, and they struggled the hardest for it. For them no educational societies were provided, and no scholarships. Could she, who had no money, build "a seminary which should be so moderate in its expenses as to be open to the daughters of farmers and artisans, and to teachers who might be mainly dependent for their support on their own exertions?"

In vain she tried to have the school at Ipswich established permanently by buildings and endowments. In vain she talked with college presidents and learned ministers. Nearly all were indifferent. They could see no need that women should study science or the classics. That women would be happier with knowledge, just as they themselves were made happier by it, seemed never to have occurred to them. That women were soon to do nine-tenths of the teaching in the schools of the country could not be foreseen. Oberlin and Cornell, Vassar and Wellesley, belonged to a golden age as yet undreamed of.

For two years she thought over it, and prayed over it, and when all seemed hopeless, she would walk the floor, and say over and over again, "Commit thy way unto the Lord. He will keep thee. Women *must* be educated; they *must* be." Finally a meeting was called in Boston at the same time as one of the religious anniversaries. She wrote to a friend, "Very few were present. The meeting was adjourned; and the adjourned meeting utterly failed. There were not enough present to organize, and there the business, in my view, has come to an end."

Still she carried the burden on her heart. She writes, in 1834, "During the past year my heart has so yearned over the adult female youth in the common walks of life, that it has sometimes seemed as though a fire were shut up in my bones." She conceived the idea of having the young women do the work of the house, partly to lessen expenses, partly to teach them useful things, and also because she says, "Might not this single feature do away with much of the prejudice against female education among common people?"

At last the purpose in her heart became so strong that she resigned her position as a teacher, and went from house to house in Ipswich collecting funds. She wrote to her mother, "I hope and trust that this is of the Lord, and that He will prosper it. In this movement I have thought much more constantly, and have felt much more deeply, about doing that which shall be for the honor of Christ, and for the good of souls, than I ever did in any step in my life." She determined to raise her first thousand dollars from women. She talked in her good-natured way with the father or the mother. She asked if they wanted a new shawl or card-table or carpet, if they would not find a way to procure it. Usually they gave five or ten dollars; some, only a half-dollar. So interested did two ladies become that they gave one hundred dollars apiece, and later, when their house was burned, and the man who had their money in charge lost it, they worked, with their own hands and earned the two hundred, that their portion might not fail in the great work.

In less than two months she had raised the thousand: but she wrote Miss Grant, "I do not recollect being so fatigued, even to prostration, as I have been for a few weeks past." She often quoted a remark of Dr. Lyman Beecher's, "The wear and tear of what I cannot do is a great deal more than the wear and tear of what I do." When she became quite worn, her habit was to sleep nearly all the time, for two or three days, till nature repaired the system.

She next went to Amherst, where good Dr. Hitchcock felt as deeply interested for girls as for the boys in his college. One January morning, with the thermometer below zero, three or four hours before sunrise, he and Miss Lyon started on the stage for Worcester. Each was wrapped in a buffalo robe, so that the long ride was not unpleasant. A meeting was to be held, and a decision made as to the location of the seminary, which, at last, was actually to be built. After a long conference, South Hadley was chosen, ten miles south of Amherst.

One by one, good men became interested in the matter,

and one true-hearted minister became an agent for the raising of funds. Miss Lyon was also untiring in her solicitations. She spoke before ladies' meetings, and visited those in high station and low. So troubled were her friends about this public work for a woman, that they reasoned with her that it was in better taste to stay at home, and let gentlemen do the work.

"What do I do that's wrong?" she replied. "I ride in the stage coach or cars without an escort. Other ladies do the same. I visit a family where I have been previously invited, and the minister's wife, or some leading woman, calls the ladies together to see me, and I lay our object before them. Is that wrong? I go with Mr. Hawks (the agent), and call on a gentleman of known liberality, at his own house, and converse with him about our enterprise. What harm is there in that? My heart is sick, my soul is pained, with this empty gentility, this genteel nothingness. I am doing a great work. I cannot come down." Pitiful, that so noble a woman should have been hampered by public opinion. How all this has changed! Now, the world and the church gladly welcome the voice, the hand, and the heart of woman in their philanthropic work.

At last, enough money was raised to begin the enterprise, and the corner-stone of Mount Holyoke Seminary was laid, October 3, 1836. "It was a day of deep interest," writes Mary Lyon. "The stones and brick and mortar speak a language which vibrates through my very soul."

With thankful heart and busy hands she watched the progress of the work. Every detail was under her careful eye. She said: "Had I a thousand lives, I could sacrifice them all in suffering and hardship, for the sake of Mount Holyoke Seminary. Did I possess the greatest fortune, I could readily relinquish it all, and become poor, and more than poor, if its prosperity should demand it."

Finally, in the autumn of 1837, the seminary was ready for pupils. The main building, four stories high, had been erected. An admirable course of study had been provided. For the forty weeks of the school year, the charges for board and tuition were sixty dollars,—only one dollar and twenty-five cents per week. Miss Lyon's own salary was but two hundred a year and she never would receive anything higher. The accommodations were for only eighty pupils, but one hundred and sixteen came the first year.

While Miss Lyon was heartily loved by her scholars, they yet respected her good discipline. It was against the rules for any one to absent herself from meals without permission to do so. One of the young ladies, not feeling quite as fresh as usual, concluded not to go down stairs at tea time, and to remain silent on the subject. Miss Lyon's quick eye detected her absence. Calling the girl's room-mate to her, she asked, "Is Miss——ill?"

"Oh, no," was the reply, "only a little indisposed, and she commissioned me to carry her a cup of tea and a cracker."

"Very well, I will see to it."

After supper, the young lady ascended to her room, in the fourth story, found her companion enjoying a glorious sunset, and seating herself beside her, they began an animated conversation. Presently there was a knock. "Come in!" both shouted gleefully, when lo! in walked Mary Lyon, with the tea and cracker. She had come up four flights of stairs; but she said every one was tired at night, and she could as well bring up the supper as anybody. She inquired with great kindness about the young lady's health, who, greatly abashed, had nothing to say. She was ever after present at meal time, unless sick in bed.

The students never forgot Miss Lyon's plain, earnest words. When they entered, they were told that they were expected to do right without formal commands; if not, they had better go to some smaller school, where they could receive the peculiar training needed by little girls. She urged loose clothing and thick shoes. "If you will persist in killing yourselves by reckless exposure," she would say, "we are not willing to take the responsibility of the act. We think, by all means, you had better go home and die, in the arms of your dear mothers."

Miss Lyon had come to her fiftieth birthday. Her seminary had prospered beyond her fondest hopes. She had raised nearly seventy thousand dollars for her beloved school, and it was out of debt. Nearly two thousand pupils had been at South Hadley, of whom a large number had become missionaries and teachers. Not a single year had passed without a revival, and rarely did a girl leave the institution without professing Christianity.

She said to a friend shortly after this fiftieth birthday: "It was the most solemn day of my life. I devoted it to reflection and prayer. Of my active toils I then took leave. I was certain that before another fifty years should have elapsed, I should wake up amid far different scenes, and far other thoughts would fill my mind, and other employments would engage my attention. I felt it. There seemed to be no ladder between me and the world above. The gates were opened, and I seemed to stand on the threshold. I felt that the evening of my days had come, and that I needed repose."

And the repose came soon. The last of February, 1849, a young lady in the seminary died. Miss Lyon called the girls together and spoke tenderly to them, urging them not to fear death, but to be ready to meet it. She said, "There is nothing in the universe that I am afraid of, but that I shall not know and do all my duty." Beautiful words! carved shortly after on her monument.

A few days later, Mary Lyon lay upon her deathbed. The brain had been congested, and she was often unconscious. In one of her lucid moments, her pastor said, "Christ precious?" Summoning all her energies, she raised both hands, clasped them, and said, "Yes." "Have you trusted Christ too much?" he asked. Seeing that she made an effort to speak, he said, "God can be glorified by silence." An indescribable smile lit up her face, and she was gone.

The English ivy grows thickly over Miss Lyon's grave, covering it like a mantle, and sending out its wealth of green leaves in the spring. So each year her own handiwork flourishes, sending out into the world its strongest forces, the very foundation of the highest civilization, —educated and Christian wives and mothers.

HARRIET G. HOSMER

SOME years ago, in an art store in Boston, a crowd of persons stood gazing intently upon a famous piece of statuary. The red curtains were drawn aside, and the white marble seemed almost to speak. A group of girls stood together, and looked on in rapt admiration. One of them said, "Just to think that a woman did it!"

"It makes me proud and glad," said another.

"Who is Harriet Hosmer?" said a third. "I wish I knew about her."

And then one of us, who had stolen all the hours she could get from school life to read art books from the Hartford Athenæum, and kept crude statues, made by herself from chalk and plaster, secreted in her room, told all she had read about the brilliant creator of "Zenobia."

The statue was seven feet high, queenly in pose and face, yet delicate and beautiful, with the thoughts which genius had wrought in it. The left arm supported the elegant drapery, while the right hung listlessly by her side, both wrists chained; the captive of the Emperor Aurelian. Since that time, I have looked upon other masterpieces in all the great galleries of Europe, but perhaps none have ever made a stronger impression upon me than "Zenobia," in those early years.

And who was the artist of whom we girls were so proud? Born in Watertown, Mass., October 9, 1830, Harriet Hosmer came into the welcome home of a leading physician, and a delicate mother, who soon died of consumption. Dr. Hosmer had also buried his only child beside Harriet, with the same disease, and he deter-

mined that this girl should live in sunshine and air, that
he might save her if possible. He used to say, "There
is a whole life-time for the education of the mind, but
the body develops in a few years; and during that time
nothing should be allowed to interfere with its free and
healthy growth."

As soon as the child was large enough, she was given
a pet dog, which she decked with ribbons and bells. Then
as the Charles River flowed past their house, a boat was
provided, and she was allowed to row at will. A Vene-
tian gondola was also built for her, with silver prow and
velvet cushions. "Too much spoiling—too much spoiling," said some of the neighbors; but Dr. Hosmer knew
that he was keeping his little daughter on the earth instead
of in heaven.

A gun was now purchased, and the girl became an admirable marksman. Her room was a perfect museum.
Here were birds, bats, beetles, snakes, and toads; some
dissected, some preserved in spirits, and others stuffed, all
gathered and prepared by her own hands. Now she
made an inkstand from the egg of a sea-gull and the
body of a kingfisher; now she climbed to the top of a
tree and brought down a crow's nest. She could walk
miles upon miles without fatigue. She grew up like a
boy, which is only another way of saying that she grew up
healthy and strong physically. Probably polite society
was shocked at Dr. Hosmer's methods. Would that there
were many such fathers and mothers, that we might have
a vigorous race of women, and consequently, a vigorous
race of men!

When Harriet tired of books,—for she was an eager
reader,—she found delight in a clay-pit in the garden,
where she molded horses and dogs to her heart's content.
Unused to restraint, she did not like the first school in
which she was placed, the principal, the brother-in-law

of Nathaniel Hawthorne, writing to her father that he "could do nothing with her."

She was then taken to Mrs. Sedgewick, who kept a famous school at Lenox, Berkshire County. She received "Happy Hatty," as she was called, with the remark, "I have a reputation for training wild colts, and I will try this one." And the wise woman succeeded. She won Harriet's confidence, not by the ten thousand times repeated "don't," which so many children hear in home and school, till life seems a prison-pen. She let her run wild, guiding her all the time with so much tact, that the girl scarcely knew she was guided at all. Blessed tact! How many thousands of young people are ruined for lack of it!

She remained here three years. Mrs. Sedgewick says, "She was the most difficult pupil to manage I ever had but I think I never had one in whom I took so deep an interest, and whom I learned to love so well." About this time, not being quite as well as usual, Dr. Hosmer engaged a physician of large practice to visit his daughter. The busy man could not be regular, which sadly interfered with Harriet's boating and driving. Complaining one day that it spoiled her pleasure, he said, "If I am alive, I will be here," naming the day and hour.

"Then if you are not here, I am to conclude that you are dead," was the reply.

As he did not come, Harriet drove to the newspaper offices in Boston that afternoon, and the next morning the community was startled to read of Dr. ——'s sudden death. Friends hastened to the house, and messages of condolence came pouring in. It is probable that he was more punctual after this.

On Harriet's return from Lenox, she began to take lessons in drawing, modeling, and anatomical studies, in Boston, frequently walking from home and back, a distance of fourteen miles. Feeling the need of a thorough course in anatomy, she applied to the Boston Medical School for admittance, and was refused because of her sex. The Medical College of St. Louis proved itself broader, glad to encourage talent wherever found, and received her.

Professor McDowell, under whom the artists Powers and Clevenger studied anatomy, spared no pains to give her every advantage, while the students were uniformly courteous. "I remember him," says Miss Hosmer, "with great affection and gratitude as being a most thorough and patient teacher, as well as at all times a good, kind friend." In testimony of her appreciation, she cut, from a bust of Professor McDowell by Clevenger, a life-size medallion in marble, now treasured in the college museum.

While in St. Louis she made her home with the family of Wayman Crow, whose daughter had been her companion at Lenox. This gentleman proved himself a constant and encouraging friend, ordering her first statue from Rome, and helping in a thousand ways a girl who had chosen for herself an unusual work in life.

After completing her studies she made a trip to New Orleans, and then North to the Falls of St. Anthony, smoking the pipe of peace with the chief of the Dakota Indians, exploring lead mines in Dubuque, and scaling a high mountain that was soon after named for her. Did the wealthy girl go alone on these journeys? Yes. As a rule, no harm comes to a young woman who conducts herself with becoming reserve with men. Flirts usually are paid in their own coin.

On her return home, Dr. Hosmer fitted up a studio for his daughter, and her first work was to copy from the antique. Then she cut Canova's "Napoleon" in marble for her father, doing all the work, that he might especially value the gift. Her next statue was an ideal bust of

Hesper, "with," said Lydia Maria Child, "the face of a lovely maiden gently falling asleep with the sound of distant music. Her hair is gracefully arranged, and intertwined with capsules of the poppy. A star shines on her forehead, and under her breast lies the crescent moon. The swell of the cheeks and the bust is like pure, young, healthy flesh, and the muscles of the beautiful mouth so delicately cut, it seems like a thing that breathes. She did every stroke of the work with her own small hands, except knocking off the corners of the block of marble. She employed a man to do that; but as he was unused to work for sculptors, she did not venture to have him approach within several inches of the surface she intended to cut. Slight girl as she was, she wielded for eight or ten hours a day a leaden mallet weighing four pounds and a half. Had it not been for the strength and flexibility of muscle acquired by rowing and other athletic exercises, such arduous labor would have been impossible."

After "Hesper" was completed, she said to her father, "I am ready to go to Rome."

"You shall go, my child, this very autumn," was the response.

He would, of course, miss the genial companionship of his only child, but her welfare was to be consulted rather than his own. When autumn came, she rode on horseback to Wayland to say good-bye to Mrs. Child. "Shall you never be homesick for your museum-parlor in Watertown? Can you be contented in a foreign land?"

"I can be happy anywhere," said Miss Hosmer, "with good health and a bit of marble."

Late in the fall Dr. Hosmer and his daughter started for Europe, reaching Rome, November 12, 1852. She had greatly desired to study under John Gibson, the leading English sculptor, but he had taken young women into his studio who in a short time became discouraged or showed themselves afraid of hard work, and he feared Miss Hosmer might be of the same useless type.

When the photographs of "Hesper" were placed before him by an artist friend of the Hosmers, he looked at them carefully, and said, "Send the young lady to me, and whatever I know, and can teach her, she shall learn." He gave Miss Hosmer an upstairs room in his studio, and here for seven years she worked with delight, honored and encouraged by her noble teacher. She wrote to her friends: "The dearest wish of my heart is gratified in that I am acknowledged by Gibson as a pupil. He has been resident in Rome thirty-four years, and leads the van. I am greatly in luck. He has just finished the model of the statue of the queen; and as his room is vacant, he permits me to use it, and I am now in his own studio. I have also a little room for work which was formerly occupied by Canova, and perhaps inspiration may be drawn from the walls."

The first work which she copied, to show Gibson whether she had correctness of eye and proper knowledge, was the Venus of Milo. When nearly finished, the iron which supported the clay snapped, and the figure lay spoiled upon the floor. She did not shrink nor cry, but immediately went to work cheerfully to shape it over again. This conduct Mr. Gibson greatly admired, and made up his mind to assist her all he could.

After this she copied the "Cupid" of Praxiteles and Tasso from the British Museum. Her first original work was "Daphne," the beautiful girl whom Apollo loved, and who, rather than accept his addresses, was changed into laurel by the gods. Apollo crowned his head with laurel, and made the flower sacred to himself forever.

Next, Miss Hosmer produced "Medusa," famed for

her beautiful hair, which Minerva turned into serpents because Neptune loved her. According to Grecian mythology, Perseus made himself immortal by conquering Medusa, whose head he cut off, and the blood dripping from it filled Africa with snakes. Miss Hosmer represented the beautiful maiden, when she finds, with horror, that her hair is turning into serpents.

Needing a real snake for her work, Miss Hosmer sent a man into the suburbs to bring her one alive. When it was obtained, she chloroformed it till she had made a cast, keeping it in plaster for three hours and a half. Then, instead of killing it, she sent it back into the country, glad to regain its liberty.

"Daphne" and "Medusa" were both exhibited in Boston the following year, 1853, and were much praised. Mr. Gibson said: "The power of imitating the roundness and softness of flesh, he had never seen surpassed." Rauch, the great Prussian, whose mausoleum at Charlottenburg of the beautiful queen Louise can never be forgotten, gave Miss Hosmer high praise.

Two years later she completed her "Œnone," the beautiful nymph of Mount Ida. This work was so much liked in America, that the St. Louis Mercantile Library made a liberal offer for some other statue. Accordingly, two years after, "Beatrice Cenci" was sent. The noble girl lies asleep, the night before her execution, after the terrible torture. "It was," says Mrs. Child, "the sleep of a body worn out with the wretchedness of the soul. On that innocent face suffering had left its traces. The arm that had been tossing in the grief tempest, had fallen heavily, too weary to change itself into a more easy position. Those large eyes, now so closely veiled by their swollen lids, had evidently wept till the fountain of tears was dry. That lovely mouth was still the open portal of a sigh, which the mastery of sleep had left no time to close."

To make this natural, the sculptor caused several models to go to sleep in her studio, that she might study them. Gibson is said to have remarked upon seeing this, "I can teach her nothing." This was also exhibited in London and in several American cities.

For three years she had worked continuously, not leaving Rome even in the hot, unhealthy summers. She had said, "I will not be an amateur; I will work as if I had to earn my daily bread." However, as her health seemed somewhat impaired, at her father's earnest wish, she had decided to go to England for the season. Her trunks were packed, and she was ready to start, when lo! a message came that Dr. Hosmer had lost his property, that he could send her no more money, and suggested that she return home at once.

At first she seemed overwhelmed; then she said firmly, "I cannot go back, and give up my art." Her trunks were at once unpacked and a cheap room rented. Her handsome horse and saddle were sold, and she was now to work indeed "as if she earned her daily bread."

By a strange freak of human nature, by which we sometimes do our most humorous work when we are saddest, Miss Hosmer produced now in her sorrow her fun-loving "Puck." It represents a child about four years old seated on a toadstool which breaks beneath him. The left hand confines a lizard, while the right holds a beetle. The legs are crossed, and the great toe of the right foot turns up. The whole is full of merriment. The Crown Princess of Germany, on seeing it, exclaimed, "Oh Miss Hosmer, you have such a talent for toes!" Very true, for this statue, with the several copies made from it, brought her thirty thousand dollars! The Prince of Wales has a copy, the Duke of Hamilton also, and it has gone even to Australia and the West Indies. A companion piece is the "Will-o'-the-wisp."

About this time the lovely sixteen-year-old daughter of Madam Falconnet died at Rome, and for her monument in the Catholic church of San Andrea del Fratte, Miss Hosmer produced an exquisite figure resting upon a sarcophagus. Layard, the explorer of Babylon and Nineveh, wrote to Madam Falconnet: "I scarcely remember to have seen a monument which more completely commanded my sympathy and more deeply interested me. I really know of none, of modern days, which I would rather have placed over the remains of one who had been dear to me."

Miss Hosmer returned to America in 1857, five years after her departure. She was still young, twenty-seven, vivacious, hopeful, not wearied from her hard work, and famous. While here she determined upon a statue of Zenobia, Queen of Palmyra, and read much concerning her and her times.

After Miss Hosmer's return to Rome, she worked on "Zenobia" with energy and enthusiasm, as she molded the clay, and then the plaster. When brought to this country, it awakened the greatest interest; crowds gathered to see it. In Chicago it was exhibited at the Sanitary Fair in behalf of the soldiers. Whittier said: "It very fully expresses my conception of what historical sculpture should be. It tells its whole proud and melancholy story. In looking at it, I felt that the artist had been as truly serving her country while working out her magnificent design abroad, as our soldiers in the field, and our public officers in their departments." From its exhibition Miss Hosmer received five thousand dollars. It was purchased by Mr. A. W. Griswold, of New York. So great a work was the statue considered in London, that some of the papers declared Gibson to be its author. Miss Hosmer at once began suits for libel, and retractions were speedily made.

In 1860 Miss Hosmer again visited America, to see her father, who was seriously ill. How proud Dr. Hosmer must have been of his gifted daughter now that her fame was in two hemispheres! Surely he had not "spoiled" her. She could now spend for him as he had spent for her in her childhood. While here, she received a commission from St. Louis for a bronze portrait-statue of Missouri's famous statesman, Thomas Hart Benton.

She was now in the midst of busy and successful work. Orders crowded upon her. Her "Sleeping Faun," which was exhibited at the Dublin Exhibition in 1865, was sold on the day of opening for five thousand dollars, to Sir Benjamin Guinness. Some discussion having arisen about the sale, he offered ten thousand, saying, that if money could buy it, he would possess it. Miss Hosmer, however, would receive only the five thousand. The faun is represented reclining against the trunk of a tree, partly draped in the spoils of a tiger. A little faun, with mischievous look, is binding the faun to the tree with the tiger-skin. The newspapers were enthusiastic about the work.

Many of the closing years of the sculptor's long life were spent in Rome, where she had a wide circle of eminent American and English friends, among whom were Hawthorne, Thackeray, George Eliot, and the Brownings. She made several discoveries in her work, one of which was a process of hardening limestone so that it resembled marble. She also wrote both prose and poetry, and would have been successful as an author, if she had not given the bulk of her time to her beloved sculpture.

After her long sojourn in Rome she spent several years

in England, executing important commissions, and then turned her face toward America. In Watertown, where she was born, she again made her home; and here she breathed her last, February 21, 1908, after an illness of three weeks. She was in her seventy-eighth year. By her long life of earnest work and self-reliant purpose, coupled with her high gift, she made for herself an abiding place in the history of art.

JULIA WARD HOWE

ALTHOUGH Julia Ward came of a distinguished and wealthy family, she never, even as a girl, traded upon that fact. She made use of her splendid talents to enrich the world. She was born May 27, 1819, in a handsome home in Bowling Green, at that time the fashionable part of New York City. Her father, Samuel Ward, was a merchant and banker of New York.

"He was a majestic person," says the daughter, "of somewhat severe aspect and reserved manners, but with a vein of true genialty and a great benevolence of heart. His great gravity, and the absence of a mother, naturally subdued the tone of the whole household; and though a greatly cherished set of children, we were not a very merry one."

Her grandfather, Samuel Ward, a graduate of Brown University, was a lieutenant-colonel in the Revolutionary War. Four of Julia Ward's ancestors were governors of Rhode Island, two Wards and two Greens. On her mother's side her ancestors were the Marions of South Carolina, her mother being a grand-niece of General Marion.

This mother, Julia Cutler Ward, was a woman of much beauty and intellect. She died at the early age of twenty-eight, leaving six little children, the fourth, Julia, only five years of age.

The blow was a distressing one to the banker and his children. For weeks he lay prostrated on a bed of sickness. Finally his wife's sister, Miss Eliza Cutler, came into the home to bring up the children as best she could.

She was a witty and talented woman, and helped to develop them in mind as well as in body.

Mrs. Laura E. Richards, the daughter of Julia Ward Howe, in her book, *When I Was Your Age,* says of Miss Cutler, "A very good aunt she was, and devoted to the motherless children; but sometimes she did funny things. They went out to ride every day—the children, I mean—in a great yellow chariot lined with fine blue cloth. Now, it occurred to their kind aunt that it would have a charming effect if the children were dressed to match the chariot. So thought, so done! Dressmakers and milliners plied their art; and one day Broadway was electrified by the sight of the little Misses Ward, seated in uneasy state on the blue cushions, clad in wonderful raiment of yellow and blue. They had blue pelisses and yellow satin bonnets.

"And this was all very well for the two younger ones, with their dark eyes and hair, and their rosy cheeks; but Julia, young as she was, felt dimly that blue and yellow was not the combination to set off her tawny locks and exquisite sea-shell complexion. It is not probable, however, that she sorrowed deeply over the funny clothes; for her mind was never set on clothes, either in childhood or in later life. Did not her sister meet her one day coming home from school with one blue shoe and one green?"

The little Julia showed great fondness for books. When nine years old she was studying Paley's *Moral Philosophy* with girls twice her age. Yet with a love for studies beyond her years, she was a child at heart, and grieved when at this age her dolls were taken from her, and she was told that "Miss Ward was too old to play with dolls any longer." "This heart-rending separation took place on her ninth birthday," writes Mrs. Howe's daughter, Maud.

Distinguished authors gathered at the Ward home, and

JULIA WARD HOWE

stimulated the young girl in her love for books. When she was sixteen she wrote, *The Ill-cut Mantell; a Romaunt of the Time of Kynge Arthur,* and gave the manuscript to her youngest sister, who relates this incident :—

"One day the young poet chanced upon her two younger sisters busy in some childish game. She upbraided them for their frivolous pursuit, and insisted that they should occupy themselves, as she did, in the composition of verses. Louisa, the elder of the two, flatly refused to make the effort; but the little Annie dutifully obeyed the elder sister, and, after a long and resolute struggle, produced some stanzas, of which the following lines have always been remembered,—

> 'He hears the ravens when they call,
> And stands them in a pleasant hall.' "

The girl did not tell her father of these desires for authorship, lest he should be disturbed by such an unusual wish on the part of a young woman. Though he loved her devotedly, and while eating his meals would hold in his left hand the hand of this daughter who sat next to him at table, she always stood somewhat in awe of him.

Julia's first published work, when she was seventeen, was "a review of a poem of Lamartine's called 'Jocelyn,' together with a translation of parts of it." She said, "The Rev. Leonard Woods, editor of one of the theological reviews, published it. Then, not long afterward, I wrote an article on a translation that had just appeared of some of the minor poems of Goethe and Schiller. This was printed in the *American Review,* edited by Charles King, afterward President of Columbia College. Both of these articles attracted attention, and encouraged me very much."

Artists as well as musicians and authors, came to the Ward mansion to visit its picture-gallery, where the father had collected many foreign works of art. It was not strange, therefore, that a sister of Julia should marry the well-known artist, Thomas Crawford of Rome, the father of Marion Crawford, the novelist.

Beside all this study and intercourse with scholarly people, there were times of merry-making at the banker's home. Mrs. Howe, in the *Forum* for July, 1893, in an article, "How the Fourth of July should be Celebrated," speaks of the laughing faces of her young brothers, who, she says, were allowed to arrange a small table, for their greater convenience, on the pavement of ancient Bond Street, a very quiet by-way in those days. From this spot went forth a perpetual popping and fizzing, varied by the occasional thud of a double-headed fire-cracker. Shouts of merriment followed those explosions. The girls within-doors enjoyed the fracas from the open windows; and in the evening our good elders brought forth a store of Roman candles, blue lights, and rockets. I remember a year, early in the thirties, in which good Gideon Lee, a Democratic mayor of New York, issued an edict prohibitive of all home fireworks. Just as we had settled ourselves in the determination to regard him thenceforth as our natural enemy, the old gentleman's heart failed him; and, living next door to us, he called to say that he would make a few exceptions to the rule for the day, and that we should count among these."

While in the prime of life, Samuel Ward, the father, died, and the family moved out of the Bond Street home, and went to live with an uncle, Mr. John Ward. Not long after, Julia, who was now a very attractive young woman, went to Boston on a visit. There she met Margaret Fuller, Horace Mann, Charles Sumner, Ralph Waldo Emerson, and other distinguished people. They were pleased with the intellectual and charming girl from New York; and she, in turn, revered the friends who gave her such a cordial welcome.

Among this band of thinkers was Dr. Samuel Gridley Howe, already noted as a philanthropist and reformer. Born in Boston in 1801, a graduate from Brown University in 1821, he espoused the cause of Greek independence in 1824, and sailed for Greece. At first he was a surgeon, and attempted to organize hospitals; then he took an active part in the war, and for two years suffered all the hardships and dangers of the conflict.

When Julia Ward met Dr. Howe, who was eighteen years older than herself, it was not strange that among many admirers he won her heart and hand. " 'Chev' was the name by which she always called our father," says her daughter Laura: "it was an abbreviation of Chevalier; for he was always to her the 'knight without reproach or fear.' "

Soon after their wedding, Dr. and Mrs. Howe made an extended journey in Europe, taking with them the bride's youngest sister, Annie, who had written in her childhood the unique poem on the ravens standing in the hall.

Arrived in England, many were eager to see Dr. Howe and his gifted young wife. They received much attention from Dickens, Carlyle, the Duchess of Sutherland, the poet Rogers, Sydney Smith, Monckton Milnes, and others.

On their return to Boston, Dr. and Mrs. Howe found a warm welcome. Soon an estate was purchased near the Institution for the Blind, of which Dr. Howe always remained the director, which the young mother, on account of its great garden and conservatories, called, half in sport, "Green Peace."

It was a roomy old house, with a large dining-room.

"On the floor," says the daughter Laura, "was a wonderful carpet, all in one piece, which was made in France, and had belonged to Joseph Bonaparte, a brother of the great emperor. In the middle was a medallion of Napoleon and Marie Louise, with sun-rays about them; then came a great circle, with strange beasts on it ramping and roaring (only they roared silently); and then a plain space; and in the corners birds and fishes such as never were seen in air or sea. Yes, that *was* a carpet! It was here we danced the wonderful dances."

"Green Peace" was a home where the literary mother, her flock of six children, and the philanthropic father, found their greatest comfort. Dr. Howe played with his children, took them with him in his morning walks, told them stories, or read to them from his favorite poets, Scott and Byron.

Mrs. Howe, with her beautiful voice, sang to the children the German songs which she and her brother had sung together after he came back from Heidelberg, or pretty French and Italian airs. When the little ones wanted a change she wrote songs of her own, composing both the music and the words, such as "Baby's Shoes," published in "Later Lyrics,"—

> "Little feet, pretty feet,
>   Feet of fairy Maud,
> Fair and fleet, trim and neat,
>   Carry her abroad!
>
> Be as wings, tiny things,
>   To my butterfly:
> In the flowers, hours on hours,
>   Let my darling lie.
>
> Like a charm which doth arm
>   Some poor mother's pain

For the child dream-beguiled
    She shall know again,

By the pet amulet
    Kept through lonely years;
Little shoe, I and you
    Would not part for tears."

In 1854, when Mrs. Howe was thirty-five, her first volume of poems, *Passion Flowers,* was published anonymously, though the authorship was soon guessed by Emerson, Longfellow, Holmes, and others.

The following year, 1855, *The World's Own,* a five-act tragedy in blank verse, was played at Wallack's Theatre in New York, Mathilda Heron and Edwin Sothern taking part in it. Two years later, 1857, a second volume of poems appeared, *Words for the Hour,* full of the spirit of the sad and earnest years which preceded our Civil War.

Both Dr. Howe and his wife were ardent workers in the anti-slavery cause. They edited an anti-slavery paper, the *Boston Commonwealth,* established by the patriotic and ever generous Mr. Stearns, and were leaders with Garrison, Sumner, Phillips, Higginson, and Theodore Parker. "It was my husband," says Mrs. Howe, "who suggested the holding of meetings in Boston for the discussion of the problem with Abolitionists on one side, and pro-slavery men on the other. Robert Toombs, who boasted that he would hold his slaves under the shadow of the Bunker Hill Monument, and Colonel Houston, I remember, came, and we had lively times."

In 1858 *Hippolytus,* a tragedy, was written for Edwin Booth by Mrs. Howe. *A Trip to Cuba* was published in 1860, giving an account of a winter spent by Dr. Howe and herself in the tropics. The next year was

written the world-famed, *Battle Hymn of the Republic*.
She has told how it came to be written.

"In the late autumn of the year 1861 I visited the
national capital, in company with my husband, Dr. Howe,
and a party of friends, among whom were Governor and
Mrs. Andrew, Mr. and Mrs. E. P. Whipple, and my
dear pastor, Rev. James Freeman Clarke.

"One day we drove out to attend a review of troops,
appointed to take place some distance from the city.   In
the carriage with me were James Freeman Clarke and
Mr. and Mrs. Whipple.   The day was fine, and everything promised well; but a sudden surprise on the part of
the enemy interrupted the proceedings before they were
well begun.   A small body of our men had been surrounded
and cut off from their companions; re-enforcements were
sent to their assistance, and the expected pageant was
necessarily given up.   The troops who were to have taken
part in it were ordered back to their quarters, and we
also turned our horses' heads homeward.

"For a long distance the foot-soldiers nearly filled the
road.   They were before and behind, and we were obliged
to drive very slowly.   We presently began to sing some
of the well-known songs of the war, and among them,—

'John Brown's body lies a-mouldering in the grave.'

"This seemed to please the soldiers, who cried, 'Good
for you!' and themselves took up the strain.   Mr. Clarke
said to me, 'You ought to write some new words to that
tune.'   I replied that I had often wished to do so.

"In spite of the excitement of the day, I went to bed
and slept as usual, but awoke next morning in the gray
of the early dawn, and to my astonishment found that
the wished-for lines were arranging themselves in my
brain.   I lay quite still until the last verse had completed
itself in my thoughts, then hastily rose, saying to myself,

'I shall lose this if I don't write it down immediately.'
I searched for a sheet of paper and an old stump of a pen
which I had had the night before, and began to scrawl the
lines almost without looking, as I had learned to do by
often scratching down verses in the darkened room
where my little children were sleeping. Having completed this, I lay down again and fell asleep, but not without feeling that something of importance had happened
to me." The poem was written at Willard's Hotel.

"One of my friends," says Mrs. Howe, "now has the
original 'scrawl' of the *Battle Hymn*. It is almost
indecipherable; if I hadn't copied it the day after it was
written, I should probably have lost it."

About this time Mrs. Howe became interested in
Woman Suffrage. Mrs. Howe says: "I think it may
have been in 1869 that Colonel Higginson wrote to me,
earnestly requesting that I would sign, with others, a call
for a woman's suffrage convention, to be held in Boston.
The war had then brought many of us out of the ruts of
established ways. It had changed the aspect of our social
world, and, will ye, nill ye, had forced us to take a larger
outlook into the possibilities of the future than it had
been our wont to do. I not only signed the call just mentioned, but actually found my way into the assemblage,
where Lucy Stone, Wendell Phillips, Colonel Higginson,
and William Lloyd Garrison occupied the platform. As
I entered and shyly seated myself, a messenger sought me
out, and invited me to sit with the friends of suffrage.

"The speeches to which I listened were calm, even, and
convincing; and when I, in turn, was requested to say a
few words, I gave in my adherence to the cause. From
that time forth I marched to the music of a new hope;
and all the years that have passed since then I have never
had occasion to regret the departure which I made then
and there."

In 1869 Mrs. Howe helped to establish the New England Women's Club, composed of several hundred able and cultured women, who met weekly to listen to some paper or discussion on educational or other useful topic. They had parlors in Park Street, Boston. Mrs. Howe was the second president of the club, and its members were never willing that she should resign.

She also founded the Boston Saturday Morning Club. With Colonel Higginson, she founded the Town and Country Club of Newport, and was its president. For many years Mrs. Howe was also president of the Association for the Advancement of Women, of which she was an original member, and to whose annual congresses she contributed valuable papers.

"In 1870," says Mrs. Howe, "the horrors of the Franco-Prussian war moved me to write an epistle 'to womanhood throughout the world,' asserting the right of women to prevent the waste of life, of which they alone knew the cost. This document was translated into several languages, and was quite widely distributed and read."

In 1873 Dr. Howe and his wife paid a second visit to San Domingo and became deeply attached to the people. The health of the former had become much impaired by his severe labors; and on January 9, 1876, he died after a brief illness. Dr. James Freeman Clarke says of Dr. Howe, in his volume of *Memorial Sketches*, "To me it seems that his last work was far greater than his first, and that the chivalry of his youth was crowned by the diviner and more gallant endeavors and successes of his manhood and age."

Mr. Anagnos, a Greek, who started the first kindergarten for the blind at the Institution, had married the eldest daughter, Julia Romana Howe, a young woman of superior mind and character, whose early death brought sorrow to a great many hearts. Her fair face and gentle presence among the blind children who loved her linger in my memory as an exquisite picture. Mr. Anagnos succeeded Dr. Howe.

The year after Dr. Howe's death, Mrs. Howe took her daughter Maud to Europe, and remained abroad two years, visiting England, France, Holland, Switzerland, Germany, Egypt, Syria, Italy, Turkey, and Greece.

Thereafter she devoted herself untiringly to everything that elevated humanity. She lectured in all parts of the United States, always showing herself to be the elegant, well-bred highly-educated woman. Some of her best-known lectures are, "Is Polite Society Polite?" "Greece Revisited," "Women in the Greek Drama," and "Reminiscences of Longfellow and Emerson."

She lectured before the Parisians in the French language, on the education and condition of women in the United States, also in Florence, Italy, and Athens. During her last visit to Rome she preached two sermons.

In her own country she preached in many pulpits. "I well remember," she says, "the astonishment of people when, a great many years ago, I preached a sermon in a Boston church. Yet at the time I did not think of the criticism that would be passed upon me for doing it. I simply felt the desire to preach, so I preached; and I have preached a great many times since in churches. . . . I have seen the barriers against women slowly broken down during the past quarter of the century; and I feel sure that the time is coming when women will have all the political and industrial privileges of men."

"I have great faith," says Mrs. Howe, "in the ministerial ability of women, and was one of a committee which held the first convention of women ministers in Boston, late in the seventies."

Mrs. Howe was a contributor to many periodicals.

For some time she was an associate editor of the *Woman's Journal*. Besides, she published several books, *Modern Society* in 1881, a *Life of Margaret Fuller* in 1883, and edited others.

When the women's department of the Cotton Centennial Exhibition at New Orleans, in the winter of 1885, needed as its head a woman of energy, brain, and polished manners, Mrs. Howe was at once chosen, and filled the position to the satisfaction of all. She was none the less warmly welcomed because she had adhered to principle in the anti-slavery days.

On her seventy-fifth birthday, 1894, a reception was given Mrs. Howe by her son, Henry M. Howe, a noted mining engineer, at his home on Marlborough Street, Boston. The *New York Critic* of June 2, said: "Notable men and women gathered to honor her. To repeat their names would be to repeat the names of the leaders of the social and literary circles. That Mrs. Howe herself enters into the last quarter of her century with the same strong physical and mental powers which have distinguished her in the past is shown by her active work on the days preceding her birthday. Last week she delivered a most interesting address before the High School Alumni, and yesterday she presided at a meeting of the woman suffragists of New England."

At the World's Columbian Exposition in Chicago, 1893, Mrs. Howe spoke before the Woman's Congress, the Parliament of Religions, the Congress of Social Purity, and in the Woman's Building.

Invited to Des Moines, Iowa, in the spring of 1894, the Iowa State Legislature, sent Mrs. Howe an official invitation to visit both houses at a stated time. They sent a carriage to bring her to the State House, where the Governor received her, and conducted her first to the Senate and then to the House of Representatives. In each of these her entrance was officially announced, the whole body standing until she had taken her seat beside the Speaker, who made her an address of welcome, to which she responded.

Mrs. Howe's friends were the eminent ones of two hemispheres. Kossuth was given a great reception at Green Peace. Agassiz was a loved and frequent visitor. Charles Sumner found the Howe home one of rest and congeniality. Edwin Booth came to a party given in his honor; and Mrs. Richards tells how "instead of talking to all the fine people who were dying for a word with him, he spent nearly the whole evening in a corner with little Maud, who enjoyed herself immensely. What wonder, when he made dolls for her out of handkerchiefs, and danced them with dramatic fervor?"

But not to the great only was Mrs. Howe a friend. Her daughter Laura says, "Our mother's hospitality was boundless. She loved to fill the little house to overflowing, in summer days, when every one was glad to get out into the fresh, green country. Often the beds were all filled, and we children had to take to sofas and cots. Once, I remember, Harry slept on a mattress laid on top of the piano, there being no other vacant spot."

Thus passed a long, busy, and useful life; and it was at the ripe age of ninety-one that it ceased. Julia Ward Howe passed away, October 17, 1910. To the last she was alert and dominant, a welcome figure at any public gathering. Her *Reminiscences,* in 1899, was her last book.

JANE ADDAMS

It is a wonderful thing to have performed a helpful service, and to have written a helpful book. The author of *Twenty Years at Hull-House* has done both, and I wish that everybody could read it. One closes the book with a resolution to carry out in life Emerson's motto, "Help Somebody," and to feel that one who does not live for others makes a failure of the present and the future.

Jane Addams who wrote the book, and who made Hull-House a power for good both at home and abroad, was born at Cedarville, Illinois, September 6, 1860, one of the younger members of a large family. Her mother died when she was a baby.

Her father owned two mills not far from their home, a flour mill and a sawmill and later was president of a bank, and member of the State Senate for sixteen years.

She was a delicate child because of a curvature of the spine, but she was a lover of nature, eager to learn, and a thinker even when young. Before she was seven years old, she showed a deep interest in the inequalities of life.

She says: "On that day I had my first sight of the poverty which implies squalor, and felt the curious distinction between the ruddy poverty of the country and that which even a small city presents in its shabbiest streets. I remember launching at my father the pertinent inquiry why people lived in such horrid little houses so close together, and that after receiving his explanation, I declared with much firmness when I grew up I should, of course, have a large house, but it would not be built among the other large houses, but right in the midst of horrid little houses like these." And all this has come true.

When she was about eight years old this desire of equality for all was put to the test. She appeared before her father in a handsome new cloak, as they were about to go to Sunday School where he taught a large Bible Class. It was so much finer than any other child had, that he advised her to wear her old one, that the children might not feel bad. "I complied with the request," she says, "but I fear without inner consent, and I certainly was quite without the joy of self-sacrifice as I walked soberly though the village street by the side of my counselor."

He told his little girl that "people might be equal in things that mattered much more than clothes, the affairs of education and religion, for instance, which we attended to when we went to school and church, and that it was very stupid to wear the sort of clothes that made it harder to have equality even there." A Quaker by descent, Mr. Addams' life of probity and high ideals necessarily bore fruit in his family. He was a friend of Lincoln, and the letters he had received from the great man made a deep impression upon his little daughter. It was said of Mr. Addams that in the trying reconstruction days after the Civil War, "he had never been offered a bribe because bad men were instinctively afraid of him." He died in August, 1881.

In 1877, when Jane Addams was seventeen, she went to Rockford Seminary, Illinois, which soon after became a college. Her three older sisters had attended there, and her father was a trustee, but she greatly desired to go to Smith College.

Miss Addams gave much time to Greek and mathematics. "My genuine interest was history" she says, "partly because of a superior teacher, and partly because my father had always insisted upon a certain amount of historic reading ever since he had paid me, as a little girl, five cents a *Life* for each Plutarch hero I could intelligently report to him, and twenty-five cents for every volume of Irving's *Life of Washington*."

Before her graduation she had decided to study medicine and "live with the poor." The winter after leaving college was spent at the Woman's Medical College of Philadelphia, but the old spinal difficulty compelled her to enter the hospital of Dr. Weir Mitchell, and to go to Europe for two years.

In these years abroad, she says, she "was irresistibly drawn to the poorer quarters of each city. She saw, as all of us have seen who are interested in the inequalities of life, the struggles of the poor in the East End of London; saw them on Saturday night, buying at auction decaying fruit and vegetables; saw one man who had bidden in a cabbage, sit down on the curb, and hastily devour it raw.

While she studied art in Dresden and in Rome, she could not forget the underpaid laborers, and the dire poverty she met. On her return she spent two winters in Baltimore attending lectures at Johns Hopkins University, and her summers at her Illinois home, where she united with the Presbyterian Church.

In one of these summers, she says: "I visited a Western State where I had formerly invested a sum of money in mortgages. I was much horrified by the wretched conditions among the farmers, which had resulted from a long period of drought, and one forlorn picture was fairly burned into my mind. A number of starved hogs—collateral for a promissory note—were huddled into an open pen. Their backs were humped in a curious camel-like fashion, and they were devouring one of their own number, the latest victim of absolute starvation, or possibly merely the one least able to defend himself against their voracious hunger.

"The farmer's wife looked on indifferently, a picture of despair as she stood in the door of the bare, crude house, and the two children behind her, whom she vainly tried to keep out of sight, continually thrust forward their faces almost covered by masses of coarse, sun-burned hair, and their little bare feet so black, so hard, the great cracks so filled with dust that they looked like flattened hoofs. The children could not be compared to anything so joyous as satyrs, although they appeared but half-human. It seemed to me quite impossible to receive interest from mortgages placed upon farms which might at any season be reduced to such conditions, and with great inconvenience to my agent and doubtless to the farmers, as speedily as possible I withdrew all my investment."

During Miss Addams' second journey in Europe she attended a meeting of the London match girls who were on strike. The low wages and their physical condition deeply affected her. "This impression of human misery," she says, "was added to the others which were already making me so wretched." She was learning more and more that culture, unless put to use for humanity, can easily become selfishness, and that it is far from soul-satisfying.

She had become convinced that it would be a good thing to rent a house in Chicago where actual needs existed, where young women who had devoted themselves to study might come in contact with life itself, and a life that required their unselfish aid. She finally found courage to talk the matter over with Miss Ellen Gates Starr, her old-time school friend, who was travelling with her, and who became deeply interested in the plan.

In June, 1888, five years after her first visit to the poor
of East London, she was visiting Toynbee Hall and the
People's Palace, and in January, 1889, on their return to
America, she and Miss Starr were searching for a suitable house in Chicago for settlement work.

After much looking, a large house was found at 335
South Halsted Street, built for a home in 1856 by Mr.
Charles J. Hull.   The lower part of it was now used for
offices and storerooms in connection with a factory that
stood back of it.   Before this it had been occupied by the
Little Sisters of the Poor as a home for the aged.   An
undertaking establishment was on one side, and a saloon
on the other.   The fine old house was repaired and furnished, and on September 18, 1889, Miss   .dams, Miss
Starr and Miss Keyser moved into it.

Miss Helen Culver, the owner, a relative of Mr. Hull,
soon gave the rent, and so much interested did she become,
that the present group of thirteen buildings added in the
past twenty years, all heated and lighted from a central
plant, is built largely on land which she "has put at the
service of the Settlement which bears Mr. Hull's name."

Hull-House, formerly in the suburbs, is now thickly
surrounded by Italians, Greeks, Russian Jews, Bohemians,
and other nationalities, Chicago ranking at one time as
the third Bohemian city in the world.

Miss Addams says of their ward at the time they moved
into Hull-House: "The streets are inexpressibly dirty,
the number of schools inadequate, sanitary legislation un-
enforced, the street lighting bad, the paving miserable and
altogether lacking in alleys and smaller streets, and the
stables foul beyond description.   Hundreds of houses
are unconnected with the street sewer."

Sweat-shops abounded.   "An unscrupulous contractor
regards no basement as too dark, no stable loft too
foul, no rear shanty too provisional, no tenement room

too small for his workroom, as these conditions imply low rental."

Among all these poor people, mostly foreigners, were some who had seen better days, but whom losses or disappointments had forced to such cheap rents.

Volunteers for the settlement work came quickly. A young lady came every morning from her home on the North Side to conduct a kindergarten in the drawing-room. Another organized a Boys' Club, "The Young Heroes" who listened to chivalrous tales, and undoubtedly resolved to become heroes themselves. On the first Christmas at Hull-House, Miss Addams says, "in spite of exigent demands upon my slender purse for candy and shoes, I gave to a club of boys twenty-five copies of the then new Carl Schurz's *Appreciation of Abraham Lincoln.*" Thus a great ideal was placed before them.

This Club has grown through all the years into the Boys' Club building, five stories high, built by one of the trustees of Hull-House "with well equipped shops for work in wood, iron and brass; for smithing in copper and tin; for commercial photography, for printing, for telegraphy, and electrical construction. These classes meet twice a week and are taught by intelligent working-men," says Miss Addams, "who apparently give the boys what they want better than do the strictly professional teachers."

The girls were gathered into sewing classes, and could carry home the garments they made. There were also classes in cooking, dressmaking and millinery. A day nursery was carried on for sixteen years. "We early learned to know the children of hard-driven mothers who went out to work all day," says Miss Addams, "sometimes leaving the little things in the casual care of a neighbor, but often locking them into their tenement rooms. The first three crippled children we encountered in the neighborhood had all been injured while their mothers were at work. One had fallen out of a third story window, another had been burned, and the third had a curved spine, due to the fact that for three years he had been tied all day long to the leg of the kitchen table, only released at noon by his older brother, who hastily ran in from a neighboring factory to share his lunch with him.

"When the hot weather came, the restless children could not brook the confinement of the stuffy rooms, and, as it was not considered safe to leave the doors open because of sneak thieves, many of the children were locked out. During our first summer an increasing number of these poor little mites would wander into the cool hallway of Hull-House. We kept them there and fed them at noon, in return for which we were sometimes offered a hot penny which had been held in a tight little fist ever since mother left in the morning, to buy something to eat with.

"Out of kindergarten hours our little guests noisily enjoyed the hospitality of our bedrooms under the so-called care of any resident to keep an eye on them." Thus the necessity of a day nursery became apparent. "With all the efforts made by modern society to nurture and educate the young, how stupid it is," says Miss Addams, "to permit the mothers of young children to spend themselves in the coarser work of the world!"

The older people were not forgotten on the first New Year's Day at Hull-House. Many of them gathered, a carriage being sent for the most feeble, and an Old Settler's Party was organized. This has been carried on each year.

For several years, knowing how aged people dreaded and struggled against the "poor-house," Miss Addams arranged a two week's vacation for many from the Cook County Infirmary. A dollar a week provided a lodging with some old acquaintance; they could have two good meals a day at the coffee-house established at Hull-House, where many factory operatives and others came for food; and they went back comparatively happy to spend a winter in remembering the bright days, and looking forward to them again.

The "residents" at Hull-House were called upon for every kind of charity. A woman would come, daily beaten by her husband. They were asked to wash a new-born baby or to conduct a funeral. All this was different from studying art in Europe, but it brought real happiness to be of service in the world.

The Working People's Social Science Club was organized in 1890, and many prominent men, like Henry George, spoke to large audiences at Hull-House.

The Jane Club, a co-operative undertaking in board for working girls, has been most successful. A friend of one of the Trustees offered twenty thousand dollars to build a house for this club. When Miss Addams learned that this man "was notorious for underpaying the girls in his establishment and concerning whom there were even darker stories," she refused the money. Later a new club house was built by an old friend of Hull-House. From the first, winter concerts were greatly enjoyed, and in 1893 Hull-House Music School was opened in quarters of its own. Loan exhibitions of pictures were given at Butler Art Gallery, which has a reading-room on the first floor, and a studio above.

Besides her great labor at Hull-House, Miss Addams has been a remarkable worker in other ways. She helped to obtain the first factory law of Illinois, regulating the sanitary conditions of sweat-shops, and fixing fourteen as the age at which a child might be employed.

This necessitated much speaking before social clubs, and other organizations to arouse public sentiment.

After the Pullman car strike, she assisted in procuring a law creating a State Board of Conciliation and Arbitration, also free employment bureaus under State control, with power by the officials to regulate private employment agencies. This law was passed by the Illinois Legislature, in 1899. It is not strange that with her womanliness, her deep interest in the oppressed, her sympathy and her good judgment, she has been one of the arbitrators appointed by the mayor in several strikes.

Hull-House has taken an active part against the wretched tenements where tuberculosis thrives. In 1902, in an epidemic of typhoid fever, it was found that their ward, with one thirty-sixth of the population of the city, registered one sixth of the total number of deaths. The sanitary inspection had been most incompetent.

Hull-House has worked for public baths for the people. It has also labored against the sale of cocaine to minors, and helped to obtain an effective law regulating such sale in 1907.

Hull-House joined actively with the Juvenile Court upon the latter's establishment in Chicago, in 1899. When the Court was housed in a model building of its own in 1907, alarmed by the amount of juvenile delinquency and crime, the Juvenile Protection Association was formed, whose twenty-two officers thereafter met weekly at Hull-House "with their executive committee to report what they have found, and to discuss city conditions effecting the lives of children and young people."

Miss Addams constantly urged playgrounds for the children, and recreation for the young who seek adventure and will have entertainment. She made an able plea for this in her book, *The Spirit of Youth and the City Streets.*

She also wrote other books; *"Democracy and Social Ethics,"* and *"The Newer Ideals of Peace."* In the latter she speaks earnestly of the duty of the State to protect its children. Of the two million children under sixteen, according to the census of 1900, who are earning their own living, she says, "We have made public education our great concern in America. It has spared no pains to make the system complete, and yet as rapidly as the children leave the schoolroom, the State seems to lose all interest and responsibility in their welfare and has, until quite recently, turned them over to the employer with no restrictions.

"At no point does the community say to the employer, we are allowing you to profit by the labor of these children whom we have educated at great cost, and we demand that they do not work so many hours that they shall be exhausted. Nor shall they be allowed to undertake the sort of labor which is beyond their strength."

Miss Addams was made a member of the Chicago Board of Education in 1905, and has for years spoken before large audiences, east and west, with convincing power and persuasion, on philanthropic and educational matters.

In 1895, after an illness from typhoid fever, she went to Europe to regain her health, meeting Tolstoy at his Russian home, and many other distinguished persons. She again visited Europe in 1900.

Miss Addams was the President of the National Conference of Charities and Correction held at St. Louis, in May, 1910. Dr. Graham Romeyn Taylor, founder of Chicago Commons Social Settlement says: "The St. Louis Conference would go down as memorable, if for no other reason than that it was the year of Jane Addams' presidency and leadership, and the occasion of her keynote utterance on Charity and Social Justice."

The outbreak of the World War found Miss Addams' sympathies strongly enlisted on the side of peace; and throughout the struggle she bent her energies to the speedy ending of the struggle and the prevention of all wars in the future. To many, even of her friends, this might seem Utopian but it is by no means the first of her dreams for the advancement of mankind. She also served on the Executive Committee of the American Union Against Militaism.

She was chosen as the first Chairman of the Women's Peace Party, and Chairman of the International Committee of Women for Permanent Peace.

A high honor came to her when she was elected President of the International Congress of Women, in 1919. She attended the Peace Conventions at the Hague, in 1915, at Zurich, in 1919, and at Vienna, in 1921.

Besides the books already mentioned she wrote *A New Conscience and an Ancient Evil,* 1911; and five years later *The Long Road of Women's Memory,* which contains many interesting side glimpses of this foremost of women for world uplift and betterment.

Miss Addams was quite active in America in the suffrage movement. But her methods were always those of conciliation. Floyd Dell, in comparing her fight for suffrage with that of Mrs. Pankhurst in England, showed how opposed they were in method (*Women as World Builders*):

"No one would call Miss Addams implacable. It is not intended to suggest that Miss Addams is one of those inveterate compromisers who prefer a bad peace to a good war. But she has the gift of imaginative sympathy; and it is impossible for her to have toward either party in conflict the cold hostility which each party has for the other. She sees both sides; and even though one side is the wrong side, she cannot help seeing why its partisans believe in it."

"If the under dog were always right," Miss Addams has said, "one might quite easily try to defend him. The trouble is that very often he is but obscurely right, sometimes only partially right, and often quite wrong, but perhaps he is never altogether wrong and pigheaded and utterly reprehensible as he is represented to be by those who add the possession of prejudice to the other almost insuperable difficulties in understanding him."

Miss Addams wrote two books on Hull-House: *Twenty Years at Hull-House,* published in 1910; and *The Second Twenty Years at Hull-House,* 1930. She was author of five other books on kindred topics, as well as numerous shorter articles.

In 1923, while visiting Japan, she underwent a serious operation which depleted her strength, and from which she never fully recovered. On the very day of the announcement that she and Dr. Nicholas Murray Butler were the joint recipients of the Nobel Peace Prize, in 1931, she went to Johns Hopkins Hospital, in Baltimore, for another operation. She died, May 21, 1935, in her seventy-fifth year.

Jane Addams was the recipient of many honors, and was repeatedly hailed here and abroad as one of the very greatest women of her time.

ALICE FREEMAN PALMER

To be born in a small country town, to earn money for an education, to help educate brother and sisters, and later become the honored and loved president of a large Eastern college, and an educational power in the land, is no small thing.

Alice Elvira Freeman was born February 21, 1855, in Colesville, New York. Her father, descended from James Knox of Washington's Life Guard, was an honest hard-working farmer, and her mother a farmer's daughter. She had been a teacher and an earnest advocate of temperance. Both parents were devoted members of the Presbyterian Church. When Alice was five years old, there were three younger children to be cared for. This burden of love she took upon herself as largely as possible for several years, while the young mother helped in the multitudinous duties of life on a farm.

When President of Wellesley College, years after, Miss Freeman told me how, loving fairy stories, she related to the children all she had read. She taught herself to read when she was three, and as books were few in the farmer's home, she improvised more tales. Bible stories, too, were great favorites, and the three little Freemans soon knew by heart, Joseph in Egypt, Daniel in the lion's den, and many others. Once she told them a bear story so successfully that she badly frightened herself and the rest, and when the parents returned at nightfall, they found the little family hiding behind doors, supperless, awaiting the expected but unwelcome animals.

There was much health and happiness in this country

ALICE FREEMAN PALMER

life, for they had the companionship of the birds, and the animals on the farm, and loved trees and flowers and brooks. But Mr. and Mrs. Freeman longed for more education and a broader field of usefulness. Could he become a physician? This was a difficult matter with a wife and four little children. But Mrs. Freeman encouraged him, and promised to carry on the farm while he was absent for two years at the Albany Medical School. All, meantime, learned rigid economy, earnest industry, and increased in desire to make the most of life in whatever surroundings.

When the father returned, after a medical course, the farm was abandoned, and the family moved to the neighboring village of Windsor. Here the young doctor prospered in his profession.

At ten years of age, Alice entered Windsor Academy, an excellent school, which Dr. Freeman had aided and developed. The girl learned quickly, excelling in whatever branch of study she took up. With a desire to help everybody, as she had helped all on the farm, she made friends and kept them. Her enthusiasm and cheerful temperament, her hope and optimism made her a leader even in her youth.

A young teacher had come to the school from Princeton Theological Seminary. To Alice he probably seemed an ideal of manhood. To the young man, the bright girl with her earnest nature and desire for knowledge seemed a fitting helper in his chosen work of the ministry, a few years later on.

At fourteen she became engaged to him, he to finish his course of study, and then she would join him in some country parish. The most natural thing happened. The girl who loved knowledge longed for a college education such as her teacher had enjoyed. Six months showed her, and possibly the young man, that she, at least, was far too young to consider marriage, and there was a mutual separation, with good will and esteem.

There was much talk concerning education in the Freeman family, but always about the one son. The surprise came when the eldest daughter said, "Father, I want to go to college."

She had taught her brother Latin, she had been an inspiration to him, but there was no money for two to be educated. Alice showed the family how necessary it was that she should not only be self-supporting, but help support and educate the brother and two sisters.

It was ascertained that Michigan University at Ann Arbor was one of the very few places of learning that thought it wise for women to be well educated, and had opened its doors to them two years previously. It seems strange now to think of the foolish arguments used: that girls would lose their health by study; that they would cease to be refined and lovely if they learned Greek and higher mathematics; that they would not marry or be sought in marriage—forgetting that the ideal marriage is always true companionship.

In June, 1872, having graduated from Windsor Academy at seventeen, Dr. Freeman took his daughter Alice on the long journey to Michigan to attend Commencement and take the entrance examinations. She did not pass! If her father thought for a moment that Alice would give up the project, the slight, ardent girl did not think of it. They talked with the noble President Angell, who, realizing that Windsor Academy was not a preparatory school for colleges, urged the examiners to give her a trial of six weeks.

She remained at Ann Arbor, rising every morning at four o'clock to study Greek, and made up her conditions, carrying on her class work at the same time.

After two years in College, money must be earned. The brave girl did not write home pecuniary troubles, but applied to President Angell for a school. This was found at the head of the Ottawa, Illinois, High School, where the hundred young men and women were nearly her own age. She won the love of the scholars, stimulated them greatly in their Greek and Latin, and was urged to remain a second year, which she declined.

These University years were a delight, with all their hardships. She writes home cheerful letters, even though she is "wearing her old black hat, buying two yards of ribbon and trimming it herself," saying, "Whatever comes, I know is best for me. It is all right. Still I believe God helps only those who help themselves. If our Father wants me to go through college, I know I shall go; and if He doesn't, I don't want to. That is the end of it. Meanwhile I am planning and thinking."

But study was not the whole of college life. She joined college clubs, distinguished herself in the debating society, united with the Presbyterian Church, taught in the Sunday School and in a Mission School, was very active in the college Christian Association, and did some tutoring in Latin and Greek.

With all the work, she kept the sunny nature which was her's through life. President Angell wrote of her, "Her soul seemed bubbling over with joy, which she wished to share with the other girls. While she was, therefore, in the most friendly relations with all the girls then in college, she was the radiant centre of a considerable group whose tastes were congenial with her own. Her nature was so large and generous, so free from envy, that she was esteemed by all her comrades, whether they cherished exactly her ideals or not."

Miss Freeman graduated in 1876, with honor, in a University of fifteen hundred students, almost all young men. In her own class were sixty-four men and eleven women. She was always an advocate of co-education. In the home, in the school, in social life, men and women had grown up together. She saw no reason why four years of study should keep them separate.

Life had not been easy at the University, and now it was to be harder still. She must earn for others, and was glad to do it. She taught for a year at Lake Geneva, Wisconsin, in a seminary for girls, and then for two years was Principal of The East Saginaw, Michigan, High School.

The health of a favorite sister, Stella, had failed through consumption. Dr. Freeman had met pecuniary reverses, and turned his property over to his creditors. The college girl now showed that with her sweetness and cheer there was great strength of character. She and her sister Ella, whom she had already aided and who was teaching, rented and furnished a house, and moved the family to Saginaw. The father resumed his practice and the son found a place in a store. Later he attended the Medical School of the University of Michigan. But all the comfort and success in the new home could not save Stella. She died in June, 1879, at the age of eighteen, deeply beloved and mourned.

Miss Freeman was not to remain long in the west. In 1875, Henry F. Durant of Boston, a noted and brilliant lawyer, having lost his only son and heir by death, opened on his estate at Wellesley, fifteen miles from Boston, a college for women. On his three hundred acres of beautiful lake, woodland, hill and valley, a great building of brick and stone had arisen in the form of a Latin Cross, covered by a Mansard roof, four hundred and seventy-five feet long, and one hundred feet broad, the whole surmounted with towers and bays and porches. Mr. Durant made the interior beautiful with famous pictures, and tropical plants. His own library of ten thousand volumes was added. When his million dollar gift was ready, and girls were eager to come, his great need was able teachers. Naturally he turned to President Angell of Michigan University, who recommended Miss Freeman among them. She was offered the chair of Mathematics in 1877, and that of Greek in 1878, but declined. In 1879, after Stella's death, she accepted the professorship of History at Wellesley.

For eight years she did wonderful work. She made the scholars in love with their studies. She taught, she gave a public lecture each week on some historical subject; she was the confidant, the advisor, the friend and leader. She used to tell the girls, "God has made you after His own plan, and He places you where He wishes you to work with Him to bring about the highest results for yourself. He has given you every opportunity. Make yourself what you will—remember it lies with you. God can make no mistakes."

Mr. Durant, far-sighted and absorbed in his great plan, soon saw, as he said, that "the little dark-eyed girl would be the next president." She was only twenty-four, but her executive ability, her ideas of what a college for women should be, and the uplift caused by her enthusiasm, all pointed to her to carry on his work. But the next year, 1880, she had a hemorrhage of the lungs, and was obliged to give up her strenuous labors for a time, and live in the open air. The following year, 1881, in October, Mr. Durant died, and Miss Freeman, the youngest of the professors, was made acting president and president in full the next year.

She showed great administrative power. During her presidency, fifteen suitable preparatory schools were opened in various parts of the country. She started the subscription for Norumbega hall, opened in 1886 The number of scholarships was doubled. More students applied by far than could be provided for.

She loved the college and spread its merits abroad. She founded Wellesley Clubs, often spoke in public for its advancement, and invited distinguished guests to address the students or attend their receptions. These were delightful occasions, which those of us who attended from Boston will never forget. We looked at the various things of interest under the many microscopes, we lingered in the Browning room, we talked with the girlish but self-poised president, who, charming in conversation, could tell an incident as interestingly as she told the bear-story to the small Freemans in the life on the farm.

Many honors came to the young, eloquent president. In 1882 she was made Doctor of Philosophy by Michigan University; in 1887, Doctor of Letters by Columbia University, and Doctor of Laws by Union University, in 1896.

In 1884 she made her first journey to England, with her father, she having been selected by General Eaton, one of three American delegates to the International Conference on Education, where she spoke most acceptably on the health of women in colleges, and upon other topics. The conference was held in London, Cardinal Manning presiding. After this she spent a few delightful weeks at the English Lakes.

In December, 1887, when she was thirty-two she was married to Professor George Herbert Palmer of Harvard University, a man of profound scholarship, an author, and in every way fitted to make her life happy. He was thirteen years her senior. He met Miss Freeman, as he says in his delightful life of the distinguished teacher, in 1884, at the house of Professor Horsford in Cambridge. The friendship soon grew into earnest affection. The loss to Wellesley College seemed incalculable, but thousands rejoiced to see her lay aside her hard work, and rest in an ideal home, in an ideal companionship. Not that she ever could or did give up her work. It simply grew broader when freed from great and wearing responsibilities.

In June of the following year, 1888, Mr. and Mrs. Palmer went abroad for fifteen months, that year being his Sabbatical year granted by Harvard each seventh year, when a professor may have half pay and rest, how and where he chooses. These months were full of comfort and peace, away from constant interruptions and unceasing calls on heart and brain from the outside world. They usually took furnished rooms, whether in Germany, France, Italy, or Greece, and visited art galleries, museums, and parks, and enjoyed natural scenery to their hearts' content. The contrast from the struggles of early life made these restful months all the more delightful. It had paid to economize, to study hard, to help others over the rough places, and now to be helped in return.

Mrs. Palmer especially loved Venice, and Grasmere in English Lakes. At Tubingen, Germany, where Professor Palmer had studied in early life, they found much to enjoy. They traveled hundreds of miles on their bicycles. She writes from Italy: "We lie in the sand, we gather the blossoming flowers, the ripe oranges and olives, and are sure that it is June and not January. Anything like this I have never experienced before, and I find it unspeakably fascinating."

On their return, Mrs. Palmer found work, as usual, waiting for her. She loved her home and its domestic life, and made it a welcome place for hundreds. Eminently social, she met her old friends and made new ones. Professor Palmer says: "From the first she was our financial manager. Whatever money was received by either of us was put into her safe-keeping; and it was she who then appropriately distributed it to tradesmen, pockets, and banks. The skilful planning of how to extract the largest enjoyment from a given outlay was a game she delighted to play, and I think her favorite volume was her classified account book."

Her variety and amount of work became very great. She was made a Trustee of Wellesley, in 1888, and her connection with the college was always very close. She was called here and there for public addresses, and her fluent speech, never written out, her magnetism, grace and dignity, and her charming personality, won for her eager listeners. If Professor Palmer promised an address and was unable to go, his wife would take his place, or he would take her's. In 1889, Governor Ames appointed Mrs. Palmer a member of the Massachusetts State Board of Education, which position she held for the remaining thirteen years of her life.

She was president for several years of the Woman's Education Association of Boston, which constantly devised means for the higher education of women. They aided Radcliffe College, and desiring degrees from Harvard, raised an endowment of $100,000, Mrs. Palmer being chairman of the Committee. When the Harvard Corporation, by a majority of one, required Radcliffe to give its own degrees, the money was returned to the givers. She also aided in raising $110,000 for Wellesley.

In 1891, Mrs. Palmer was appointed by the Governor one of five on a Board of Managers for Massachusetts, for the World's Fair at Chicago. On this Board she did most efficient and valuable work.

She was deeply interested in Foreign and Home Missions as well, and was president of the Woman's Home Missionary Association. She was also president of the International Institute for girls in Spain.

Both Professor and Mrs. Palmer were members of the Equal Suffrage Association, believing "no doubt" as he says, "that eventually women will vote as naturally and with as little disturbance to the community as do men." He quotes a letter from his wife to a friend: "How much time must a woman spend on her political duties? If she belongs to the well-to-do class and hires others to do her domestic work, she has time for whatever interests her most—only let her interests be noble. If she does her own house work, she can take ten minutes to stop on her way to market for voting once or twice a year. She can find half an hour a day for newspapers and other means of information. She can talk with her family and friends about what she reads. Study of the vital questions of our government would make them better comrades to their husbands and friends, better guides to their sons, and more interesting and valuable members of society. Women have more leisure than men; they are less tied to hours of routine; they usually have more years of school training, and in this country their conscience and loyalty compare favorably with men's."

Mrs. Palmer labored among the poor, helped in the "No-license" campaigns for Cambridge, and was willing to aid everybody who needed advice or help. Professor Palmer wittily says: "I think she did not know a bore when she saw him—and she saw him under every guise. Sometimes he appeared as the crazy schemer, anxious to hitch his rickety wagon to her auspicious star. . . . These direct contacts with persons through calls and letters she valued extremely; and large as was the draft they made on her time, they were probably worth while."

Chicago University, founded in 1892, urged both Mr. and Mrs. Palmer to accept, one the Professorship of Philosophy, the other of History and Dean of Women. Though the salary offered was three times what was then received at Harvard, and though both believed in co-education, they declined the offer.

President Harper finally prevailed upon Mrs. Palmer to become Dean of Women, without teaching, with no obligation to reside in Chicago for more than twelve weeks each year. After three years, she resigned in June, 1895, and went to Europe, but always retained the warmest interest in the University.

When both Professor Palmer and his wife were tired of constant work, they hastened to his country home at Boxford, twenty-five miles north from Boston, and six miles from the sea, where his family had lived for eight generations, since the Indians owned the farm. Here among the flowers, and pines and brooks and woodland, both were supremely happy. They read together and studied, and wrote and rested. She wrote many poems here, some religious, some on nature, and some showing her happy married life. They loved the birds and the wild flowers. "It made a kind of festival," writes Professor Palmer "when I brought her the first columbine, the first wild rose, the first cardinal, or the first blue gentian."

It seemed a hard thing that this idyllic life should be broken; that Boxford should have but the memory of one who seemed a part of its sunshine, and the song of its birds. But it came suddenly. In 1902 the Sabbatical year was due Professor Palmer. Though hating to leave Boxford, they sailed the first of October, spending a little time at the English Lakes, and then about the first of November going to Paris. During this month Mrs. Palmer suffered from seeming indigestion. No one thought of danger until five days before her death. An operation was decided upon, and brave and calm, knowing that it would probably prove fatal, she was carried to the hospital on Wednesday forenoon, and on Saturday morning, December 6, 1902, fully conscious to the end, passed gently into the last sleep. Only forty-seven and so much accomplished!

Thousands were saddened when the brief, noble life ended. Wellesley erected in her college chapel an exquisite monument by Daniel Chester French. The college has also a full-length portrait painted by Abbott Thayer in 1890, and a bust by Anne Whitney, carved in 1892. Chicago University placed a chime of bells in Mitchell tower to honor the sweet-voiced leader. There are ten bells, the largest weighing over two thousand pounds. The Collegiate Alumnæ Association founded a fellowship in her name, and Wellesley College did likewise. Mrs. Durant had already, in 1888, erected Freeman College.

One of the chiefest and most lasting monuments to Alice Freeman Palmer is the loving and able portrayal by her husband, of her beautiful life.

CLARA BARTON

THE renowned old county of Worcester, Massachusetts, has long been famous for its production of marvelous "doers." Here was given to the world the inventors of the sewing machine and the cotton gin; Morton, the man who discovered ether; Slater, the great loom and spindle maker who revolutionized the mills of the world; Dorothea Dix, the founder of insane asylums, Bancroft, the historian; John B. Gough, the great temperance orator; Edward Everett Hale, Luther Burbank, and others equally well known to fame. And here, on Christmas Day, 1821, was born a little babe who was one day destined to become our nation's heroine, Clara Barton, "the angel of the battlefield." Every boy and girl in the land to-day who has rallied round the American Red Cross banner,—that banner whose white field symbolizes its founder's purity and whose deep red cross blazons anew her bravery, courage, and self-sacrifice—knows something of the life and work of Clara Barton, and would fain know more. She was one of the world's greatest humanitarians, and her life story is intertwined with national and international history.

Her farmer father served on the Western frontier, under Mad Anthony Wayne, side by side with William Henry Harrison—"Old Tippecanoe"—and Richard M. Johnson, then lieutenants in the army, and later president and vice-president of the United States. He was present at the slaying of Tecumseh, and marched home through the wilderness, meeting here and there in the field with a variety of adventure which ever held a breathless interest for little Clara. She was her father's pet, the baby of the household. Seated upon his knee, she fought over and over again his battles and learned "every shade of military etiquette." Here, too, she got her first ideas of the government, and it is recorded that when her sister Sally, ten years older, inquired of her privately what she thought the vice-president was like, she answered promptly: "A great green man about the size of our school-house!"

Besides these two little girls, the family numbered an older sister Dorothy, seventeen when Clara was born; a grave older brother, Stephen, fifteen; and harum-scarum David, thirteen,—the "Buffalo Bill" who undertook Clara's riding education, taking her to the pasture with him where they had the maddest kind of bare-backed gallops on their father's high-bred Morgan colts. And this training served her well. "Sometimes in later years," she tells us in *The Story of My Childhood,* "when I found myself on a strange horse, in a trooper's saddle, flying for life or liberty in front of pursuit, I blessed those wild gallops among the beautiful colts."

Clara Barton never had a doll. Her mother was too staunch a Puritan to permit such nonsense. There were animal pets, and later flower and garden beds to tend, little household tasks, and sewing for the poor. "A level head" was what the mother sought to give her daughter. And there is plenty of proof that she succeeded, though she often said that among all the girl's other teachers she had little chance. Certain it is that her training stood Clara in good stead when she had to be a "mother to an army and a little sister to the soldiers." Then, as she herself has said, she "became a notable housekeeper, if that might be said of one who had no house to keep, but lived in fields and woods and tents and wagons with all out-of-doors for a cooking range, mother earth for a kitchen hearth, and the winds of heaven for a chimney. At Antietam, so the story runs, a dying soldier longed for a custard pie, "one crinkly around the edges," just to remind him of home. The great nurse listened to the plea with swimming eyes, and a few moments later, herself made the pie, with quick supple fingers that stamped the "crinkly edges" with a touch which none but one skilled in the art could have achieved.

Clara's brothers and sisters were a family of school teachers. "All took charge of me, all educated me," she once said, "each according to his personal taste." She seemed not to be able to remember when she could not read. In spelling, arithmetic and geography, too, she had made some progress before the winter of her seventh birthday, when Stephen hoisted her on his broad shoulders and carried her off to the district school. Here for one year a stranger was her teacher; thereafter Stephen taught the school in the winters, and one or the other of her sisters had it in the summers, until Clara left for the High School at Oxford.

When she was eight years old, Clara's father moved his family down the mile-long slope to what shortly proved a place of enchantment for the child. "Here the woman who later was to cross the pontoon bridge at Fredericksburg under fire and with skirt shot away, learned to cross the winding river on teetering logs at its most dangerous depth. Later, when this sport had become tame, she would go to the mill and ride out on the saw carriage twenty feet above the stream and be pulled back on the returning log." [1]

Her first opportunity to show the talent which was later to make her the greatest of war nurses and the founder of the Red Cross in America came the summer she was eleven years old. Her brother David was

[1] *The Life of Clara Barton, Epler.*

seriously injured in a barn-raising. For two years Clara scarcely left his bedside night or day, "almost forgetting that there was an outside to the house." And then her devotion and some new remedies conquered. David became as good as new, and the family now realized with a start that they had another patient on their hands. Clara was worn out—a mere bundle of nerves, and so little! In the two years she had not grown an inch nor gained a pound! Moreover, she had become a perfect little hermit. Always shy, she was now more sensitive and bashful than ever, and preferred nothing so much as to be let alone. Sally, to divert her sister's mind from herself, started her on a stiff course of Scotch and English poetry, which she made so interesting that the little maid was captivated at once. While David, himself delighting in the open, coaxed Clara out with him on every possible pretext.

To encourage horseback riding, of which he felt there could not be too much, her father made the girl a present of a beautiful brown Morgan colt. Never was there a better-trained saddle-animal than Billy! "He could change from a single foot to a rack, pace, or trot," and could get over the ground so swiftly that not a horse around could outdistance him. Such gallops as the two had together! Shortly there was a new light in Clara's big dark eyes, and the tint of health in her dusky cheeks. But the two years of quiet housing had stunted her growth. She never grew any taller—five feet and three inches—and her figure was always slight and frail. Nor did she seem to conquer her timidness.

"Perhaps a boarding school might help her," the family concluded, and so she was sent away to an academy conducted by Colonel Stone, her first teacher, of whom she had always been very fond. But the experiment did not work. Clara was miserable among the one hundred and

fifty strange girls, and the idea had to be abandoned.
But not so her education. Home instruction went on as
before at the hands of Stephen and Sally. Later a new
tutor was secured to round off the corners they had neglected, and after this Clara mustered up courage to attend a famous district academy that had opened up south
of North Oxford, her home town. Here among other advanced studies she took up philosophy, chemistry, and
Latin, and here, best of all, she discovered the tonic which
she felt would henceforth banish worry and breakdown.
It was *Work!* She needed to be kept too busy to think
of self. She proposed to enter the cloth mills managed
by her brother, and learn to master the flying shuttle.
But to this her mother strenuously objected, and the
matter would have been dropped had not Stephen taken
up the cudgels.

"We have always kept Clara reined in too tightly," he
declared. "A few years ago she wanted to learn to
dance; this was considered too frivolous and improper;
now she wants to work. She needs some outlet for her
energies, and I, for one, am willing to let her try her skill
at the loom."

And to Clara's delight matters were finally arranged.
But she was not long permitted to enjoy her new labors.
Inside of two weeks the mills burned down, and her oc-
cupation was gone. What next should she do?

"Let her teach school," said a friend of the family.
"Nothing will help her to overcome her sensitiveness and
timidity more than responsibility for others."

And Clara finally consented to make the attempt. At
fifteen, she "let down her skirts and put up her hair,"
and in May set out to walk to her first school. As was
to be expected from a family of teachers, she was a success from the very beginning. Eighteen years, one-fifth
of her life, Miss Barton spent in the school-room, ten

CLARA BARTON

years being given to a school which she herself established among the humming factories in North Oxford. While here she found time also to keep her brother Stephen's mill books, and to read and study extensively. Daily, as her horizon broadened, Miss Barton felt the need of a better education, and finally she decided, as she said, "to break away from her long shackles" and enter the Clinton Liberal Institute, in New York State, one of the best known girls' seminaries. There were no colleges open to girls in those days. Not yet had the blessed labors of Susan B. Anthony, Elizabeth Cady Stanton, Mary Lyon, and Elizabeth Blackwell reached their pinnacle of success. "Every girl to-day should bless these pioneer women in their daily prayers," Miss Barton once said. She got all the Institute could give her, and then began to look about for a field of action. Her mother was now dead, the home was broken up, and she was free to go where she pleased. Fortune took her to Hightstown, New Jersey. As yet there were no public schools in this State, and prejudice against them ran high—"free schools for paupers" they were styled, and the few attempts to start such free schools had ended in dismal failure. Bordentown, a nearby village, had some two hundred children in school, the remaining four hundred ran wild, and Clara Barton's great heart yearned over them. She determined to go to this place, and herself open a public school.

"Give me a building," she said to the town authorities, "and I will teach three months. If at the end of that time the school is not an established success, you need not pay me a cent."

School began in a tumble-down, ramshacklety building, with six bright-faced, harum-scarum boys for pupils. Not a mother would trust her girls in such a place! But Clara Barton understood boys, and in short, as she wrote later, "Teaching was my trade. We got on well together. In five weeks our building was too small. In a year, I stood in a new building, built for me at a cost of $4000, and my six pupils had grown to six hundred. . . . At length, broken in strength, with a complete loss of voice, I was compelled to leave them. A few years later I found them all over the Southern fields standing firmly behind their muskets or lying in their blood; but every one remembered. They remember to-day, those pupils; gray-haired men of business all over the land and seas, their letters come faithfully to my table."

How hard it was for Miss Barton to leave her chosen field, only those who have known and loved the work as she did will understand. But with her voice gone and her health undermined, it was evident that she must seek elsewhere for occupation. And she must work or die, that she had decided long ago! What could she do? Some work with her hands, that was evident. As she wrote with great legibility and had a considerable knowledge of bookkeeping, she decided to go to Washington and look for a "clerkship." As Washington to her meant the Government, what more natural than that she should seek a Government position? Through the influence of the Representative from Massachusetts, she received an appointment in the Department of the Interior, during Franklin Pierce's administration, and was *the first woman to be employed by the Government.* Shortly she held a confidential desk in the Patent Office, at a salary of $1400 per year. Here she stayed until after the election of President Buchanan, in 1856, when the departments were swept clean of every one who held anti-slavery sympathies. But so well did she understand her business, and in such a muddle did the affairs she had controlled get, that at the end of two years she was recalled.

Now the war clouds were fast thickening and settling

in a pall over Washington. Buchanan, anxious to pacify
every one, satisfied none. Everywhere was division of
opinion and indecision. But not so with Clara Barton.
Accustomed always to think clearly and to reason things
out for herself, her mind was already made up. She
knew just where she stood, and in a letter written to her
niece, just after the firing on Fort Sumter, she said:
"I think the city will shortly be attacked. If it must be,
let it come, and when there is no longer a soldier's arm
to raise the Stars and Stripes above our capitol, may God
give strength to mine."

On April 15, 1861, Massachusetts responded to Lincoln's call for 75,000 troops by offering four regiments;
one of these, the sixth set off at once for Washington,
and in spite of mob opposition arrived in time to save
the Nation's capital from the hands of the enemy. As
the men detrained, Clara Barton was there to receive
them! For the boys of the sixth were largely her own
early friends and schoolmates, and she was bursting with
pride and gratitude for their swift response. Now for
the first time she bound up war wounds, and saw blood
which had been shed in combat. Nor did it set her reel-
ing, sick and faint, as had the sight of even the blood from
a chicken in her early girlhood days. When their supply
of handkerchiefs was exhausted, Miss Barton and her
helpers rushed to her home—the comfortable retreat of
one large room and several smaller ones which she kept in
a lodging house—and tore up her sheets for bandages,
towels, handkerchiefs, and the like. Nor did she stop
there. The next day the amazed church-goers met her
leading a procession of five husky negro porters carrying
hampers containing comforts for "her soldiers," and in
the Senate chamber, where they had gathered, she spread
a feast before them and contributed to their further entertainment by reading the home news to them from the

Worcester Spy. As she read, an inspiration came to her. This bore fruit in an announcement in the next issue of the *Spy.* It stated the need of various supplies for the valiant Sixth, and added that *Clara Barton* would be glad to receive any contributions in money or goods for their relief. How nobly Worcester responded! And the other cities and towns of Massachusetts were not slow in following; so that presently Miss Barton's rooms were filled and overflowing, and a warehouse nearby was hired.

Now indeed Clara Barton had work in plenty. Following the Peninsular Campaign, when the wounded came pouring in from the swamps of Chickahominy, Clara Barton met them at the wharf. As she washed those loathsome, running sores, and did all she could with first-aid methods, while the poor fellows waited in the burning hot sun for the slow-moving ambulances to take them to the hospitals, her heart overflowed with pity. So much of this awful suffering could have been relieved by quick attention on the field. Here were her early comrades and later her schoolboys of both Massachusetts and New Jersey. It was terrible that there was no one to go to them! Could she do it? Aye! But would the people be scandalized and her reputation gone, if she tried it? It would be considered right while she ministered to those who knew and loved her. But no good woman was to be found unprotected among rough and strange soldiers; and there were, moreover, strict army regulations which she must needs overcome. Should she try it?

It was her brave old soldier father who settled the question from his death-bed. "Go, my child, if duty calls you," he said. "I know soldiers, not a man but will respect and honor you for your errand of mercy."

A few months longer Clara Barton worked and waited,

caring for the wreckage from the opening battles of the Army of the Potomac, and with each arrival of the wounded her purpose grew. She *must* go to the Front! Finally came the eight thousand wounded and bleeding sufferers, with their heart-rending tales, from the line of McClellan's seven days' retreat, and the noble woman could wait no longer. Determining to take no rebuff, she finally won her way to Assistant Quartermaster-General Rucker, and laid her plans before him. Tears welled in this great-hearted man's eyes, as he listened to the plea of the slender little woman, and he blessed her with a sympathy and insight that sent her flying to get her stores loaded. For at last she had all the authority necessary! She was to be not only the first woman on the field, but the first person to take organized aid where it was most needed.

She arrived the day after the battle of Cedar Mountain, and never was human succor more welcome. For five days and nights, with only three hours' sleep, she worked like a Spartan, and then came the news of the terrible casualties on the old Bull Run field. Instantly Miss Barton left for the scene in a rude freight car, arriving about 10 o'clock Sunday morning, in the midst of acres and acres of wounded, lying sore and famishing on beds of hay. A terrible sight it was! Yet within fifteen minutes, Miss Barton and her helpers had coffee and hot soup ready and had begun on their mission of mercy.

"I never realized until that day how little a human being could be grateful for," said Miss Barton later. "A bit of bread sufficient to cover a gold eagle was worth more than the gold itself. And how we watched and pleaded and cautioned, lest some unwary searcher fire the hay with his candle, as we worked and wept that night! How we put socks and slippers upon cold damp feet, wrapped blankets and quilts about them, and when we had no longer these to give, how we covered them in the hay and left them to their rest!"

At daylight on Monday, the trains began to arrive for the wounded, but as they left filled, no appreciable vacancy showed among those sodden beds; for wagons were even yet steadily arriving with poor sufferers who had lain for three days unfed and unattended on the battlefield. It was impossible to dress a third of the wounds, the enemy hovered in the hills, any moment the firing might begin, and the place must be evacuated as speedily as possible. Miss Barton knew that if these last poor fellows were put on the trains without food, a large number could not live to reach Washington. So she sought out the commanding officers and begged that the wagons might pause at a certain point. Thereafter she made it her business to feed with her own hands each new arrival until he expressed himself satisfied.

All day the clouds had been gathering black and murky, and about four o'clock, when Miss Barton who had not paused to taste food since Saturday noon, now found a moment for this purpose, "God's artillery and man's" broke out together in a fearful crash. "Chantilly with all its darkness and horrors had opened in the rear." Imagine what it meant to keep on in that pouring flood, as darkness descended, amid lightnings and gun flashes and the deafening noise of the volleys creeping nearer and nearer! But somehow Miss Barton clung, administering such food as she had left—army crackers, pounded to crumbs, and stirred into a mixture of sweetened wine, whiskey and water. "But whether," as she said, "it should have been classed as food, or, like the Widow Bedott's cabbage, as a delightful beverage, it would puzzle an epicure to determine." Nor did it matter, so long as it imparted strength and comfort, and put heart into the poor fellows to face the jolting journey ahead.

At last, the wagons ceased to come, and the last train left, clearing the fields, but the faithful nurse dared not leave, for daylight would bring more wounded. One of her two women helpers had gone into Washington with a train of desperate sufferers, the other, worn out, lay sleeping on a pile of boxes. Miss Barton could find no place for herself, and had not strength enough left to make one. Suddenly she remembered that a little tent had been pitched for her a few rods away on the hillside. Its gleaming whiteness offered a safe shelter from trampling beasts and wagons, and she recalled that the grass there was long. Could she reach it? Never did she forget that attempt. How many times she fell from sheer exhaustion, to rise again presently and struggle onward until the welcome grasp of the canvas was in her hand, and then she found to her dismay a little brook rushing forth to meet her!

No further effort was possible. Stumbling across the water, she half-lay, half-propped herself on her arm on the farther side, where the ground was higher, and telling herself that she dare not sink down or the water would run in her ears, she drifted off to sleep! For two hours only—then the rumbling of the incoming wagons roused her, and she saw that tired nature had had its way. She lay flat on the ground, and oh, how she had rested! Springing up and wringing the water from her skirts, she went forth to those awful loads, filled alike with the wounded, the dying and the dead.

Thus until the plaintive wail of a fife and the muffled drum sounded retreat, and the enemy's cavalry skirting the hills warned them that they must leave or be taken prisoners. Yet it was impossible to desert the wounded, and with the heart of desperation they struggled on. Finally an officer burst upon the scene.

"Miss Barton, can you ride?" he demanded, breathlessly. She could indeed, thanks to David and those wild, irrepressible Morgan colts. "Then you are safe for another hour," he cried. A blessed hour! All too quickly passed, but it served to put the last wounded men on the train. Then, again came the officer. "Try the train," he ordered briefly. "It will get you through, unless they have taken the bridge. In that case, I shall be on hand with a horse, and you must take your chances with the army." .But the bridge was safe; midnight found the nation's heroine in Washington, and ready for the next call of duty.

So it was with variations on through the four years of war. In May, 1864, the government honored Miss Barton by creating for her the Department of Nurses, to be stationed at City Point, Virginia, and making her superintendent, feeling that such an act would not only show the country's appreciation, but give her sufficient authority to carry out her ideas. All the offices in the world, however, could not keep Miss Barton away from the firing line. And there she stayed until after the siege of Petersburg. Then, with the close of the war, came the burden of the missing men, and the wail of the grief-stricken multitude seeking them pressed close to her heart. For four years she did her best to find missing ones, using some $8,000 of her own means, until the Government at length awoke to the importance of what she was doing, and voted $15,000 to reimburse her funds and to aid in the further search.

All over the country were people who wanted to know the real facts of the war, and at length Miss Barton went upon the lecture platform, as the best means of answering them. Here she was an unbounded success, but the hardships of this tour, coupled with those years of unsheltered days and nights, the unending fatigue and lack of proper food, brought a heavy toll. Her voice failed, as it had long before when she was forced to leave the schoolroom, and she became a victim of nervous prostration. All winter she lay helpless in Washington, and then in the spring her doctor ordered her off to Europe to rest.

Two delightful weeks she had in Bonny Scotland, a day or two in Paris, a brief trip across southern France, and then Switzerland, where she was to rest for three years, according to home verdict. Rest! In less than a month after her arrival in Geneva, she was visited by the "International Committee for the Relief of the Wounded in War." Why was it that the United States had all along refused to join this humane movement?

Miss Barton was amazed. She had never heard of the Commission, and she was sensible enough to realize that America as a people never had either! Twenty-two nations were on the roll; in short not a civilized people in the world but ourselves was missing! Miss Barton's national pride was ashamed and humiliated. She went over the nine articles of the Treaty, the work of the World's Red Cross Convention, of 1864. Surely it was such a document as America should be proud and glad to sign! And then and there she registered a determination to see that this was done. But some months were to elapse before opportunity offered. The Franco-Prussian War was at hand, and presently the Grand Duchess of Baden and the Red Cross societies had drawn Miss Barton into their campaign of relief.

Of course, she went into it with her whole soul, and somehow had strength to carry on, but in the end her poor eyes, blinded by the stinging cannon smoke of two wars, gave way, and her nerves with them. Weary months of illness followed, many of them with bandaged eyes in a darkened room, and it was not until October, 1873, that Miss Barton landed on home soil, filled with her strong determination to establish the American National Red Cross. To this end, she proposed to settle on Capitol Hill to be near the seat of her activities, but her physician vetoed this with his most emphatic *No*. More months of illness and utter prostration followed the death of her beloved sister Sally, and she was forced to put in ten years in a sanitarium at Dansville, New York. But these were not altogether idle years. She was busy with her pen preparing the public mind for the advent of her Red Cross campaign.

With the election of Garfield, Miss Barton gathered hope. She had stood side by side with him in the rain of shell for their country's cause, and she felt that he would understand. Nor was she disappointed. He had followed the path of her pen, and his whole noble soul was fired with the glory of Red Cross work. When she went to see him, he called in Secretary Blaine and after the three had gone fully into the details of the plan, the Secretary himself enthusiastically agreed to lay it before the cabinet. Here two more men—William Windom and Robert T. Lincoln—became its champions, and the "American Association of the Red Cross" presently came into being, with a constitution drafted by the Hon. William Lawrence, of Ohio, the First Comptroller of the Treasury of the United States.

All along, the principal argument against a Red Cross for America was that we had no wars, nor were we likely to have any. Miss Barton pointed out that granting and hoping this, we were not proof against national disasters,—floods, fire, famine, and plagues: and here the Red Cross would be invaluable. The new constitution made a feature of this, and Garfield promised to recommend the cause in his message. That message alas! was never written. Garfield fell by an assassin's bullet. But President Arthur came valiantly to the rescue, and promptly carried out all of his predecessor's promises.

At length, thanks to Miss Barton's untiring perseverance, the signature of the United States was affixed to the World's Treaty, America became a member of the International Red Cross, and the fact, owing to Miss Barton's cable, was proclaimed by bonfires in the streets of Switzerland, France, Germany, and Spain. At home, the intelligence had only a four-line announcement in the Congressional report of the day's doings in the Washington *Evening Star!* Thus was the American Red Cross "left in obscurity to make its own way and live its own hard life." But, with Miss Barton as its president, it could not fail. For a quarter of a century she upheld its banner in the field through flood and fire, cyclone, famine, epidemics, and the vicissitudes of the Cuban War, and this without a falter, though she was sixty-one years of age when she began—an age when most women, especially those with delicate health, consider their working days over and retire to the chimney corner.

Clara Barton was the best known national and international figure of her time—for she made several trips across the water in the interests of the Red Cross. She numbered five of our presidents—Lincoln, Grant, Garfield, Arthur and McKinley—as well as a large number of our greatest statesmen, among her closest friends. Kings, emperors, dukes, Imperial chancellors, and European diplomats of the first rank knew and honored her—nay more, they waited with respect and deference for her wise judgment. At her death, which occurred April 12, 1912, newspapers throughout the length and breadth of the land vied with one another in their words of love, honor and esteem.

But her proudest monument, and the one which will endure for all time, is the American Red Cross.

SUSAN B. ANTHONY

SUSAN B. ANTHONY has many times been called the "Moses" of the movement for Woman's Rights. She led her sex out of the Wilderness of Utter Subjection to the very gates of the Promised Land, and there, like the Great Leader, died within sight of the prize. But there can be no doubt that to her, more than to any other of the noble women who shared her work, is due the enviable position of the American women in the world to-day. No woman has done so much for other women as she did, and when the recording angel is asked for the names of those who loved their fellow-women best, her name will lead all the rest. "No wrong under which women suffered was too great for her to dare attack it, no injustice too small to enlist her pity and her attempt to remedy it."

To Susan B. Anthony, herself an old maid, is due the entire remodeling of the marriage law, and the development of the modern axiom that "what is the husband's is also the wife's—what is the wife's is her own." She found women almost without recognition before the law—with no property rights, not even the control of their own wages and the custody of their own children; she left them safeguarded in this respect, and in four states in the Union women had equal voice with men in making the laws that govern them. She found the doors of nearly all avenues of learning closed to women, and the woman who desired an education hounded as a freak and a menace to "civilization." She left the doors of all seats of learning wide open to women, and parents eager

269

to educate both sons and daughters alike. She found only three vocations for the woman forced to earn her own bread: "hired girl," mill-hand, and school teacher. She left no bounds set to a woman's achievements save those made by her own lack of energy or ability.

To be sure, Miss Anthony did not accomplish all these herculean efforts alone and single-handed, but she was head and front of the great movement for Woman's Emancipation, and with the meeting of the first Woman's Rights convention, in 1848, the status of women began to ascend. But it was not easy! For more than sixty years "Aunt Susan's" life was one of constant battle, and she died fighting, with her face bravely turned to the last of the foe—those who opposed the ballot for women. What she endured in the earliest years—ridicule, cat-calling, vegetable-throwing, all manner of scorn and abuse— seems impossible to us now in the warmth of our enlightened outlook. "It was my good fortune," said Dorothy Dix, in the New York *Evening Journal,* on the occasion of the death of Miss Anthony, "to once stand beside the dear old liberator when an audience composed of the most brilliant and distinguished people of a big city, rose and cheered her until they were hoarse, and pelted her with roses until the frail figure in its black silk dress, and with its white silk shawl slipping from the shoulders, was standing almost knee-deep in flowers. When the applause had died away and the audience gone, she turned to me and with a smile that trembled between a laugh and a tear, she said, 'Time brings strange changes. In this very city that has pelted me with roses I have been pelted with rotten eggs for saying the very things that I have said to-night.' "

Susan Brownell Anthony was born in the Berkshire Hills, February 15, 1820,—a region famous for its loveliness of scenery, purity of air, and the birthplace of noted people, among these being William Cullen Bryant, Maria Sedgewick, the Goodale sisters, Cyrus W. Field, Jonathan Edwards, Mark and Albert Hopkins, and many others in a list too long for quoting. Oliver Wendell Holmes, whose grandfather was a Berkshire man, once wrote: "Berkshire has produced a race which, for independent thought, daring schemes and achievements that have had world-wide consequences, has not been surpassed. We claim, also, that more of those first things that draw the chariot of progress forward so that people can see that it has moved, have been planned and executed by the inhabitants of the nine-hundred and fifty square miles that constitute the territory of Berkshire, than can be credited to any other tract of equal extent in the United States."

And one of the first in these ranks was Susan B. Anthony! She was the second child of a love-match, the courtship of her father and mother being a delightful New England romance. Daniel Anthony, her father, was a Quaker school teacher, and Lucy Read, her mother, was his most brilliant and beautiful pupil. The Reads were Baptists and the Quakers were not permitted to "marry out of meeting." Moreover, Lucy Read had been brought up most liberally; she loved to dance and to wear pretty clothes, and above all to sing—a thing which was especially frowned upon by the sober, straight-laced Friends. Could she give up all these for her lover? For, of course, in those days, no one had ever dreamed of a husband adapting himself to his wife's views!

Shortly after the marriage, for love triumphed then as now, a committee of Friends waited upon Daniel, and Lucy always laughingly declared that to save himself he told them that *he was sorry he had married her!* To this the husband always replied quickly: "No, indeed. I told them that I was sorry that in order to marry the woman I loved best, I had to violate a rule of the religious society I revered most!''

Somehow this excuse appeased the elders. The Anthonys had ever stood strong in their midst, and David was a most likely young man. Moreover, they soon learned to love Lucy, for the young wife quickly adapted herself to the Friends, though she never used the "plain language" or wore the Quaker garb, and she *would* sing to her babies, which in truth delighted her Quaker relatives as much as it did her husband, and they only asked her gently why she did it.

A busy work-a-day life was Lucy Anthony's. She was the mother of eight children, and for many years she not only did all the cooking, washing and ironing for her own brood, but boarded and "did" for anywhere from eight to a dozen of her husband's factory hands as well, and this without complaint, and entirely as a matter-of course. It was the way of those days! Her spare time, and how little this must have been during her early married life, was given to reading. She loved history, Dickens and Scott, knew by heart "The Lady of the Lake," and had read the Bible from cover to cover many times. In old age, when her mind wandered, she talked with characters she had known in books, as of persons she had known in youth. Always her highest interest was in her home; she loved to have her house swept and garnished, and to provide a bountiful table; and her husband and children were ever sure of her affectionate interest in everything that interested them. "Do not mind me," she often said to Susan, in her last days, when that affectionate daughter would have tarried by her side, "Go, and do all the good you can!"

Little Susan was a remarkably bright and intelligent child. She learned her letters, and to pick out a few words, at the age of three, while she was staying at Grandmother Read's while the third baby was being made welcome at home. Susan, and indeed all the little Anthonys loved Grandma Read. They always visited her on the way both to and from school, and she never failed them in the matter of cookies, caraway cakes, maple sugar, cheese curd, and "left overs." When Lucy Anthony remonstrated, as mothers will, little Susan replied quickly, "Why, mother, grandma's *potato peelings* are better than your boiled dinners!" There was no treat to be compared with the "coffee" the good dame brewed for them—a beverage compounded by pouring boiling water, sweetened with maple-sugar, over the crust of brown rye or Italian bread. Another favorite was hasty pudding, heaped in a great cone, with its center hollowed out and filled with fresh butter and honey or maple syrup.

Early in life, Susan learned to do her share of the day's household tasks. On the occasion of a new baby, when the older sister Guelma—named for William Penn's wife who was an Anthony connection—was fourteen, Susan twelve, and Hannah ten, the three little girls did all the work for the family and some ten or a dozen mill hands, cooking the food and carrying specimens frequently to the mother's room to see if it was nicely prepared, as well as taking for her inspection the pails packed with the factory force's dinner. When Susan went away to boarding-school, one of the severest reprimands she received, was for climbing up on the teacher's table, with a broom in hand, to sweep the cobwebs out of the corner of the room; for alas! for her housewifely zeal, her heavy shoes crushed in the table top! There are many references in old letters to Susan's "tip-top dinners," and in her seventieth year, when she went to housekeeping in the old home at Rochester, New York, nothing delighted her more than to entertain a few friends at a meal which she herself had prepared.

At fifteen, Susan began her career as a school teacher, receiving two dollars per week and the doubtful privilege of boarding around. And for fifteen years thereafter she was in the harness, gradually rising in her profession, and more often than not successfully succeeding men who had been dismal failures, and receiving in return only one-fourth of the salary. It roused her fighting blood. Why should not a woman receive as much as a man for work which she performed as well or better than he did? Then and there was born her desire to wage a campaign for equal pay for equal work. Moreover, as she sojourned in home after home, she came firmly to the conclusion that she preferred a life of spinsterhood, and to those who sought to convince her otherwise, and they were many, for Susan was a handsome young woman, quick of speech and keen of wit, she turned an exceedingly cold shoulder. Married women had no life of their own, they were mere chattels, the slave to man's desires. She used often to cite with a good deal of scorn an incident which she declared was typical of woman's sphere. Her cousin Margaret's husband, in whose home she lived for two years, one day complained of a headache, and demanded quiet and a darkened room.

"Why," said Margaret, quickly, speaking from the burden of her heavy household tasks combined with ill-health, "I have had the headache constantly for two weeks."

"But my headache is different," returned her lord and master promptly, "mine is a real pain; yours is just the ache of consequence."

Poor, beloved cousin Margaret, however, gave her life because of this steady drain of "consequence!"

Again, when her father failed in business, Susan saw his creditors claim not only the things her mother cherished as relics of her girlhood's home, but her wedding presents, and even all but the barest necessities of the clothing of herself and children. Only the wit and resourcefulness of her brother, in holding the property left to Lucy Anthony by her father, kept it from falling into the maw.

"We should have a law whereby what is the wife's is her own," concluded Susan, and she added this to her growing platform of woman's rights.

For years she and her school-teacher sister, Hannah, carefully saved every penny they could spare to aid their father in paying his debts, and he, honest, scrupulous Quaker that he was—though the Friends had now cast him off because his ever-broadening creed had brought him to attend the Unitarian Church—kept a record to the last cent, and gave them his notes, which he ultimately redeemed. When Susan found herself growing daily more dissatisfied with her limited round of usefulness in the schoolroom, and turned with longing to the causes of temperance and abolition, none gave her more encouragement and hearty God-speed than her father. His mother and sister, Hannah Anthony, were "high seat" Quakers, the latter an eloquent and well-known preacher. He, himself, had long held that daughters should be trained for self-support as well as sons. He and his wife and daughter Mary attended the first Woman's Rights convention, held in Seneca Falls, and signed the declaration demanding equal rights for women. Susan was away teaching, and it was at his own suggestion that she presently came home for a year and superintended the Rochester farm, where the family now lived, while he himself devoted all his energies to his insurance business in Syracuse.

Anthony wanted his daughter to find herself, and that year, 1850, was in truth one of transition. The Anthony home teemed with liberal-minded visitors, and on Sundays when her father was at home, frequently as many as twenty sat down to the bountiful dinner, prepared by Susan, under the divided agony of "being a successful cook, and not missing a word in the parlor!" Hither came Garrison, Channing, Frederick Douglass, Pillsbury, Phillips, and scores of others who had become leaders in abolition, temperance, and Woman's Rights, and it was inevitable that Susan B. Anthony should be drawn into the reform movement.

In midsummer, the Quaker girl went up to Seneca Falls to do what she could toward getting the new People's College funded for girls as well as boys. She was the guest of Amelia Bloomer, the lady whose name, much to her own protest and chagrin, had been indelibly affixed to the "sensible costume" which she devised for women, and which for a few ill-starred years featured more or less extensively in the Woman's Rights campaign, being adopted by various of its fair champions. While Miss Anthony waited on a street corner with her hostess, who wore the bloomer costume, who should appear but another lady in bloomers, Elizabeth Cady Stanton. The latter was at once taken with the sensible young lady in grey, "the very perfection of neatness and sobriety," and she asked her at once to dinner in her own home to meet Lucy Stone and Horace Greeley, assuring Miss Anthony that the last-named spirited champion of young people would have more to do with the making of the constitution and by-laws than anybody. It was a memorable dinner, and the beginning of a life-long friendship among the three women, who were to do so much for the cause of their sex, and yet, as we are told in the

Life and Work of Susan B. Anthony, by Ida H. Harper, "There was certainly nothing formidable in the appearance of the trio: Miss Anthony, a quiet dignified Quaker girl; Mrs. Stanton, a plump, jolly, youthful matron, scarcely five feet high; and Lucy Stone a petite, soft-voiced young woman who seemed better fitted for caresses than for the hard buffetings of the world."

It is impossible in this brief sketch to follow Susan B. Anthony in her sixty-year battle for the right—a period longer than the lifetime of the average person. We can only say that she permitted nothing to daunt, or divert her. "This one thing I do," was her watchword, and she did it with a sympathy, persistence, and business-like directness which won victory and untold laurels in the end. Like Lincoln, her logic, tact and wit went hand in hand, and she could settle a discussion in almost as few words as he. On one occasion, Horace Greeley, it is said, took rather heated exception to her statement that woman's rights could only be secured by the ballot:

"See here, Miss Anthony," he demanded, sharply, "If women vote, they must fight. Are you ready to do that?"

"Yes, sir," replied Aunt Susan, with vigor, "Just as you did in the late war,—at the end of a goose quill!"

Miss Anthony was an exceedingly interesting speaker. She never soared to heights of rhetoric or flowers of fancy. What she had to say was briefly and plainly told in a simple fashion, which none could fail to understand, and those who heard her once were eager to do so again. Always she was frank and unpretentious—delightfully genuine and modest to a degree. Anna Howard Shaw in her *Memoirs* relates a little happening which shows the real Aunt Susan. One evening, shortly after the tide had begun to turn in her favor, the dear white-haired old lady walked out upon the platform, to the accompaniments of deafening cheers, which she did not in the least understand.

"What is it? What has happened?" she queried of Miss Shaw.

"*You* happened, Aunt Susan," returned her assistant, happily.

"Nonsense," said the sturdy old reformer, "they wouldn't be cheering *me!* It's the *Cause!*"

And with that she herself joined in the cheers. Needless to say, it brought down the house!

Miss Anthony died at the ripe old age of eighty-six, March 13, 1906, and the press on both sides of the water united to do her honor. Death claimed her before the dream of her life, universal equal suffrage for men and women, was realized, but to-day that hour is very near. Humanity now knows the debt it owes to this staunch and courageous woman, who "dared to take the blows and bear the scorn that other women might be free."

Every college girl to-day, every woman working in her chosen sphere, every wife protected in person and property, every mother blessed with the custody of her children, owes these prized and sacred privileges to Susan B. Anthony beyond all others. "No one ever served a cause more unselfishly than Miss Anthony served the cause of woman," says one of her dearest friends, in rendering her last tribute. "She had wonderful executive ability; she had untiring industry; great genius in many lines— all the things the world is most willing to pay for, and yet she gave them all and asked no reward for herself."

ANNA HOWARD SHAW

MORE than threescore years ago, in the days when the old-time school exhibitions held their full and interesting sway, a young girl rose to "speak a piece." But, ere half a dozen lines had been given, she toppled over in a faint, completely overcome by stage fright. She was carried into the hall and revived, and might easily have escaped any further ordeal had she been so minded. But a strong mixture of spunk and vim had been handed down to Anna Howard Shaw from a long line of Scottish Highlanders, and all her fighting forces rose in arms against her cowardly heart. She would deliver that recitation or die in the attempt! So back she marched to the stage, and succeeded in acquitting herself very creditably. Moreover, she thenceforward stuck so manfully to the guns, that she eventually developed a genius for public speaking, and such a tireless capacity for work, that she became a great American personality—an indefatigable worker in her chosen field as a minister of the Gospel, and on the lecture platform in the great causes of temperance and woman's suffrage.

Anna Howard Shaw was born at Newcastle-on-Tyne, England, February 14, 1847. When she was very young her family emigrated to the new Land of Promise, and found a home presently at Lawrence, Massachusetts. And here, shortly after the courageous event recorded above, the call of "Westward Ho!" stimulated Mr. Shaw to a further emigration. With his eldest son, James, he went to the wilderness of northern Michigan and took up a claim of three hundred and sixty acres of land. This, he reasoned, would in time become a fine estate, a place which his sons would inherit and later pass on to their sons—a vision always dear to the Englishman's heart. Staying only to build the bare walls and roof of a rude log cabin, and its huge fireplace of stone, he left James, a sturdy young man of twenty years, in charge, and returned to Massachusetts for his wife and four younger children; while he himself and two other sons remained behind to earn the money necessary to keep the family clothed and provisioned.

Such a journey and a home-coming as that was for the semi-invalid, town-bred English wife and her brood! At Grand Rapids, Michigan, one hundred miles from the "new estate," the railroad ended, and the rest of the way must be made by wagon. James Shaw was on hand to meet them with a dilapidated old prairie schooner and a raw-boned team,—a hired outfit, so disreputable-looking that twelve-year old Anna and her two elder sisters, Eleanor and Mary, were too proud to have any one think they were in any wise connected with it! So they started out on foot, their heads high in the air, and refused even to look at the lumbering old conveyance until the town had been left far behind. Then, when they would have entered the vehicle, there was alas! small room, so filled was it with bedding and provisions, not to mention a box of hungry, squealing little pigs! There was no furniture. This was to be made when the new home was reached.

Seven days it took to make that one hundred miles, and every step of it James walked ahead, leading the team, while one or more of his sisters, and sometimes the small brother Harry, the baby of the family, eight years of age, took turns in keeping him company. To the youthful Shaws the expedition supplied no end of adventure, and it was of small moment to them whether they had shelter at night at the homes of the settlers where they stopped, or failed to find it. They were strong and hearty, and there was an abundance of food with them to supply their ravenous appetites, while the strange and unusual sights aroused their interest at every turn. Not once did they fathom what their delicate mother endured, as they went deeper and deeper into the wilderness, fording innumerable streams, and often sinking so deeply into the mud that the wagon had to be unloaded before the struggling horses could pull it free.

At length, late in a memorable afternoon, they drove into the little clearing which surrounded the new "country home." And such a home! Only an unchinked log frame, with a roof, it is true, but with yawning openings where the doors and windows were destined to be, and its floor also a "thing of the future." Without a word, the mother crossed the threshold and stood looking around her. Then, smitten by the utter desolation of it all, and the thoughts of herself and children there alone in the wilderness, forty miles from a postoffice, and surrounded by Indians, wolves and wildcats, with her nearest neighbors six or eight miles away, she sank in a heap on the ground, and buried her face in her hands, not sobbing, her despair was too deep for that. Her children, frightened, stood by not knowing what to do, all their pleasure in the cabin, if indeed they had been able to find any, swept away by their mother's collapse. Never before had they known her to lose courage, and for the time being their world was chaos.

But not for long did they stand helpless. Sensible James, young lad though he was, had all the true pioneer's instinct. Rousing his elder sisters, he got them at supper preparations, over the great bed of coals which he soon had in the wide fireplace, the one comfortable feature of the huge, barn-like room. Then, with Anna and Harry as his willing helpers, he piled boughs into the corners for beds, spread them with blankets, and tacked

up more blankets at the doors and windows, as the dusk
drew close. Filled with the cheery firelight, and appetizing odor of the steaming food which Eleanor and Mary
spread upon the table—a broad, rough slab on top of
two barrels—the room needed only the sound of happy
voices to make a promise of home.

But these were stilled; for the mother yet sat silent
and unseeing. Outside, James had stationed the horses
close between the cabin and "the schooner," and was now
busy lighting the piles of brush which encircled the small
clearing. The reason for this was soon made apparent,
for the howl of wolves and the not-far-distant screech of
a panther filled the room, and startled little Harry into
wails of terror. Then, and not till then, did the mother-
heart rouse.

"But," said Anna, writing years later of this awful
night in the new home, "though my mother took up her
burden resolutely, her face never afterward lost the deep
lines those first hours of her pioneer life had cut upon it."

And small wonder. Such a host of perplexing problems as crowded close with the dawn of the new day!
Food they had, and a place to cook it and firewood in
plenty. Water was not so easy, but it could be carried
from a creek some distance away. Furniture was an
immediate necessity, and James was soon busy making
rude bunks, benches, stools and tables. Doors and windows, too, were an imperative need. There was a small
saw-mill nine miles away, and with the help of "the
neighbors" and their ox-teams, enough lumber was presently hauled not only to fill the yawning apertures and
lay a floor, but to build partitions, dividing the cabin into
four rooms and an attic. It was too late in the season
for plowing and planting, but there was plenty of wild
fruit to be gathered and dried, and Anna and Harry soon

became expert fishermen, while later they vied with the squirrels in storing away nuts.

In the Spring, James fell ill and had to go back East, and the Shaws would have been in despair, had not Anna stepped so confidently into the breach. She and Harry planted a garden, and made one hundred and fifty pounds of maple sugar and a barrel of syrup. Then the sturdy young woman began to dig a well! She finished it, too, with a little help from a neighbor boy, and ever afterward regarded it as the height of her wilderness triumphs. In the meantime there were various encounters with wild animals and Indians, which served their full share in developing courage and mettle. For the satisfaction of her deep longing for knowledge, Anna fell back on the copies of the New York *Independent,* which her father sent each month.

By the time she was fifteen years old, enough settlers had arrived to demand a district school, and Anna was the first teacher, receiving two dollars a week and the privilege of "boarding round." As this was the first school in the township, no appropriations had been made for school funds, and it was voted to pay the teacher's salary from the dog tax! Nearly all the school-books were Anna's own meager few. Hymn books and almanacs served the young pupils in lieu of readers.

In the second year of her teaching, news came that Ft. Sumter had been fired on, and that Lincoln had called for troops. Almost at once, Anna's father and her brothers, Jack and Tom, who had joined them, marched away, and she was left once again as the head of the household. Of those bitter years of war there is no need to write, for the struggle to keep alive the Shaw home in the wilderness was reflected in other homes all over the country. Sorrow, too, crept in. Eleanor died, and the sister Mary married and went to Grand Rapids to live. But through the monotony of the daily grind, broken only by messages from the Front, somehow Anna managed to keep unscathed a determination which had settled strong upon her. Someday she was going to college.

With the close of the war, and the blessed return of father and brothers, the first step toward this ambition was realized. Mary had married a successful man; and she now offered Anna a home with her, and a chance to attend the Grand Rapids High School. Most thankfully the girl accepted, and on the evening of the first day she poured out her further hopes to the principal, Lucy Stone, to whom she was greatly attracted. Nor was her confidence misplaced, for though her communication was most astonishing, in that she said she had long felt the desire stirring within her *to preach,* Miss Stone listened with perfect equanimity. As she heard of the numerous times when the child Anna and later the young backwoods teacher had stood upon stumps and harangued the unresponsive trees on all manner of subjects, one might have thought women preachers were an every-day occurrence, instead of an almost unknown quantity. And prompt indeed was she to meet the issue. Anna Shaw was at once placed in the speaking and debating classes, and given every opportunity to test her eloquence.

Nor was this all. When the young woman had again and again proved her undoubted ability, Miss Stone [1] invited her to dinner, and had as a second guest, Dr. Peck, the presiding elder of the Methodist Episcopal church. A delightful evening followed, and at its close Dr. Peck asked Anna Shaw to preach the quarterly-meeting sermon, at Ashton.

[1] Miss Stone was herself a warm advocate of Women's Rights, and, in 1869, became the founder of the American Woman's Suffrage association.

"For a moment," records Dr. Shaw, in her grippingly interesting memoirs, *The Story of a Pioneer*, "the earth seemed to slip away from my feet. I stared at him in utter stupefaction. Then slowly I realized that, incredible as it seemed, the man was in earnest."

At first the thing seemed impossible, but Dr. Peck stuck to the point, and finally an agreement was made. Six weeks intervened before the important day, and it is impossible to say how many times that first sermon was written and rewritten. Sleeping and waking it was always before Anna Shaw's eyes, but she said nothing of it to her family or friends until three days before, when she confided in her sister Mary.

Words cannot portray the latter's dismay, nor the prayers and tears with which she strove to prevail upon Anna to give up her wild notion of disgracing the family! She was powerless, however, to sway her sister's resolution, and on the morning of the fateful day the two boarded the train together. But Mary sat in the rear of the car, as far from her sister as she could get. Her destination was the bosom of her family, and she wept throughout the entire journey!

The text and subject of that first sermon have long since been forgotten; but it was listened to by a curious eager crowd, who, after the first few words, found themselves entirely in sympathy with the young girl, who trembled so violently that the oil shook in a glass lamp on a stand at her side, not alone from her natural timidity but from the thoughts of the family conclave to which Mary had gone. She knew her father, mother, brother, too, would disapprove of her course even more than her sister had done, and it was hard to go on. She felt that she was in all probability alienating herself from her family forever. But the call to preach was strong, and she felt that she was right in heeding it; so that, when Dr. Peck came

to her commending her effort, and assuring her that the
sermon had been better than his first one, at the same time
urging that she go on and preach in the thirty-six ap-
pointments which made up his circuit, she could not refuse.
Her decision was soon to be sorely tried. Her family
summoned her to a solemn council; they could not bear
the course she had set, and if she would give up all
thoughts of preaching forever, they would send her to college, and pay the entire expenses of a four years' course.
They suggested Ann Arbor, and this was a severe temptation to the college-longing girl. But in the end she
stood firm. She must heed the voice which urged her to
preach.

A sorry, unhappy time it was. Anna Shaw went from
the family circle with a heavy heart; but though her sister
Mary's love and approval were henceforth denied her,
her home was not, and she continued on in her High
School course, going out to preach at stated intervals,
as Dr. Peck desired. Finally the day came when she had
completed the circuit, and the thirty-six ministers met to
vote on her application for a license to preach. As yet,
no woman had been ordained in the Methodist ministry,
and there was an unusually large attendance at the conference, among them being Anna Shaw's father who
came to see how his daughter passed. When the majority of the ministers present voted on her name by
joyously raising both hands, Mr. Shaw rose and slipped
away. Those nearest him said that he looked pleased,
but no word came to Anna, either of congratulation or
forgiveness.

Being a licensed preacher now enabled the young
woman to enter the Methodist College with free tuition,
and she prepared at once to take advantage of this. One
thing troubled her, she had never studied United States
history, and she feared she could not pass the entrance

requirements in this branch. In a chance conversation
with the president of the institution she betrayed this
fact, and he invited her into his office, with the purpose,
Miss Shaw felt later, of kindly breaking the news to her
that her preparations for college were insufficient. As a
beginning he began to talk of history, and for some time
they discussed not only our own country but "the governments of the world, the causes which led to the influence
of one nation on another, the philosophical basis of the
different national movements westward, and the like,
Miss Shaw drawing upon what she had read long ago in
the *Independent* for her share of the conversation.
When she finally sensed the passing of time and rose to
go, Dr. Josclyn smilingly detained her, while he filled out
a card. To her astonishment this proved to be a pass on
the entire historical course of the college! Their conversation, the president said, had satisfied him of her knowledge on the points required, more fully than a written
examination could possibly have done.

Fees from preaching in country churches and school-
houses, and an occasional five dollars per night for a temperance lecture, kept Miss Shaw's expenses paid through
college, and then she went to the Boston University to begin her theological course. She was now twenty-seven
years old, and had for three years been a licensed
preacher. Thus far she had worked and studied in a
community where she was fairly well-known; now she
was to experience what it meant "to step from a solid
plank into space." Grim months were to be hers in
Boston, months in which she was often to go to bed cold
and hungry and to wake in the same state, with no hope
of conditions growing easier. Many times she almost
lost her faith that it was the Lord's hand guiding her,
and came to feel that her mad attempt to secure a university degree on nothing was but an "inheritance from

her visionary father," to whom "an acorn was never an acorn but a staunch grove of young oaks."

She was the only woman in a class of forty-three. When the city ministers required help, they invariably chose some of the young men. Opportunities to preach and lecture were, by her own account, "rarer than fire-light and food." Nor was there any hope of help from her family, for they had hotly objected to her coming away East to live by herself. More than ever she was disgracing them! As was inevitable, the day dawned when her last money was gone, and only one small box of crackers stood between herself and starvation. For some time now she had been living on crackers and milk, and her courage dwindled as her stock of supplies ebbed. Must she give up her career and seek work to support herself? At this juncture came an appeal from a local minister to help in a week of revival meetings. It seemed like a providential straw, and Anna Howard Shaw grasped it determinedly. If it yielded enough money to replace her shoes, which were bursting at the sides, and to feed her for a few days, she would struggle on with her theological course. If it did not, she would give up the fight.

Into the effort of the next seven days she put "not only her heart and soul, but the last flame of her dying vitality." They had a rousing revival, and somehow Anna lived on the excitement and her trembling hopes, "mildly aided by the box of biscuits." Then, the campaign over, weak and trembling, she sank into a chair to await her fate from the pastor whom she had assisted. It came in a copious, heart-felt flow of thanks. She had served the cause most nobly, and had earned at least fifty dollars. But alas! notwithstanding the spiritual uplift, the collections had been exceedingly small, the good man could not give her fifty dollars. Indeed, he could give her nothing at all but his thanks, and again these were showered upon her!

How the poor girl reached the street she never knew. Faint and ill with her disappointment and the crushing feeling that the Lord had not found her worthy, friendless, penniless, all but starving, she stumbled blindly down the steps, and at the foot was caught in the arms of a little, old woman, who clung to her crying softly. Miss Shaw did not know the woman, but it seemed fitting enough to be wept over just then. Indeed, she tells us that if all the people on the earth had suddenly broken into wailing it would have seemed most meet! But the darkest clouds have a silvery lining, and Anna Shaw was soon made aware that hers were turning inside out. The little old lady's tears were tears of joy! Anna's arguments and prayers had converted a wayward grandson, and as a token of her delight and appreciation, the woman pressed a bill into the girl's hand. "It is little enough," she said humbly, "only five dollars. But I want you to have it, Miss. I know life is often very hard for young students."

"It is the biggest gift I ever had in my life!" the girl assured her warmly. "Big enough to carry my whole future on its back!"

And she laughed joyously, feeling her whole heart singing within her. God had not forgotten! He still wanted Anna Howard Shaw for His servant, and nothing else in all the world mattered!

The next day another proof came. A woman who had an office on the same floor where Anna roomed called her inside. A friend had been watching her, she said, and she felt sure Anna was overdoing. If she would give up her preaching during the school year, and give her whole time to her studies and the care of her health, three dollars and a half would be paid to her each Saturday night. How gratefully Anna accepted this gift only she herself knew; for had not the kind Heavenly Father prompted the donor?

We have not space here to record the facts of the next few years, but the corner was turned. In due time Anna finished her theological course, and later took a degree of medicine at the same university. She held charges in various Massachusetts towns, and was the first ordained woman to preach in Denmark, Germany, Holland, Sweden Hungary, Italy, and Norway. In 1893, Miss Shaw was chosen to make the address on Woman's Day at the World's Fair, Chicago, and then, and not until then, did her father, who was present, at last express his appreciation of "my little Anna." Full well now the family realized that instead of disgracing them, as they had wailed, Anna had made known and honored the name of Shaw. When she presently gave up practising both her professions as minister and doctor of medicine, to enter upon her work of prison reform and the causes of temperance and woman's suffrage, she had their hearty approval. But it was Susan B. Anthony who finally decided Miss Shaw's vocation.

"You can't win two causes at once," she said. "You are merely scattering your energies. Win suffrage for women, and the rest will follow."

To clinch her argument, she took Anna Shaw with her on her Kansas campaign, and thereafter the two worked shoulder to shoulder until Miss Anthony's death, eighteen years later. Indeed, so entirely in harmony were the two, that often Miss Anthony, whose voice failed more and more as the years went on, would stop abruptly, and signal for Miss Shaw to finish her speech. Calmly the latter would rise, complete the broken sentence and go on with the line of argument as though it were her own! This was all the more remarkable, as neither one ever wrote out her speeches. It was Miss Shaw's custom to name her fingers for the points she wanted to make.

In 1892, she was elected vice-president of the National Woman Suffrage Association, and in 1904 she became the president, which office she held for more than ten years, planning nation-wide campaigns and doing much both at home and abroad for the uplift of women and of humanity. All her splendid talent was given whole-heartedly to the cause she served, and she had her reward in the ever-widening triumph of political equality, in the increased interest taken in the passage of good laws for the home, and above and beyond all, in the foundation of the spirit which swept the International Woman Suffrage Alliance Congress, which met at Geneva, in June, 1920. Here delegates from thirty-five countries were gathered to celebrate the enfranchisement of the women of twenty-two nations, and to outline a campaign to bring the remaining outsiders into the fold. And here the key-note of the hows and wherefores of this proceeding, when summed up, was found to sound the one word— *Love!* the kinship of mother-hearts,—which had always been the principal plank in the campaign of the two grand pioneers in suffrage—Susan B. Anthony and Anna Howard Shaw.

Miss Shaw passed away, July 2, 1919, leaving behind her a life full of struggle, but crowned with victory for her cherished aims.

FRANCES ELIZABETH WILLARD

"THE best-loved woman in America" first saw the light of day, September 28, 1839 at Churchville, New York. This little babe was to become the woman who, following her noble motto, "For God and Home and Native Land," was to bind the White Ribbon of temperance, not only across her own beloved United States, but around the world as well. Frances Elizabeth she was christened, but her brother Oliver and sister Mary called her "Frank."

The Willards had both been teachers in the Empire State, and their home was a delightful place—"a richly nurtured child-garden, where the sturdy small plants struck deep root and spread wide leafage to the air, catching every drop of pure knowledge and every beam of home-love falling within its rays." But when "Frank" was still a child they removed to Oberlin, Ohio, where the father taught in college.

Presently the college life at Oberlin was broken by the failing of the father's health. He must get out into the free open air, away from all studious pursuits, and the physicians strongly recommended a farm home. "Why not?" asked the mother, "Saint Courageous," as Frances called her in later years. Big, white prairie schooners, headed westward, were a daily occurrence; all the world, it seemed, was stirred with the impulsive movement, "Westward Ho!" There new homes and fortunes were to be carved out, and there the Willards shortly determined to go. Accordingly, three of the quaint, white-hooded vehicles were loaded with such things as the little family felt that they could not leave behind. The father

led the way. Next came young Oliver, proud indeed of
his responsibility and the strong, gentle horses he guided.
While the mother, with her baby girls comfortably pil-
lowed on father's old-fashioned desk, brought up the rear.

For three weeks they journeyed steadily, pausing only
for their Sunday "rests," which were faithfully kept;
on through Chicago, "then chiefly notable as a place in
vast need of improvement," and away to the northwest,
until at length the little caravan reached the neighborhood
of the beautiful Rock River, not far from Janesville,
Wisconsin. Here, it seemed to both parents, was the
ideal site for the new home nest—the very spot of their
dreams!

Camp was soon made, and here in due time rose the
home which for twelve happy years sheltered "an idyllic
life of love and labor, play and study and prayer." "Forest Home," how often Miss Willard loved to picture it:
"The bluffs, so characteristic of Wisconsin, rose above
it on the right and left. Groves of oak and hickory were
on either hand; a miniature forest of evergreens almost
concealed the cottage from the view of passers-by; the
Virginia creeper twined at will around the pillars of the
piazza and over the parlor windows, while its rival, the
Michigan rose, clambered over the trellis and balustrade
to the roof. The air was laden with the perfume of
flowers. Through the thick and luxuriant growth of
shrubbery were paths which strayed off aimlessly, tempt-
ing the feet of the curious down their mysterious aisles."

"At first," we are told, in Miss Gordon's *"Beautiful
Life of Frances Willard,"* "the visitors were chiefly the
chipmunks and birds, change of season and turn of day."
But these were quite sufficient. No one ever had a dull
day at Forest Home. There was a wealth of imagination to season piquantly the hours of work as well as
those of play. The children organized a club, whose main

object was, naïvely set forth by Frances, "to tell what great things we have done ourselves, or what Oliver and Loren or the Hodge boys have, or Daniel Boone, or anybody else." Of the two dogs on the place, "Fred" was chosen the "club dog," but a clause provided "Carlo" as a substitute, in this wise : "Once in a while we may take Carlo—Carlo can go when he has sense enough." A wise provision truly! And a forerunner of the diplomatic genius of Frances, who was the recognized leader in nearly all their enterprises. She it was who was the editor-in-chief of the *Forest Home Weekly,* and to her masterly guidance was entrusted the command of the Fort, when a great mock Indian raid was in progress, and the mother and the two girls sought to hold out against the terrible attacks of the wily enemy, consisting of two boys and a dog! One piece of strategem here was ever after quoted with no little amusement, it was so much the tactics of Frances throughout her eminently successful career. "Have ready a nice piece of juicy sparerib to entice the dog, and so weaken the enemy's advances!"

An old oak on the edge of the garden bore this rather formidable placard :

THE EAGLE'S NEST—BEWARE !

High in its gnarled and twisted branches was the outdoor study of the "aspiring Frances," who often perched there hours at a time, secure from interruption, and busy with the "long, long thoughts of youth." Here her flying pencil set down many a praiseworthy bit of verse, and here was written a marvelous novel of adventure, some four hundred or more pages in length!

At first Mrs. Willard was her children's only teacher, but as the little family became more prosperous and the neighborhood more established, Mr. Willard fitted up a room with desks and benches which he himself had made, and a young lady, fresh from the schools of the East, came in daily to teach the little Willards and others of the neighborhood children whom the good mother could not bear to see growing up without educational advantages. Delightful times they had here, and much solid, careful study as well. Then, when Frances was fourteen, a little schoolhouse was built in the woods, about a mile distant. Tiny and brown and plain it was, "a sort of big ground-nut," Frances afterward wrote. There were pine desks built along the wall, girls on one side, boys on the other, as was the custom in those days, and "a real live graduate from Yale was the teacher."

Happy, happy schooldays! They passed all too quickly. By and by, Oliver went away to college, and later Frances and Mary became students in the Milwaukee Female College, where Mrs. Willard's youngest sister, the beloved "Aunt Sarah," was the graphic, stimulating Professor of History. Here the girls formed a charming circle of companions, and here, as she had been in the home study and in the district school, "Frank" was soon the ring-leader, and so much in harmony with the college atmosphere that she was "downright sorry to go home," as she said, at the close of the year.

Both girls fully expected to return to Milwaukee in the Fall, but their father was a staunch Methodist and so decided to send them to his church school, located at Evanston, Illinois. Here, again, their charm and personality made quick friends, among them being Miss Mary Bannister, who was the closest life-long "heart-friend" of Frances, and later the wife of her brother Oliver. And here again "Frank" was the acknowledged leader in all things. During the summer vacation of this year, Miss Willard taught her first school, in the little "brown nut" schoolhouse, to the extreme satisfaction of herself and everybody concerned. It was a period, she often looked back upon with mingled regret and pleasure, for it was the last of the happy days at Foest Home. In the Fall, a tenant took possession of the beloved home, and the family removed to Evanston.

Changes now came thick and fast. Soon college days were over. Frances, in search of a position where she "must be alternately the hammer that strikes and the anvil that bears," in order to grow "strong and earnest in practice" as she had always been in theory, decided to take up teaching as her life work, it being in her opinion the best of the few paths then open to women. Her father was not at all in favor of this. He believed that woman's place was in the home. To the men belonged the stern financial battles of life, and he was ready and willing to care for his own precious three.

"But, father," argued Frances, with all his own spirit, "single-handed and alone I should like to try my powers, for I have remained in the nest a full-grown bird long enough, and too long. It is an anomaly in natural history."

She was twenty-one years old, and so full of the independence she had declared on her eighteenth birthday, that now "she did not need to obey any laws but those of God thereafter!' So, though her father argued and advised, he did not command, and Miss Willard had her way. Nearly all the schools were then engaged, but after looking carefully about him, the Superintendent of Cook County found a teacherless little red schoolhouse away out on the plains. Here Frank arrived on that never-to-be-forgotten Monday to find a most desolate place indeed, with broken windows, dirty floor and benches, walls plentifully besprinkled with paper wads, and a group of little foreigners heartily engaged in a "free for all."

The business of the day began with a chapter from the Bible, and the song "I want to be an Angel!" How

FRANCES E. WILLARD

Miss Willard laughed about it later, but then the occasion had anything but an amusing side. The pupils soon found, however, that though "teacher" could sing and pray like a seraph, she could also wield the rod. Order emerged out of chaos, and the school presently became a fair model. For Miss Willard led here as she had else-where, and each one of the twenty was her adoring slave. Before this happy state came about, however, it is safe to say, as Miss Gordon observes, that "the brave young spirit got more discipline than her pupils." The hammer blows were swift and sure, but the metal rang true, and before Miss Willard gave up Harlem, she and a girl-friend whom she found in this out-of-the-way corner had established a Sunday school in the little old school-house. To-day this is represented in a prosperous Metho-dist church in what is now River Forest, one of the charming little suburbs of Chicago.

More years of teaching followed for Frances, part of the time with her dear friend Mary Bannister in the public schools of Evanston. Then Oliver, now a full-fledged young minister, and Mary Bannister his bride went away to their first charge in the far West. The sweet young sister Mary died, and other changes followed with bewildering rapidity. Both Forest Home and Swampscott, the newer house by the lake were sold, and the parents went to make a home at Rest Cottage, in Evanston. For two years, Frances kept them company, teaching in the Northwestern Female College, from which she had graduated. Then a better position was offered her in the Pittsburgh Female College, and here Miss Wil-lard, in the hours that had formerly been given to little home duties, wrote her exquisite memoriam of her sister Mary, *Nineteen Beautiful Years*.

A year in the Grove school at Evanston, a private academy for the children of the "best-born," where Miss

Willard put into practice her pet theories for student government; three terms at Genesee Wesleyan Seminary, at Lima, New York, thirty miles from her old birthplace; and then Miss Willard received a most delightful surprise. One of her teacher friends, Miss Kate Jackson, invited her to go on a two-year tour of Europe, all expenses paid. Miss Willard was indeed overwhelmed, and hesitated to accept, until Miss Jackson's father added his entreaties to his daughter's, saying that nothing would give him greater pleasure than to pay all bills. He had long desired to send his daughter abroad, but until then had never found any one to accompany her in whom he felt complete confidence. One strong obstacle yet stood in the way. Miss Willard's father had died but a few short months before, and she felt that she could not leave her mother. When "Saint Courageous" heard of the project, however, she was all for it. She delighted in the prospect of so much culture and happiness for her child; as for herself, she dismissed that matter summarily. She would go and stay with Oliver and Mary, who were now living at Appleton, Wisconsin.

For the story of those delightful years abroad, there is no place here. Miss Willard came back "with a picture gallery in her heart" far exceeding the riches which crowded the most marvelous galleries of Europe. While in her mind surged one burning question: "What can I do to better the condition of women everywhere?"

But for this question the answer was not yet.

Shortly she was back into the harness again, this time at the head of the Evanston College for Ladies, *being the first woman president of a college in America.* Here as elsewhere she was successful because she was faithful. But teaching, much as she loved the work, was more and more becoming an irksome task. To be "tied to a bell rope" was "an asphyxiating process," she says, "from which I vainly sought escape, changing the spot only to keep the pain." Her pupils could not help loving her, she was so lovable, drawing always from a richly-stored mind and sparkling with wit and humor. Not one of her girls would consciously have done anything to give her pain. She believed in them, trusted them, stood by them, often in the face of the most discouraging circumstances; the shy ones found in her a friend who understood, and she never failed to win them and inspire them with confidence.

All in all, Miss Willard was first an educator. She gave fifteen years of her life to teaching, in eleven different institutions, in six different towns, in four different states. And at the last she left college, not to engage, as many suppose, in the new work which was beginning to fire her soul, but because a conflict of opinion arose between her and the new president of Northwestern University over the relation the Woman's College and the University should sustain to each other. In her own language the situation was thus explained. "Dr. Fowler has the will of a Napoleon, I have the will of a Queen Elizabeth; when an immovable meets an indestructible object, something has to give way." Therefore, she gave up her position and means of support, deeply grieved, because her power and usefulness had, as she felt, been curtailed beyond endurance.

The story of her life since that eventful day, June 13, 1874, has become common property of the English-speaking people of the world. She had previously had a wonderful religious experience. After that she longed for a more unrestricted field of usefulness. This she found in a Crusade which was slowly rising against the terrible Dragon which imperiled the earth. Up and down throughout the land this loathsome creature was destroying thousands of human lives and millions of dollars' worth of property every year.

Surely if she could succeed in helping to slay this Dragon, this loathsome, hideous fiend Strong Drink, she would be doing a service as noble as any that had been rendered in the thirty or more Crusades that had been waged to make the world better! She read everything she could find bearing upon the new movement, and presently her interest in the Crusade drew her to the East to confer with its leaders. What she saw in the slums of New York filled her heart with pity, and the stimulus of the first Gospel Temperance camp meeting, held at Old Orchard, Maine, did the rest. Heart and soul she was alive to the burning need and righteousness of the Temperance Cause.

Miss Willard was a born organizer, and she saw clearly that what the Women's Christian Temperance Union most needed was a leader, a guiding hand upon the reins. Moreover she felt that she was eminently fitted to step into the place, and that she could lead the band to victory. Only one thing stayed her eager hands: it required money to be a philanthropist and a reformer, and she had so little, that even as she longed to enter the work and sat seeing visions of its possibilities, there was in the background a fear that if she and her mother remained much longer at that expensive Portland hotel, there would not be money enough left to defray their homeward expenses! In the emergency, she turned to her Bible seeking guidance, and lo! it opened to these words: "Trust in the Lord and do good; so shalt thou dwell in the land, and verily thou shalt be fed."

But she was not yet fully decided. She wanted, oh! how she wanted to dedicate her life utterly to the Cause.

Willard prudence—that staunch heritage from her father
—bade her to be very sure she was right before she went
ahead.   Moreover, her nearest and dearest, even warm-
hearted "Saint Courageous," who so loved to help others,
urged against the course they knew she longed to pursue.

"Temperance workers needs must *give* their time,
Frank," counseled her brother.   "You would suffer for
the very necessaries of life, I fear.   Better stick to your
girls and the higher education, and do what you can in
your own place.   Indeed, it has occurred to me that if
every one should do his best, *each in his own place,* the
Dragon would be short-lived."

So it would.   But Frank knew this was an idealist's
view.   It would never be brought about until the crying
need of such a course was urged from the house-tops!

Meantime offers of new positions came pouring in,
the best of these being the offer of Lady Principal in one
of the most select schools for young women in New
York City, salary $2400 and her own choice of the sub-
jects she wished to teach.   With it, in the same mail,
came a letter from Chicago, begging Miss Willard to accept the presidency of that branch of the W. C. T. U.
"It has come to me as I believe from the Lord," said the
writer, "that you ought to be our president."   And the
die was cast!   Forthwith came Frances E. Willard's determination to dedicate her life to the cause of humanity.
Moreover she set her mark high.   She would accept the
post offered, and urge the blessed appeal to the best that
was in women everywhere, and together they would wind
the White Ribbon with its lofty ideals around the
globe!

A noble resolution, most nobly carried out!   Her sacri-
fices at the beginning were heroic.   Many days she went
without her dinner and walked long distances in Chicago

in the prosecution of her work, because she had no money. Far and wide sounded her plea to the women of the church, the home, and the school to band together—

> "For the cause that lacks assistance,
> For the wrong that needs resistance,
> For the future in the distance,
>   And the good that you can do!"

"Alone we can do little," she said. "Separated, we are the units of weakness; but aggregated we become batteries of power. Agitate, educate, organize—these are the deathless watchwords of success. The fingers of the hands can do little alone, but correlated into a fist they become formidable. The plank borne here and there by the sport of the wave is an image of imbecility, but frame a thousand planks of heart of oak into a hull, put in your engine with its heart of fire, fit out your ship, and it shall cross at a right angle those same waves to the port it has purposed to attain. We want all those like-minded with us, who would put down the dramshop, exalt the house, redeem manhood, and uplift womanhood, to join hands with us for organized work according to a plan. It took the allied armies to win at Waterloo, and the alcohol Napoleon will capitulate to a no less mighty army."

From the platform of every city of over ten thousand inhabitants, and in many smaller places in the Union, her eloquent, silvery-toned voice, which was often likened to that of the distinguished Wendell Phillips, the prince of American orators, urged the call, and those who listened never forgot her vivid power and self-possession. More than any other speaker, perhaps, she possessed the rare gift of firing others with the thought of what they might accomplish, and the faith to dare and to do.

Miss Willard literally wore herself out in her public work. She passed away in her fifty-ninth year. Her death occurred in New York City, February 18, 1898.

"She was a conscience aglow with divine light," Mr. Little said, in the opening sentences of his splendid funeral address above her bier, and those words in truth most fittingly described the great worker who "made the white ribbon God's olive branch of peace."

At her death Miss Willard was the "Best Loved Woman in America," and president of the Woman's Christian Temperance Union of the World. Abroad, her position as a household guiding star is best revealed in the beautiful and pathetic trust of the poor Swedish woman, who, lonely and bereaved, somehow made her way to this country, and to Willard Hall, "the Temple" of the W. C. T. U. in Chicago. "Home!" she breathed happily, as she sat herself down and looked delightedly around. It was the one English word she knew, but it was enough. Where Miss Willard reigned was indeed home!

Two sentences in her *Glimpses of Fifty Years* give us the secret of this peerless woman's untiring zeal, and the inspiration which led her to devote her beautiful, unselfish life to humanity. "As I follow in these later years the thorny path of a reformer," she says, "I sometimes think how good and pleasant would have been the quiet life, so universally approved, of a teacher of girls. But confident belief gives me grace and courage to go on, and it is this:

"My bark is wafted to the strand
  By breath divine,
And on the helm there rests a Hand
  Other than mine."

ELIZABETH BLACKWELL

In her last days Elizabeth Blackwell once observed that "no one who was not alive sixty years ago can realize the iron wall hemming in on every side any young woman who wished to earn her own living, or to do anything outside of the narrowest conventional groove. Such a woman was simply crushed. Those who were of a character not to submit without resistance, had to fight for their lives, and their fight broke the way through for the others to follow."

And a battle royal was that waged by Elizabeth Blackwell! Indeed, the story of her onslaught against the walled entrance of prejudice and public opinion forms a tale of courage and successful pioneering that has seldom been equaled by man or woman. Girls of to-day can but read it with mingled wonder, delight and indignation, intermixed with a strong feeling of thankful gratitude for the wide avenues now open to all manner of opportunities for women—avenues for which such pioneers as Elizabeth Blackwell, Frances Willard, Susan B. Anthony and Anna Howard Shaw first blazed the trail.

Elizabeth Blackwell was born in 1821, and lived the first eleven uneventful years of her life in Bristol, England. She was the third daughter in a family of nine brothers and sisters, and always stoutly maintained that it was a great advantage to have been born one of a large family group of healthy, active children, surrounded by wholesome influences, where goodness, gentleness, and reverence were inseparably blended with breezy commons, lovely woods, clear streams, and the reading of charming books.

The father was a sugar-refiner, whom business reverses finally sent to America, in August, 1832. The family located in New York, and Mr. Blackwell, who had been an ardent member of the Independent body at home, soon found himself drawn into the anti-slavery struggle. William Lloyd Garrison was an especial friend, and always doubly welcomed by the children in the home, who delighted in the numerous tales he told for their benefit, and in the long-drawn selections from Russian poetry with which he was wont to conclude his entertainment.

Six years in the seething atmosphere of abolition and its free speech and fierce antagonisms, then Mr. Blackwell removed his family to Cincinnati, Ohio, where he hoped to establish himself in the beet sugar business. But the Fates forbade; in a few months he passed away, leaving his large family totally unprovided for, and strangers in a strange land. It was a crushing blow, this sudden removal of "their earthly Providence," but stern necessity soon roused to action the three elder daughters, of whom Elizabeth, then just turned seventeen, was the youngest. They had been well educated, by governesses at their home in England, and later in a school in New York, and now decided to open a day and boarding school for young ladies. Uphill business this was, but it kept a roof over their heads and the wolf from the door, and served to bring on the younger children and keep the home together until the boys of the family were old enough to put their shoulders to the wheel; then the school was abandoned, and Elizabeth went to Kentucky to take charge of a girl's district school.

This was her first contact with the slow-going, slower-served Kentuckians of that period, and she did not like it. Her disgust began on the first day of her journey, when the sleepy-eyed captain put his boat down the river at the rate of three miles per hour; it increased at sight of the straggling, dingy, uninteresting, dog-overrun town of her destination, and "the hole" to which she and her trunks were first taken. Indeed, the general easy-going conditions on every hand well-nigh maddened her.

"Begin to teach on Monday? This was utterly impossible! The idea seemed to them preposterous, the schoolhouse was hardly selected, the windows were broken, the floor and walls filthy, the plaster fallen off, the scholars unnotified of my arrival; no, 'twas impossible, I must wait a week." [1]

But Elizabeth Blackwell was of no such mind. This was her first trip away from home. She felt that she would die of homesickness, if she had to wait there inactive for a whole week! So she rose up and argued and demanded to such purpose that presently a committee of "Responsibles" came to see her, a negro was dispatched to mend the windows, and another to clean the floor, and there was at least a hope that school might begin on Monday. But Miss Blackwell had yet to learn that slave labor could do nothing without supervision. When towards evening she went to look at her schoolroom, "nothing had been done but mischief. The old negro had flooded the muddy floor with water and gone away, leaving the place like the bed of the Nile." It was Saturday night, and no hope of getting anything done the next day. School could not begin before Tuesday, but begin then it certainly should! And Miss Blackwell stuck so firmly to her resolution, that one of the "Responsibles" later told her that Monday was an epoch in the history of Henderson!

As for the school, it was limited to twenty-one pupils, but such was the impression Miss Blackwell created that she soon had a full roll. "I teach ten hours, three days of the week," she wrote to her sister, "and wish the other three were similarly filled; but it is small remuneration

[1] *Pioneer Work,* by Dr. Blackwell.

for such an outlay of breath, and as soon as I have the
opportunity I shall fly off to some other point of the com-
pass, where I may learn myself while teaching others.
Carlyle's name has never even been distantly echoed here,
Emerson is a perfect stranger, and Channing, I presume,
would produce a universal fainting-fit."

Moreover, Miss Blackwell's abolition sympathies made
her more and more intolerant of the domestic conditions.
"I suppose," she wrote, "that I see slavery here in its
mildest form.   I have heard of no use being made of the
whipping-post, nor any instance of downright cruelty.
(It was really meant as an act of hospitality when they
placed a little negro girl as a screen between me and the
fire the other day!)   But to live in the midst of beings
drudging on from earliest morning to latest night, cuffed
about by every one, scolded all day long, blamed unjustly,
and without spirit enough to reply, with no consideration
in any way for their feelings, with no hope for the future,
smelling horribly, and as ugly as Satan—to live in their
midst, utterly unable to help them, is to me dreadful, and
what I would not do long for any consideration.   Meanwhile I treat them civilly, and dispense with their services as much as possible, for which I believe the poor
creatures despise me."

Considering, then, all these points of repugnance, it
speaks considerably for Miss Blackwell's resolution and
self-command that she stuck it out to the end of the
term.   But, having once gone home to Walnut Hills, and
the neighborly atmosphere of the Lane Theological Seminary, conducted by the Beechers and Professor Stowe,
nothing could have persuaded her to return to Kentucky.
She was soon engrossed in the study of music and German
and the friendship of Lucy Stone, who presently became
the wife of her brother Henry, but who by mutual consent retained her maiden name, a proceeding hitherto

unheard-of in those times. Perhaps it was the vigorous, active life of these two, engrossed heart and soul in the crusade for Woman's Suffrage, that shortly put a wedge of dissatisfaction in Elizabeth's horizon. She was not getting enough out of life, she must have some all-absorbing pursuit.

"You are fond of study, and have health and leisure; why not take up medicine?" suggested an invalid friend. "If I could be treated by a lady doctor, my worst sufferings would be spared me."

A lady doctor! The idea appealed to Miss Blackwell, even though at first she thought she had not the spirit for it. She had always had a horror of illness, and could not bear the sight of a medical book. But, undoubtedly, a lady doctor could do a great deal of good. Moreover, the struggle to win recognition as such promised no end of an interesting fight. It was a good idea, a very good idea, said all the physicians to whom she put the query, but there were so many obstacles in the way of such a course, that it would be impossible of execution.

"Is that so?" said Miss Blackwell shortly, and being just in the mood to begin a crusade of her own, she decided at once to go in and win a doctor's degree.

But where was the money to come from? All her advisers solemnly warned her as to the expense necessary. She would teach school and hoard the money for future use. Diligently she began to cast about for a place where she might teach and study. This was found at Asheville, North Carolina, where the principal, who held a doctor's degree, agreed to supervise her medical studies. And so in sympathy was the family with her plans, that two of her brothers volunteered to drive her over the mountains to begin her unknown career. Of the eleven interesting days of this trip, and of the subsequent time spent in Asheville and later in Charleston, carrying out her schedule, there is no place here to record. Daily the rightfulness of her purpose grew stronger, and she knew that no matter what opposition she encountered, she would not give way.

At length, in the summer of 1847, Miss Blackwell felt that the sum of her carefully hoarded earnings would admit of a beginning, and she accordingly took passage for Philadelphia in a sailing vessel, that city being then as now the Mecca for the medical profession. Here she began anatomical studies in a private school, while making application one after another to the medical colleges for admission. One staunch old Quaker, Doctor Warrington, was her tireless sponsor. He allowed her to visit his patients, attend his lectures, and use his library, while he continually recommended her course to the medical profession; but it was all to no purpose. The colleges refused to open their doors; the prejudice against a woman intruding herself into the doctors' ranks was too strong, and following this lead museums, hospitals, and other sources also turned such a cold shoulder that Dr. Warrington exclaimed in despair: "Elizabeth, it is of no use trying. Thee cannot gain admission to these schools. Thee must go to Paris and don masculine attire to gain the necessary knowledge."

Following this advice, the head of one of the largest Philadelphia medical colleges, who was wholly in sympathy with her desires, suggested to Miss Blackwell that she dress as a man and enter his college, saying that he would entrust the secret to two or three of his students in whom he had entire confidence, and that a watch would be maintained so that she could withdraw if at any time her disguise was suspected.

But Miss Blackwell shrank from entering a medical college, either at home or abroad, in any way that was not just and true. She had entered on a moral crusade.

Her course must be openly pursued and with entire public sanction to accomplish its end. Nor was she to be dissuaded from her purpose.

The schools of Philadelphia were not the only medical schools in the United States! She might fare better elsewhere. Forthwith Miss Blackwell began writing for various prospectuses and getting out applications to all the schools which seemed desirable. At length her perseverance brought its reward. She was admitted to the Geneva University, in New York State. And here she subsequently became a nine days' wonder in the town! As she walked back and forth to the college, the women whom she met invariably stopped and stared at her as at a curious animal or hastened on with averted faces, feeling that she was either a totally bad woman or an insane one, who might break out at any moment. Behind the great doors of the college only did she find peace, for the students and the faculty, one and all, accorded her the "admirable courtesy of true Christian gentlemen."

In due time Miss Blackwell was graduated, one of her brothers going on for the express purpose of accompanying her to the church and seeing that she did not feel embarrassed and alone. But, though Elizabeth fully appreciated the love and sympathy which prompted him, there was now no fear of censure and hostile glances. Public opinion had turned. The ladies of Geneva had come to the conclusion that Miss Blackwell was pursuing a most noble course, and they turned out *en masse* to see the first woman doctor get her diploma, while all over the land the press very generally recorded the event, and spoke favorably of it. Going shortly afterward to Philadelphia, Miss Blackwell was cordially received by the learned doctors who had before refused admission to their halls, and was freely invited to attend a number of important lectures and to visit the hospitals.

But she was not yet ready to begin the practising of her profession, and presently set sail for a tour of European study. Here she experienced another battle against closed doors, and here, too, she had a serious illness and lost an eye, but her purpose remained unchanged. Shortly now she was to be *the first woman surgeon in the world.* Everywhere, strange as it now seems, Miss Blackwell encountered much stronger opposition from women than from men. "Prejudice," said she once, "is more violent the blinder it is!"

Returning from her studies in Paris, Miss Blackwell spent some time in London, doing the rounds of the hospitals, and making a number of friends who helped greatly to cheer the somberness of her life. Among the most distinguished of these were Faraday, Lady Noel Byron, Mrs. Jameson, and Florence Nightingale. To the latter Miss Blackwell said that she owed chiefly her awakening to the fact that "Sanitation is the supreme goal of medicine, its foundation and its crown." For awhile Miss Blackwell entertained serious notions of setting up as a practitioner in London. Two things deterred: lack of funds, and the fact that her sister Emily had begun a medical career, and looked forward to establishing a hospital with her.

Back in America, with offices in University Place, New York, life took on once more the grim guise of battle. Few patients came to consult her. The medical profession stood aloof and society followed suit. Insolent letters occasionally arrived by post, and as a final cap-sheaf poverty hounded close on her heels. To America's shame be it said, Miss Blackwell's sole inspiration in these dark hours came to her from her English friends who sent such warm-hearted encouraging letters of sympathy that, years later, their memory still burned deeply enough to draw her back to her native land to await the final summons. How her noble heart bled in secret over her lot is recorded in her memoirs: "Ah, I am glad I, and not another, have to bear this pioneer work. I understand now why this life has never been lived before. It is hard, with no support but a high purpose, to live against every species of social opposition."

At last in sheer desperation over her loneliness, Miss Blackwell went to the city orphan asylum and adopted a little girl. This proved to be the most fortunate act of her life, so far as her happiness was concerned, for the orphan girl, Katherine Barry, proved a treasure indeed. All her time was given to a warm-hearted devotion of her foster-mother, and moreover their loving example so stimulated Miss Blackwell's two elder sisters, that both went and did likewise, and from the physician's ability of Dr. Elizabeth and Dr. Emily to read character and faces, both alike drew hearts of purest gold.

In 1856, the cherished idea of the Blackwell doctors took shape in "The New York Infirmary for Women and Children." And it, too, met with such a flood of opposition that for a long time its maintenance was a severe burden. Bazaars, lectures, concerts, every available means for collecting money was resorted to, and many times it seemed to the few friends that the effort would have to be abandoned. But Dr. Elizabeth and Dr. Emily refused even to think of this. "They slept in the garret, and dined in the cellar," as the latter said, "when they dined at all."

At length they triumphed; for everywhere women students were beginning to demand enlightenment, and there was need for a general hospital where nurses and young doctors might be trained. When Lincoln's call for troops fired the North, the Blackwell doctors called a meeting to see what could be done toward supplying the nurses that they knew would be needed, and from this effort grew the National Sanitary Aid Association which did such effectual work throughout the war. At its close, the Blackwell Infirmary was recognized, on the advice of leading New York physicians, and a female college of medicine added. Here Dr. Elizabeth Blackwell held the chair of hygiene, and among her other duties included the work of sanitary visitor in the homes of the poor—a field in which she was again the pioneer.

On the day when her diploma was handed to her at Geneva, Elizabeth Blackwell spoke these heartfelt words to Dr. Webster, the president, and her valued friend: "Sir, I thank you; by the help of the Most High, it shall be the effort of my life to shed honor upon your diploma." How nobly her life reflected that promise! Never did the college cease to rejoice that she had been a graduate of it. Today her name is perpetuated there in the Elizabeth Blackwell House. The Blackwell Medical School, of Rochester, New York, also does honor to the noble woman pioneer whose long years of toil and opposition paved the way for the establishment of medical schools for women both at home and abroad; her portrait hangs in the London School of Medicine for Women. In these days when scientific work and studies in medicine are available to women everywhere, let none forget at what price of courage, perseverance, and fortitude they were gained.

Elizabeth Blackwell lived to the advanced age of eighty-nine, quitting her earthly labors in 1910. During the long span of her life she was permitted to see many if not all of the things for which she had fought, made a reality in the lives of all other women who desired to do their share of the work of the world.

HELEN KELLER

In the little town of Tuscumbia, in the northern part of Alabama, June 27, 1880, Helen Keller was born. Her father, Arthur H. Keller, a Captain in the Confederate Army, was descended from Caspar Keller of Switzerland, who settled in Maryland, and on his mother's side from Alexander Spotswood, Colonial Governor of Virginia.

Helen's mother, Kate Adams, was descended from Benjamin Adams of Newburg, Massachusetts, and is a relative of the Everetts from which family came Edward Everett and Dr. Edward Everett Hale.

The home called "Ivy Green" because covered by English ivy, was set in a garden of roses, honeysuckles, jessamine, clematis, and all those fragrant flowers familiar to anyone who has lived in the South.

"But the roses," says Helen Keller in *The Story of My Life,* "they were the loveliest of all. Never have I found in the greenhouses of the North, such heart-satisfying roses as the climbing roses of my Southern home. They used to hang in long festoons from our porch, filling the whole air with their fragrance, untainted by any earthy smell; and in the early morning washed in dew, they felt so soft and pure, I could not help wondering if they did not resemble the asphodels of God's garden."

For nineteen months the baby Helen was a joy to the proud parents. She walked when a year old, she could speak a few words, and her eager, active infancy gave great promise. Then came congestion of the stomach and brain, and the light and sound went out forever from the little sufferer.

She was dumb because she could not hear, and the few spoken words were soon forgotten. She could feel the boxwood hedges in the garden, and by the sense of smell could find the first violets and lilies, but she was never again to hear the birds sing, nor see the beauties of the world about her.

Several years went by. At five she learned to fold and put away the clean clothes when they were brought from the laundry, and she could distinguish her own from the others.

With a little colored girl, Martha Washington, the child of their cook, and Belle, an old setter, they hunted the eggs of the guinea-fowl in the long grass. The horses and the cows were a never-ending source of pleasure.

Dolls, too, helped to pass away the hours, and one, which Helen afterward named Nancy, became the especial object of her love and of her temper as well. The child was restless under the bondage of silence and darkness.

Finally the grieved mother remembered that in Charles Dickens's *American Notes* she read of Laura Bridgman, deaf and blind, educated by Dr. Samuel Gridley Howe of Boston. But he had died ten years before.

When Helen was six, she was taken by her parents to Baltimore to an eminent doctor, but he could do nothing for her. He, however, advised Mr. Keller to see Dr. Alexander Graham Bell of Washington, who, in turn, urged him to write to the Perkins Institution for the Blind, in Boston, under the charge of Mr. Anagnos, who had married the gifted daughter of Dr. Howe. Mr. Keller did so, and a teacher was selected, who reached the Keller home March 3, 1887. "The most important day I remember in all my life," wrote Helen Keller afterward, "is the one on which my teacher, Anne Mansfield Sullivan, came to me."

Miss Sullivan entered the Perkins Institution in 1880,

the year Helen was born, when she was fourteen years old, almost totally blind, but later her sight was partially restored. She graduated in 1886, and was soon ready for her important work.

The little blind children at the Perkins Institution had made a doll for Helen, and Laura Bridgman had dressed it. When Miss Sullivan gave it to her, she slowly spelled the word d-o-l-l in her pupil's hand. The child did not know that things had names, but she liked this finger play and at once tried to imitate it. Then she ran downstairs, held up her hand to her mother and made the letters for doll. Later, Miss Sullivan says, she planted the doll in the dirt in the garden to have it grow tall like her teacher!

On April 5th, Miss Sullivan spelled in her hand the word "water," letting the water from the pump run over her hand. "At once," says Miss Sullivan, "a new light came into her face. She spelled 'water' several times. Then she dropped on the ground and asked for its name and pointed to the pump and the trellis, and suddenly turning round she asked for my name. I spelled 'teacher.'" The child was greatly excited and in a few hours learned thirty new words.

Soon after, in the pump-house, she found five little puppies with one of the setter dogs, and at once learned the words "puppy" and "mother-dog." In three months Helen had learned about three hundred words and many common sentences. At the end of August she knew six hundred and twenty-five words.

With rare skill and sympathy Miss Sullivan unfolded the child's bright mind. She made raised maps in clay to show her about mountains and rivers. "I built dams of pebbles, made islands and lakes, and dug river-beds, all for fun, and never dreamed that I was learning a lesson," Miss Keller said later. "She is much interested," writes Miss Sullivan, "in some little chickens that are pecking their way into the world this morning. I let her hold a shell in her hand and feel the chicken 'chip, chip.' Her astonishment when she felt the tiny creature inside, cannot be put in a letter. The hen was very gentle and made no objections to our investigations. Besides the chickens we have several other additions to the family, two calves, a colt, and a penful of funny little pigs. You would be amused to see me hold a squealing pig in my arms, while Helen feels it all over and asks countless questions. After seeing the chicken come out of the egg, she asked, 'Did baby pig grow in egg?' She was also much interested to learn, 'who put the chickens in eggs?'"

Helen soon learned to read in raised letters, made for the blind, and also to write. When she received a letter she used to read it to Belle, the dog, spelling the sentences out on her fingers. When Belle walked away, uninterested, Helen would make her lie down and listen, or watch the busy fingers. She wrote later concerning Belle: "I made a chain for her neck out of the lovely blue Paulownia flowers and covered her with great heart-shaped leaves. Dear old Belle, she has long been dreaming among the lotus-flowers and poppies of the dog's paradise."

In May, 1888, when she was eight years old, Miss Sullivan took Helen to the Perkins Institution in Boston. The big rag doll, Nancy, went with them. "She was covered with dirt," said Miss Keller years afterward, "the remains of mud pies I had compelled her to eat, although she had never shown any special liking for them. The laundress at the Perkins Institution secretly carried her off to give her a bath. This was too much for poor Nancy. When I next saw her, she was a formless heap of cotton."

Helen was delighted to find that the little blind children could talk to her with their hands. "I remember the surprise and the pain I felt as I noticed that they placed their hands over mine when I talked to them and that they read books with their fingers."

She learned her first lesson in history at Bunker Hill, and climbed the monument, counting the steps. She took her first voyage in a steamboat to Plymouth and learned about the Pilgrims. The first vacation was spent at Brewster on Cape Cod where the ocean was a constant delight. She asked, at once, "Who put salt in the water?"

In the autumn, Helen and her teacher went back to Alabama, and to her parents' summer cottage about fourteen miles from Tuscumbia, called Fern Quarry. Here she rode her pony, which she called Black Beauty as she had just read the book, and carried on the studying for which her eager mind was always ready. A deep affection had grown between teacher and pupil. "Her heart," said Miss Sullivan, "is too full of unselfishness and affection to allow a dream of fear or unkindness. She does not realize that one can be anything but kind-hearted and tender." She was distressed one morning to find that one of the dogs had a block tied to her collar so that she could not run away. So at every opportunity Helen carried the block, so that Pearl, the dog, should not have the burden of it. A gentleman in Cincinnati said, "I have lived long and seen many happy faces, but I have never seen such a radiant face as this child's before to-night."

In 1890, when Helen was ten years old, she learned to speak. She had long known from the motion of the lips and throat that all persons did not use the sign language for speech. When one of Laura Bridgman's teachers, after a visit in Norway, told her of a deaf girl who could speak, Helen says, "I was on fire with eagerness. I would not rest satisfied till my teacher took me for advice and assistance. Miss Sarah Fuller, principal of the Horace Mann School for the Deaf, in Boston, began with Helen, March 26, 1890, and gave her eleven lessons. She let Helen feel the position of her tongue and lips when she made a sound. In an hour, she had learned six elements of speech, M. P. A. S. T. I.

Miss Sullivan and Miss Fuller could understand her, "but most people," she says, "would not have understood one word in a hundred. She was often discouraged, but she practised constantly." She talked to her "toys, stones, the moon, birds and dumb animals."

Her great desire was to speak to her parents when she returned to the South. The whole family were at the Tuscumbia station to greet her. "My eyes fill with tears, now," writes Miss Keller, "as I think how my mother pressed me close to her, speechless and trembling with delight, taking in every syllable that I spoke, while little Mildred (her sister) seized my free hand and pressed it and danced, and my father expressed his pride and affection in a big silence. It was as if Isaiah's prophecy had been fulfilled in me. 'The mountains and the hills shall break forth before you into singing and all the trees of the field shall clap their hands.' "

When Helen was twelve, she wrote a brief account of her life for the *Youth's Companion*. In 1893, when she was thirteen, she went to Niagara Falls, and to the World's Fair. At the Falls she "felt the air vibrate and the earth tremble."

Dr. Alexander Graham Bell went with Helen and Miss Sullivan to the World's Fair. Helen enjoyed everything. She had permission to touch the exhibits "and with an eagerness as insatiable as that with which Pizarro seized the treasures of Peru," she writes, "I took in the glories of the Fair with my fingers."

She was fascinated with the French bronzes. She felt of the machinery in motion in the Cape of Good Hope exhibit, to see how diamonds were weighed, cut, and polished. She examined telephones, phonographs, and treasures from all the world.

After this she began to learn Latin, and French, Miss Sullivan spelling the teacher's lessons into Helen's hand. For two years she studied at the Wright-Humason school for the Deaf in New York City. Beside lip-reading and vocal culture she studied arithmetic, physical geography, French and German. "Before the end of the first year," she says, "I read *Wilhelm Tell* with the greatest delight," but she "regarded arithmetic as a system of pitfalls." She enjoyed Central Park, sailed on the Hudson River and walked through "Sleepy Hollow."

In October, 1896, the year her father died, she entered the Cambridge School for Young Ladies, to prepare for Radcliffe College. Such an undertaking seemed marvelous for a deaf and blind girl. There were few books among the many which she needed, that were in the raised type for the blind. Miss Sullivan with great labor and patience had to spell into her hand all that the teachers said. Mr. Arthur Gilman, the principal, learned the finger alphabet to aid her in his instruction.

Miss Keller's daily themes, examinations, and the like, were done by herself on a typewriter which she used with great skill. In 1900 Miss Keller had passed, with credit, her difficult examinations in advanced Greek, Latin, German, Algebra and Geometry, the same as the Harvard examinations, and entered Radcliffe. She was urged by Dean Irmin to take a special course, but she wisely determined to follow that taken by others at Harvard and Radcliffe, who can both see and hear.

These were fruitful and wonderful years. Discouragements came, but she said, "I soon recover my buoyancy and laugh the discontent out of my heart, for, after all, every one who wishes to gain true knowledge must climb

© 1903 by Whitman

Helen Keller

the Hill Difficulty alone, and since there is no royal road to the summit, I must zigzag it in my own way. I slip back many times, I fall, I stand still, I run against the edge of hidden obstacles, I lose my temper and find it again and keep it better, I trudge on, I gain a little, I feel encouraged, I get more eager and climb higher and begin to see the widening horizon. Every struggle is a victory. One more effort and I reach the luminous cloud, the blue depths of the sky, the uplands of my desire."

Miss Keller graduated from Radcliffe in 1904. In *McClure's Magazine* for June, 1905, in "An Apology for going to College," Miss Keller says: "I discovered that darkness and silence might be rich in possibilities, which in my turn I might discover to the world. In other words I found the treasure of my own island. . . . I felt and still feel that the demand of the world is not so much for scholarship as for service. The world needs men and women who are able to work, and work with enthusiasm. . . . The idea of college education is not to give miscellaneous instruction, but to disclose to the student his highest capacities and teach him how to turn them to account. By this ideal, those who labor in darkness are brought to see a great light, and those who dwell in silence shall give service in obedience to the voice of love."

While Miss Keller is a prodigious reader of all the best in English, French and German literature, she is exceedingly fond of nature, loves to row and swim, and delights in trees and flowers. She lives at Wrentham, Massachusetts, with her teacher, and loves the country more than the crowded city. "Several times," she says, "I have visited the narrow, dirty streets where the poor live, and I grow hot and indignant to think that good people should be content to live in fine houses and become strong and beautiful, while others are condemned to live in hideous, sunless, tenements and grow ugly, withered and cringing.

The children who crowd these grimy alleys, half-clad
and underfed, shrink away from your outstretched hand
as if from a blow.   Dear little creatures, they crouch in
my heart and haunt me with a constant sense of pain."

Miss Keller loves animals, and says: "Whenever it is
possible, my dog accompanies me on a walk, or ride, or
sail.   I have had many dog friends—huge mastiffs, soft-
eyed spaniels, wood-wise setters and honest, homely bull
terriers.   At present the lord of my affections is one of
these bull terriers. . . . My dog friends seem to understand my limitations and always keep close beside me
when I am alone.   I love their affectionate ways and the
eloquent wag of their tails."   A book concerning Miss
Keller's pets would be very interesting reading.

She has had many distinguished friends, Phillips
Brooks, who wrote to her beautiful letters about God,
Oliver Wendell Holmes, Whittier, Howells, Mark Twain,
Dr. Edward Everett Hale and many others.

Before Miss Keller graduated from college, her *Story
of My Life,* had been published in 1903, and *Optimism*
the same year.   She preaches a beautiful gospel of
cheerfulness.   She says: "I have found out that though
the ways in which I can make myself useful are few, yet
the work open to me is endless.   The gladdest laborer in
the vineyard may be a cripple.   Even should the others
outstrip him, yet the vineyards ripen in the sun each year,
and the full clusters weigh into his hand.   Darwin could
work only half an hour at a time; yet in many diligent
half hours he laid anew the foundations of philosophy.
I long to accomplish a great and noble task; but it is my
chief duty and joy to accomplish humble tasks as though
they were great and noble.   I love the good that others
do; for their activity is an assurance that whether I can
help or not, the true and the good will stand sure."

Miss Keller shows how most of the great men of

thought and action have been optimists. "The recognition of the right of all men," she says, "to life, liberty and the pursuit of happiness, a spirit of concilation such as Burke dreamed of, the willingness on the part of the strong to make concessions to the weak, the realization that the rights of the employer are bound up in the rights of the employed—in these the optimist beholds the signs of our times."

After graduation from college, what should she do? Naturally her thoughts turned towards the blind and how to help them. She was made a member of the Massachusetts Commission for the Blind, and served on several Advisory Boards for the blind and deaf. This was not new work for her. When she was eleven years old, through her friends and letters in the newspapers she raised $1600 to help educate Tommy Stringer, a poor child who became blind and deaf when he was four years old. His mother was dead and his father too poor to take care of him. Helen's dog, Lioness, had been killed and her friends decided to raise money to buy her another dog. All such persons she urged to give money for Tommy, who was sent to the Perkins Institution in Boston. When she was twelve, she raised over $2000 for the Kindergarten for the Blind by a tea which she gave in Boston.

In the *Outlook,* April 28, 1906, Miss Keller urged that the blind have a chance to be self-supporting, self-respecting citizens. She says: "Almost nothing has been done for industrial education, which is necessary to alleviate the tragic condition of blindness. . . . What the blind of America need to open the door of usefulness and keep it open, is organized aid and intelligent encouragement. Europe affords good types of such organized aid for the blind."

After giving reports of work done in Germany, France

and Great Britain, agents finding employment for the blind after their industrial training, she says: "At the Glasgow Asylum for the Blind the average annual sales for three years was 29,000 pounds. . . . Not only do the women make bedding for the institution, but they have secured contracts with shipping firms and other institutions. . . . There is a tea agency in London, the managers of which are wholly or partially blind. Hundreds of blind agents sell its teas, coffees and cocoas all over England. Finally, 85 per cent. of the graduates of the Royal Normal College and Academy of Music in London are self-supporting. What shall we say when we contrast this with the report of the New York Commission for the Blind, which finds that only one per cent. of our sightless countrymen are in workshops?"

Miss Keller receives letters from Texas, South Africa, Arizona, Japan, Sweden, India, Germany, England, Spain, "from wherever the heart of man is warm and sympathetic," she says. Some ask to translate her books; others wish aid for various good causes. A blind boy asks, "How to become a writer?" which she answers in *World's Work,* April 10, 1910. "I believe the only place to look for the information you desire is in the biographies of successful authors. As far as I know, one fact is common to them all. In their youth they read good books and began writing in a simple way. They kept the best models of style before them."

Sometimes Miss Keller speaks to audiences, and her voice, says Mr. Macy, "is low and pleasant to listen to." She talks to others, but of course can only have communication from them by feeling the motion of their lips, or by their making the letters in her hand. Her face has great animation, and her heart is as kind as her mind is remarkable. Charles Dudley Warner says, "When a policeman shot dead her dog, a dearly loved companion, she found in her forgiving heart no condemnation for the man; she only said, 'If he had only known what a good dog she was, he wouldn't have shot her.' "

Miss Keller's book, *The World I Live In,* was published in 1908, the articles having appeared in the *Century Magazine.* It is full of beautiful thoughts, often wonderfully expressed. "My hand is to me what your hearing and sight are to you," she says. "The delicate tremble of a butterfly's wings in my hand, the soft petals of violets curling in the cool folds of their leaves or lifting sweetly out of the meadow grass, the clear, firm outline of face and limb, the smooth arch of a horse's neck and the velvety touch of his nose, and a thousand resultant combinations which take shape in my mind, constitute my world."

Again she says: "My fingers are tickled to delight by the soft ripple of a baby's laugh, and find amusement in the lusty crow of the barnyard autocrat. Once I had a pet rooster that used to perch on my knee and stretch his neck and crow. . . . In the strength of the human hand, too, there is something divine. I am told that the glance of a beloved eye thrills one from a distance; but there is no distance in the touch of a beloved hand."

In the chapter on "The Finer Vibrations," she says: "The thousand soft voices of the earth have truly found their way to me—the small rustle in tufts of grass, the silky swish of leaves, the buzz of insects, the hum of bees in blossoms I have plucked, the flutter of a bird's wings after his bath, and the slender rippling vibration of water running over pebbles. Once having been felt, these loved voices rustle, buzz, hum, flutter, and ripple in my thoughts forever, an undying part of happy memories."

Miss Keller's education has been an untold blessing to her. She says: "The only lightless dark is the night of ignorance and insensibility. . . . The calamity of the blind is immense, irreparable. But it does not take away our share of the things that count—service, friendship, humor, imagination, wisdom. . . . While I walk about my chamber with unsteady steps, my spirit sweeps skyward on eagle wings and looks out with unquenchable vision upon the world of eternal beauty."

What a buoyant, beautiful life! and much good Miss Keller has done already, and will do in the years to come. The *Century Magazine* well says, "The workings of this unique mind are beyond comprehension, but for ourselves, whatever other qualities it may show, it always seems as free as the sky-searching lark, and as elate."

LADY ASTOR

THAT "Virginia is the mother of Presidents" has been a much-quoted aphorism; that she may one day be further recognized as "the father of stateswomen" one may well believe who follows the wonderfully interesting and stimulating career of her distinguished daughter, Lady Nancy Astor, the first woman Member of Parliament, who so steadfastly urges all women to concern themselves in politics as a matter of duty. "I don't mean that every woman should go in for a political career," she says in her whimsical, confidential fashion, "that, of course, would be absurd." But that women should use the ballot to aid in raising and building up moral standards she makes very clear. "I believe," she says,—and how true rings her strong, courageous spirit, the voice of her Virginian ancestry—"I believe the women can help to bring to the world the real peace—the spiritual peace, the peace which passeth all understanding.

"Always remember St. Paul's words," she advises further; "they apply particularly to women: 'God hath not given us the spirit of fear, but of power and love and of a sound mind.' We can only bring this spirit into world politics if we have got it in our hearts. Let us prove to all nations that we are not talkers, but doers."

"Fair play and no favor," is her slogan as it is that of every true American sportsman, backed up by the staunch spirit of a whole line of politicians on her mother's side—Nancy Langhorne Astor plainly is heir to all that she ascribes. She was "born and raised" in the South—

in the Blue Ridge Mountains, not far from Charlottes-
ville, Virginia. "Mirador," the Langhorne home, was
just such a beautiful old Southern colonial mansion of
square, brick type as one may see in dreams, located in the
center of stately grounds and gardens fragrant with the
breath of magnolia, honeysuckle, and jasmine. "Aristo-
cratic and land-poor" sufficiently catalogs the Lang-
hornes. As for Miss Nancy herself, a distinctive type
of the far-famed Southern belle, but departing from the
usual in being very fair and slender, her own words
perhaps may best characterize her position: "I am sure
I was very gay and flirtatious. I know that I never
thought of a career outside of marriage and devotion to
my family. In those days Southern girls did not think
of politics. However, like all well-brought-up girls we
were trained in altruism, were kind-hearted, and wanted
to do good and to make miserable people less miserable.
In a callow way I intended to improve the world a great
deal, all in good time. Still, I certainly had no priggish
objections to parties or beaux."

Nancy Witcher Langhorne, as her parents christened
her, was one of a group of sisters who early became
noted for their wit and beauty. The "Langhorne girls"
are a tradition in Virginia to this day. One of them became the wife of Charles Dana Gibson, the artist.

Nancy as a child was not physically as strong as her
sisters, and she grew to be a small, slight woman, not at
all of the statuesque type of Mrs. Gibson. But she was
more than their equal in riding, driving, hunting, and
other sports. She was more or less of a tomboy, con-
fides a chum of the old days, and it was no unusual thing
to find her playing football in the street with the boys of
Richmond. Her tongue was as quick as the rest of her
young body. None was spared her good-natured sallies.
But as she grew up her feminine side asserted itself.

"She was different from the rest of us," says this early friend, Mrs. Lewis C. Albro. "It was no unusual thing for her to act as nurse-maid when she thought the situation demanded it. She would go into a train dressed as the Langhorne girls knew how to dress, and find a tired old mother wearily taking care of half a dozen children. Nancy would look at the woman, then at the young tribe of unwashed youngsters, and decide immediately that there was something she could do in the way of evening things up a bit. In spite of the expostulations of the embarrassed mother she would bundle the children off into another section of the car and tell the woman to take a nap. Nancy took care of the children, and Nancy loved it. So did the children, I might add.

"There is a little girl in the Sheltered Arms Hospital in Virginia who has for years received an annual income from Nancy Langhorne. Nancy didn't want her to feel that she was just a charity patient. When Nancy comes to Richmond, one of the first visits she pays is to this girl.

"After Nancy married into the Astor family, we wondered what her attitude would be when she came back to visit her home in Virginia. We didn't have to wonder very long. It was the same old Nancy Langhorne whom everybody adored. She visited her old school-teacher and 'sassed' her in the old way. When she came to visit us—our home was next door to hers—one of her first questions was: 'How is the old Home-Ruler?' She was referring to an old Irish maid of ours from whom she used to wheedle cookies."

It is not generally known that Viscount Astor is her second husband. Nancy Langhorne was married in 1897, to Robert Gould Shaw, 2nd, of Boston. He came of approved Back Bay stock with abolitionist traditions. She was a Virginian of strong Southern prejudices. It

was fore-ordained that they should not "hit it off"—
so at the end of six years they "agreed to disagree" and
were divorced.

She tried to forget it all in a whirl of social gayety,
and a few months later met Viscount Astor, the son
of William Waldorf Astor, who had forsaken America
for England, and there become a peer of the realm. Lord
Astor was very ambitious for his son, and disapproved
this Virginia marriage. He wanted the young man to
marry the daughter of some old English house; but
later was not only reconciled but heartily approved his
son's choice; for few could withstand Nancy Langhorne's "sass."

One of her first conquests, on going to her new English home, was King Edward himself. It is related that
at an afternoon reception he was hugely enjoying a bit
of repartee with her, to the manifest annoyance of several
English ladies who felt that he was devoting too much
time to this young parvenu.

"Will your Majesty join us in a game of bridge?"
finally some of them asked.

"I will if Viscountess Astor will join us also," he replied
gallantly.

Now Viscountess Astor did not play bridge, and was
not blind to this maneuvre. "Please excuse me, your
Majesty," she replied; "but the truth is, I don't even know
a king from a knave!"

The monarch's loud laugh was heard clear across the
hall—and he also refused the game of cards.

On the death of Lord Astor, his son, formerly
the Viscount, fell heir to his immense wealth and position. Thus it chanced that the Virginian belle became
Lady Astor, and henceforth, like Alice in Wonder-
land, her life, as she says, became "curiouser and
curiouser." For, according to British law, when Lord

Astor stepped into his inheritance and his father's title, he was transferred to the House of Lords and his seat in the Commons was vacant. It was his own idea that his wife should make a campaign to succeed him. Speaking before the National League of Women Voters in Baltimore, on a visit to America, Lady Astor told how it happened.

"My entrance into the House of Commons was not, as some thought, in the nature of a revolution. It was simply evolution. It is interesting how it came about. My husband was the one who started me off on this downward career—from the home to the House. If I have helped the cause of women, he is the one to thank— not me. He is a strange and remarkable man. First, it was strange to urge his wife to take up public life, especially as he is a most domesticated creature; but the truth is, he is a born social reformer. He has avoided the pitfalls which so many well-to-do men fall into. He doesn't think that you can right wrongs with philanthropy. He realizes that you must go to the bottom of the causes of wrongs and not simply glide over the top. For eleven years I had helped him with his work at Plymouth. I found out the wrongs and he tried to right them. It was a wonderful and happy combination, and I often wish that it was still going on.

"Plymouth," she informed further, "is an ideal port to sail from or to. It has bidden 'God speed' to so many voyagers. I felt that I was embarking on a voyage of faith, but when I arrived at my destination some of the Honorable Members looked upon me more as a pirate than a Pilgrim! A woman in the House of Commons! It was almost enough to have broken up the House. I don't blame them, but it was as hard on the woman as it was on them. Pioneers may be picturesque figures, but they are often rather lonely ones. I must say though for the House of Commons, they bore their shock with dauntless decency. No body of men could have been kinder and fairer than they were. When you hear people over here trying to run down England, please remember that England first gave the vote to women, and that the men of England welcomed an American-born woman in the House with a fairness and justice which this woman, at least, will never forget."

The details of how the different Members received Lady Astor would make most interesting reading. To begin with, Parliament found her difficult to understand. She didn't care "a tuppence" about political conventions, and she frequently went against her party when they backed measures she could not conscientiously support. She was ever on the alert, and so quick in retort that never a slip but was shown up by her ready tongue. "Joan of Arc," they called her privately, when they found how staunchly she could support the lone cause, and it is recorded that in the early days of the new labor government, so unrelenting were her efforts that more than once the Speaker of the House was constrained to say: "I must ask the honorable Member for Plymouth to listen to other Members."

Gradually, however, it was borne in upon the M. P.'s that she was for the cause and the cause alone. As one Member put it: "You fight us and we fight you back. But somehow we know it isn't us but our idea that you are fighting. And we appreciate your attitude." A remark for which Lady Astor said she was grateful with all her heart. "I love being a politician and getting into fights," she admitted apropos of this, but she added that she could not go into a fight with any gusto unless it was for a measure that she felt would do a great deal of good, and one so important that it made her blood boil to think that anyone was cold-blooded enough to oppose it.

"When I believe so fiercely in some reform," she says, "I can display a great deal of nerve and ferocity. But I am not enough of a politician to put up a fight for a bill I don't approve of, because it will further the interests of my party."

Lady Astor's speeches are always brilliant, dynamic and straight to the point, and she frequently expresses her delight in being able to champion things in which she believes strongly. "To be a good politician," she says, "one must be able to hate. Although in private life I think that to hate is wicked, dastardly, unchristian, in politics I allow myself this luxury. At least, I allow myself a sort of pseudo-hatred which stimulates me to put up a good fight. You see, really I hate only ugliness, brutality and injustice."

One such "fight" where she espoused the unpopular side is that of temperance. Yet she never has hesitated to unfurl her true colors. "Temperance is not a popular subject," she admits. "A deprecatory and rather embarrassed expression comes over the faces of really respectable people, when you begin talking to them about drink. They wish you would leave it alone, and not ask them to face up to such a controversial subject as the drink problem." In 1922, she introduced a bill in Commons giving people the right to decide for themselves as to the sale of liquor—a vague reform measure but better than nothing. The next year she carried through a bill against public drinking by minors.

She has also been interested in bettering living conditions in England, and as a practical beginning she offered to furnish a site in Plymouth and put up model workers' homes. The Town Council after some delay accepted her offer, in 1924, and she at once submitted further plans, with her personal check for £20,000, "as a starter." Plymouth now realizes that she is in earnest.

Nancy Langhorne Astor came home from England in
1922 to speak before the National League of Women
Voters, and—to visit old Virginia.   She stayed a month
and she *made forty speeches,* talking bravely about the
League of Nations—a thing they told her "over there"
she would better not mention—and the duty of women—
and incidentally of men—of the English-speaking race
everywhere.   The people packed every hall she spoke in,
and wires came from all over America begging to arrange dates.   She was accompanied by her husband, and
the route lay from New York to Baltimore, Washington,
Philadelphia, Virginia, then Chicago—"a wonderful
place—" and lastly to Canada, where as Lady Astor later
told home folks, "everyone was kind, from the Prime
Minister down, and most of my friends were down."
All along the line, in fact, Lady Astor was continually
summoned from the train to meet an enthusiastic reception from the soldiers who had landed in Plymouth from
France, and who before being allowed to sail for home
had often stayed weeks on end at Lady Astor's own
special quarters for wounded soldiers, the hospital at
Cliveden, on the magnificent Astor estate near Taplow, in
Buckinghamshire, about twenty-five miles from London.
"But I told them," Lady Astor said, smiling through the
tears at her beloved Devon constituents, "that I realized
that in thanking me, they were just thanking all the
women of England."

Nor did she forget to give her husband a loyal share
of the honors.   "We traveled far and wide, the two
Plymouth M. P.'s of the Upper and Lower Houses," she
said.   "The Member of the Upper House was a far
greater success than the member of the Lower House.
They were slightly prepared for my democratic outlook,
but they were totally unprepared for his.   Imagine their
surprise when they found him more progressive and

democratic than most of the people that they saw about them."

It was Independence Day in America on the occasion of her home-returning address at Plymouth, and brave Nancy Langhorne Astor had no hesitation in mentioning the fact. "Little American children are burning their fingers with fire-crackers today," she said. "American orators are burning their audiences with oratory. . . . Let us all remember that the American War of Independence was fought by British Americans against a German King and a reactionary Prime Minister for British ideals, and that a large part of the British nation sympathized with the rebels. The same old British fighting always for freedom! The great American of that day was a Virginian—George Washington. Someone described him as one of England's greatest sons. He was a Virginian with only British blood—I am just the other way around—a British M. P. with only Virginian blood. I am no leader, no general, and no statesman, but I hope I am a fighter, especially when it's a fight for peace."

Lady Astor is deeply patriotic; every nerve of her slender, soldierly figure thrills with love of her *"two countries."* "It takes a good deal of prayer to keep me humble," she said in Chicago. "To be born in Virginia and to represent Plymouth is enough to turn a stronger head than mine. The Good Book tells us to love all men, also the greater the loving the greater the life. I am fortunate in loving two great countries, but their greatness will be tested by their attitude to lesser countries."

Unable to remain quiet herself for long, Lady Astor is impatient with those who are prone to lay measures on the table. "I fear bombs in politics far less than I do apathy," she proclaims. On duty in the House of Commons, she wears a neat uniform, a stylish one-piece black dress with white turnover collar and cuffs, and a black hat. She is so very small and slender that she would give an impression of frailness did not her very alertness shout to the contrary. Her strongest "planks" are the mother-woman's point of view—she has six children of her own for stimulus in getting the right viewpoint here—the necessity for the abolition of war, and for an association of nations based upon human sympathy and co-operation. Moreover, as one gazes upon her standing vitally erect, ready at every turn to meet thrust with parry, it is evident that she manifestly "has a heart." We have her own word, too, that she puts her trust in that organ. "I usually do speak from my heart, for I have tried my head and found it wanting," she averred wittily at a dinner given in her honor in New York during her American tour.

How must all present have shortly admired and envied this "heart sense," which proved itself so capable of putting the fundamental truths of political philosophy in a common-sense fashion that none could fail to understand or perhaps hope to equal. "We are new brooms," she pleaded; "let us see that we sweep the right rooms," and her call was that the band of women voters be interested "in something bigger than any party." Common-sense and humanity she has since sounded as the most practical things in the world; and her cry today is for confidence, co-operation, and conference—fitting mottoes for men and women voters alike.

She by no means lost her interest in her *home* when she entered the *House*. Fortunately her home is not far from London, and her duties in Parliament do not keep her away for long periods. She is very proud of her brood, and loses no good opportunity to boast of them when "on the stump."

The home place itself, "Cliveden," is an imposing pile of white stone, fitted out without regard to expense but most tastefully. Viscount Astor holds enormously valuable real estate in New York City, and is so wealthy that he might easily spend a life of selfish indolence. But like his energetic Virginia wife, he finds his greatest enjoyment in service for others. During the World War, the doors of Cliveden were open to returning American soldiers, and the "boys" have a warm spot in their hearts for her.

Another pleasant story is told of the visit to London of a Richmond merchant, one whom she had known as a girl. He was invited to Cliveden, and shown about the beautiful grounds with as much consideration as if he had been a peer of the realm.

That Lady Astor's political career has not been plain sailing has been evidenced by many anecdotes, some humorous, others verging on the tragic. It was not so long ago that she became the innocent storm center in the staid old House of Commons all because of a picture. It has been customary to hang paintings of historic episodes, such as coronations and battles, on the walls of the Parliament house. A painting by Charles Sims merely entitled "The First Woman Member," was thus hung. It showed Lady Astor being escorted by Balfour and Lloyd George to her seat, and was really excellent likenesses of the two statesmen also. But many conservatives strenuously objected, and the offending picture was taken down.

It is stated that she receives and answers over eight hundred letters every month, chiefly from her constituents imploring her to take up this, that, or the other cause. They feel that with her for champion the cause is half won.

As Lady Astor comes up for re-election from time to time, the campaign always becomes picturesque—for she is at her best when being heckled. Her ready wit never fails her. And she always has the crowd with her "from the jump." A cable dispatch in October, 1924, says: "Tonight hundreds failed to get admittance to the hall in which a convention adopted her once more. Lady Astor faced her audience confidently. A few hecklers gained admission to the hall, and she promised them a 'hot time for a fortnight.' The first thing she did on entering the hall was to lean across a rail of the platform and call at the top of her voice: 'Are we downhearted?' The 'no' given in response could be heard far outside the hall."

Lady Astor is a firm adherent of the League of Nations, and lost no opportunity while in America of driving her views home. She may be characterized as a progressive with conservative views.

"The more I see of life," she observes sagely, "the more I see that the only way is the narrow way and the broad view. . . . The safe policy for politicians and nations is not to do others, but to do unto others as you would they should do unto you. . . . Things which are worth while are made only by great ideals in the hearts of the common people. . . . It is hopeless trying to go forward when you are looking backward."

MADAME CURIE

Madame Marie Sklodowska Curie, that great woman scientist to whom mankind is indebted for vast progress in scientific realms and for inestimable relief of human suffering, is herself a very modest woman. A few years ago, when she was being repeatedly importuned to write the story of her life, she had but one answer:

"I feel that it would not be much of a book," she said simply. "It is a very uneventful tale. I was born in Warsaw, of a family of teachers. I married Pierre Curie and had two children. I have done my work in France."

A simple enough statement truly! And yet, as one of her earnest admirers points out, "When most of us shall have been forgotten, when even the great World War shall have dwindled to a few pages in the history books, when Governments shall have fallen and risen and fallen again, the work of Marie Curie will be remembered." But of Marie Curie herself the world must be content with only the briefest glimpses. Her philosophy, simply lived, is "Truth, for the truth's sake," and she concerns herself with little else.

Marie Sklodowska was born in Warsaw on November 7, 1867. Left motherless as a child, she was brought up by her father, a teacher of physics and mathematics. She got her first glimpses of science in her father's laboratory. Times in Poland in those days were very strenuous. In 1861, the land had been taken over by Russian right of conquest. Nothing but the Russian language was allowed in the schools; nor was any mention of the good old days when Poland had her own government permissible. Indeed, such an indiscretion might have meant exile for the speaker to the bleak, hard land of Siberia. In the Sklodowska home, however, Polish was always spoken; evenings the professor used to read Polish poetry aloud, and often in the summer vacation he took his family southward where Austria ruled less rigorously, and where the children could romp and race in the fields and call out in their native tongue without danger of arrest.

At sixteen, Marie was graduated with honors from the gymnasium. Since this course not only included high school, but two years of college as well, it will be seen that the girl had done very well indeed. Her intention had been to teach in the free schools of Warsaw, but no position being available, she finally took a situation as governess in the family of a Russian nobleman. This meant the beginning of a new life for Marie: for now she must leave her father's roof, and go so far away on the train that she could return but seldom.

However, resourceful and busy as she always was, the girl did not succumb to homesickness, as her family feared. She had her private reading and studies, and she soon made a place for herself in her new home. The eldest daughter of the house was a girl about her own age, and the two had such a similarity of tastes that they soon became fast friends. Together, they started a little school for the poor children of the village, and here they spent a few hours every day, doing no little good in a small way.

Marie stayed three years in the nobleman's family. Then her pupils were quite grown out from under her hand, and she was no longer needed. What now? She had hoarded her earnings with all the craft of a miser, hoping to save enough to enter some school where she could obtain her degree. But after all, the salary of a governess in those days was but a mere pittance. So she was obliged to take another position. Here she remained for one year, and then went home to be with her father, who was now the only one left in the home nest. Back in Warsaw, Marie kept house, taught a few private pupils, and found several hours each day to carry on her own studies. Some of her cousins directed a little laboratory, and here the girl went on with the experiments in chemistry which she had begun some time before under her father's direction.

Advancement of the Polish people was still frowned upon by the Russian government. So Marie, in company with a number of young students, formed a secret society, with the object of educating the peasants and workmen. Every evening one of the members of the society taught in this free school, each one presenting the subject in which he was the most interested. The school met with considerable favor among the down-trodden Poles: for many felt that education was the key-note to success. If only their people could become sufficiently enlightened, the nation must be uplifted, and perhaps one day they might come back into their own. So the little school was soon running at full capacity, and most pleasantly for those who were fortunate enough to attend. One special thing it did for Marie: it gave her a glimpse of how much there was to be learned, and stimulated anew her desire to obtain an education. Shortly, then, she was off for Paris, but on applying for entrance into the university school of chemistry, was much disappointed, to find that there was no room for her.

Did the girl give up, and turn to something else? Not Marie Sklodowska. At least, only for the time being. In tiny quarters high up above the surrounding roofs in a dreary enough tenement, she dragged out what some would have found a wretched existence, cooking her chocolate and eggs over a little alcohol lamp, and carrying her small pittance of coal up six flights of stairs. But Marie was happy. Her books kept her mind occupied, and in her absorbing studies she lost all sight of her dingy surroundings.

A day came, however, when her enjoyment was seriously shattered. Her money, of which there had been little enough in the beginning, was nearly all gone. So Marie put on her coat, and sallied forth determinedly, going from one laboratory to another, trying to find some place where an assistant was needed. "For," she said to herself, "if I am fortunate enough to find an opening in my own line, then I can learn as I earn."

Men, however, looked askance at a slender young girl seeking such unusual employment. What could she know about science? Women had no minds for such work. They might be painstaking enough, but how about exactness? No. It would not do. Marie was advised to find a place to do housework.

Housework! The very idea, when all her being was set on ferreting out the truths of science! Squaring her shoulders significantly, the girl went on with the search. Laboratory work was filled with many plodding details: surely she would find an experimental scientist soon who was too busy and important to bother with the small necessities. Eventually, of course, perseverance won; moreover, her own wistfulness and determination were her best references.

"I can see that you might prove very useful," said a professor in the Sorbonne research laboratory. "You may start at once, if you like."

Marie could scarcely find words to express her gratitude, but the professor knew that it was not for lack of brains behind that high, arched forehead. Her face fairly shone with happiness as she fell upon the place and after several hours of washing and scouring, evolved order and shining neatness out of the messy chaos. Moreover, she showed such intelligence and familiarity with the tools of the craft, that the professor privately thanked his lucky stars. Here was just the helper that he had been wanting! And he lost no time in setting her at some minor experiments whose results he needed to complete a certain detail.

How happily the hours now flew by! For shortly, through the professor's intervention, Marie was admitted to the chemistry class to which she had been denied, and with her studies and experiments each moment was packed to the brim. In two years, she had completed her work at the university, and had taken her degree with high honors.

What next?

Life was ready with the answer. "Be my wife," said Pierre Curie, a young professor of research, and Marie, realizing full well that she could find no more worthy and beloved companion, consented joyously.

The first home of the Curies was an extremely simple one; just a little apartment of three rooms, not far from the School of Physics. Its chief claim to pretensions was its view of a really delightful garden—a spot which never failed to spur Pierre Curie's tiring spirits. For he loved the quiet and freedom of secluded spots—the opportunity to think the "long, long thoughts" which were being constantly shifted into the background under the incessant demand of his teacher's existence. Knowing how much such periods of undisturbed concentration meant to him, we see why Marie Curie bought two bicycles with the money which a relative sent to her to outfit their little home.

In the intervals of teaching, Pierre was making experiments tending to discover the secrets of crystals—a work which later brought him considerable renown. Marie, who found time to go to her husband's laboratory every day, became interested in investigating the magnetic properties of steel. Later, when both she and her husband became deeply involved with the problems of radioactivity, Marie performed a large part of the experiments, while Pierre was busy with his classes, testing not only the simple compounds, but also a great number of minerals. Of them all, uranium and thorium produced a radioactivity which seemed abnormal. "Why?" questioned the young scientists. And then came the further startling discovery that pitchblende, the parent mineral from which uranium was obtained, exhibited a degree of radioactivity four times as great as that given off by all the pure uranium which could be extracted from the sample itself. What could this mean? There was but one answer: pitchblende must contain some other element more radioactive than uranium itself.

To find this marvelous element was the next thing. And such an interesting, all-absorbing occupation as the search afforded! Presently a strong radioactive element was found, which Madame Curie named *polonium* in honor of her homeland. But that there was a much greater power hidden in the pitchblende was certain. So the investigations went on with an ever mounting enthusiasm which the serious lack of appliances could not dampen. Thus, in 1898, the Curies finally brought out the long-sought element, and in the subsequent tests proved it to be two hundred and fifty million times more radioactive than uranium.

You know, of course, that this new element was radium, and that shortly the whole scientific world was aflame with the discovery. It was found so potent as to darken photographic plates, to ionize any gas with which it came in contact, to excite phosphorescence, to produce various chemical changes, and to destroy minute organisms—the latter feature suggesting it as a specific treatment for cancers, ulcers, and other malignant growths. Since the least touch of radium will produce a severe burn, it is not possible to handle it with bare hands. It is said that Madame Curie's own hands have been made numb from working so much with radium, and that when not on actual duty she has acquired a certain nervous little habit of rubbing the tips of her fingers over the pad of her thumb to start the circulation.

It was the hope of the Curies to own a little home of their own one day, with a small garden for vegetables and flowers. But this was never realized. For always they yielded to the demands of science, and the money which might have been used to purchase comfort for themselves went into supplies for their beloved experiments. Indeed, Pierre Curie, struck down by a motor truck, passed from life at the age of forty-nine, without ever having anything like an adequate laboratory in which to work. He had recently been appointed to the new chair in physics, created especially for him in the Sorbonne, and a laboratory was to have been set up for his use—a laboratory to which he looked forward with kindling enthusiasm, and the plans for which he never tired of discussing.

Crushed by the sudden blow which had removed her closest companion and dearest friend, Madame Curie yet struggled to bear up, knowing that Pierre would want her to go on with her scientific work. But, turn as she might, she could not see her way clear. At this juncture, she was offered the position which her husband had occupied, and which at first she felt she could not accept, so deeply painful had been the cruel circumstances of its coming. No woman had ever before held a like position of trust and honor, and the responsibility would be very great. But Marie had now to be the bread-winner of her little family. So, after much hesitation, she decided to accept the offer. From the very first, as those who knew of her exceptional painstaking ability were well assured, Madame Curie's professional work was a success. Her classes were very popular, and when it came to be fully known that "the truth, and nothing but the truth" was desired, a number of very earnest students allied themselves with research work.

The discovery of radium had brought about a new branch of medical science, called radiumtherapy, which was developing rapidly, with results of more and more importance for the treatment of several diseases, and particularly of cancer. Imagine the joy Madame Curie felt in realizing that the discovery which she and her husband had brought about was not only of great scientific importance, but that it was destined to become a powerful and efficient factor in the control of human suffering and the ravages of a terrible disease! Moreover, only a beginning had been made in the use of the wonderful rays of radium light! Nobody could even surmise as to its importance in future years.

The first factor in the success of radiumtherapy lay in securing a primary standard, so that the quantity of radium used might always be accurately gauged. To Madame Curie was appointed this very delicate mission, an accurate result being secured in 1911. The standard, a thin glass tube, of a few centimeters in length, contains the pure salt used in determining the atomic weight. It is deposited in the International Bureau of Weights and Measures, at Sevres, near Paris. Several secondary standards have been made by comparison with the primary one. In France, the control of radium tubes, by the measurement of their radiation, takes place in Madame

Curie's laboratory, and here any one may take radium to be tested. In the United States, the Bureau of Standards does this work.

In 1903, the Nobel prize for the greatest contribution to science was made jointly to Henry Becquerel and the Curies as co-discoverers of radioactivity and the new radioactive elements. In 1911, the award was made to Madame Curie alone, for her great work in the preparation of pure radium. Though she was in very poor health, she yielded to the demands made upon her, and went to Stockholm to receive the prize. Here she was most delightfully welcomed, but the rites connected with the delivery of the gift took on almost the nature of a national ceremonial, and Madame Curie returned to Paris so thoroughly fagged that she was obliged to keep to her bed for several months.

Then, in 1912, came an offered honor which the quiet woman of science appreciated very much. A laboratory of radium had been created at Warsaw, where she was born, and Madame Curie was asked to come and be its director. She could not leave her work in France to go back to her native land, but she was glad to give advice in planning the new curriculum and to attend the inauguration fêtes, feeling a distinct pleasure that she had been instrumental in helping to found a useful work on her native heath.

Shortly now came the knowledge that the Pasteur Institute wished to be associated with the Curie laboratory in Paris, and Madame Curie was happy to welcome it, since this would mean increased funds and greater opportunities. The World War intervened, however, before all the combining arrangements had been satisfactorily completed. In the great conflict, Madame Curie soon found her own particular activity, doing a work which was of the utmost value and which absorbed the greater part of her time and efforts. This was the establishment of radiology stations, and teaching the use of X-ray machines in finding the location of projectiles which had entered the body, and showing up lesions of bones and injuries to the internal organs. The radiologic trucks which proved such a boon at the far front were Madame Curie's own idea. These she fitted up in collaboration with the Red Cross. Nor did she stop just with the building and equipping of these essential first aids. She went into the zone of the deepest military action, and saw them set up and in operation. More than this, she drove one of the trucks herself, and her slender, capable person was hailed with joy by the hard-worked surgeons in many smoking, battle-scarred areas. She went to the relief of front-line hospitals at Amiens, Calais, Verdun, Nancy, Compiegne, and many other points where those in charge found themselves facing the most intensive work with almost no surgical appliances. Often Madame Curie was accompanied by her daughter Irene, who studied nursing and learned radiology, in the hope of being able to lighten her mother's cares.

In 1921 came a very precious encouragement to the noble woman of science. She was asked to come to the United States to receive a gift of radium which the women of this country had succeeded in buying to further the great work in which Madame Curie was engaged. For the Curies with their deeply ingrained honestness had never kept any of their discovery for themselves. Nor had they taken out any patents for their own protection. "We were working in the interests of science," Madame Curie once said, when questioned on this point. ",Radium was not to enrich any one. It is an element. It belongs to all people."

The thimbleful of radium, subscribed to Madame Curie by the American women, represented one gramme in weight, and to secure it five hundred men had worked for six months to separate the radium from the ore. Ten thousand tons of distilled water had been used, a thousand tons of coal had been burned, and five hundred tons of chemicals had been used. All for a thimbleful of radium! Think of it! No wonder that such a product is more to be valued than rubies, or diamonds, or platinum.

Madame Curie received the deed of gift, a beautifully engraved scroll, with mixed emotions, and presently her generosity gave voice to the feeling that was uppermost: "I can not have this precious fortune left in this way," she protested earnestly. "Not only does this gramme of radium represent a great deal of money, but it is the contribution of the women of America to science. It must not be deeded to me. It must be consecrated to science for all time. Please have a lawyer draw up a paper that will make this very clear."

Nor was she content when assured that the matter would be attended to within a few days.

"It must be done to-night," she exclaimed. "Suppose that I should die before morning! The radium would go to my estate. My daughter Eve is not of age; some time would thus elapse before the radium could lawfully revert to its proper channel. Too much is at stake. Let it be done to-night, please."

And so, notwithstanding the lateness of the hour and the consequent difficulties, the transfer was arranged,— a lawyer finally being found who settled the matter satisfactorily from a draft which Madame Curie herself prepared. Mrs. Calvin Coolidge was one of the witnesses of the document.

Because of Madame Curie's always rather frail condition she could not enter into nearly all the plans made for her while in America. But she saw a great deal of our country, and interested herself in the work of many

schools and colleges, sailing for home finally, filled with
enthusiasm for what she yet hoped to do for science, and
with a renewed courage which promised much from one
of her dauntless resources. Still she was constantly
handicapped for lack of funds, and prone more than ever
now, as she naively said, after seeing so much of American business methods, "to feel compelled to give thought
to a very fundamental question concerning the view a
scientist ought to take of his discovery."

Had she and Pierre Curie been right to yield all the
profits of their discovery of radium to science? They
had taken out no patents of any kind on their process of
isolating the element, and the methods first introduced by
them are still used. Even the radium which they had
themselves prepared had been given outright to the Institute where they were employed. Had they used what
the public termed "practical business sense," not only
could they have faced the world with adequate personal
means, but they would have had funds available for
building and equipping such a laboratory as the needs of
science demanded! Undoubtedly humanity has great
need for practical men, who can safeguard their own
interests, the while the general need is not forgotten.
But dreamers, too, are in demand; folks like Sir Hum-
phrey Davy and Michael Faraday, with a long vision and
a willingness to delve deep into truth for truth's sake,
and when a great principle comes to light, to leave its ex-
ploitation to capital and pass on to further revelations.
The latter had been the course of the Curies. And, reason as she might, Madame Curie could not feel that their
initial decision should have been different. The world,
to-day, is fast coming to see that it is the part of governments, financiers, and educational institutions to go to the
root of such matters. A fund should be forthcoming for
the protection of the investigators in science; they should

not have to turn and contrive, as Madame Curie has been forced to do, going without all the pleasures and most of what people in general term the necessities of life, in order to pursue the threads of research. Huxley, speaking on this point, once declared: "A Faraday at a million dollars a year would be dirt cheap!" and of this there can be no gainsaying.

With the gramme of radium given to Madame Curie, in 1921, went a gift of money, which was intended by the donors to make life easier for the great woman of science who had for so long lived in such straitened circumstances. But did Madame Curie avail herself of it? No, indeed. With characteristic singleness of purpose, she used it to rent radium for the Warsaw Cancer Hospital in her beloved homeland. Finding this out at length, the women of America again interested themselves in Madame Curie's behalf, with the result that an invitation soon went to this great woman scientist of the world to come once more as our nation's guest, and receive the gift of a second gramme of radium to be transferred to Warsaw.

On October 15, 1929, a little lady in black came slowly down the gangplank from the liner *Ile de France*. Her steps were carefully guided by Ambassador Charles Dawes, who had arrived on the same steamer, and the bustling, chattering crowds on the pier fell silent as the frail figure advanced, and the whisper went round: "It is Madame Curie." A crowd of reporters and photographers drew back respectfully. Not for their rude onslaughts was that worn, all too apparently fragile woman. For to-day Madame Curie is no longer young, and her condition is anaemic and enfeebled, brought on, it is said, by constantly working with radium. En route the ship's captain anxiously studied special wireless reports of the weather, prepared to change the course of the ship if rough seas threatened. But the crossing was smooth, and Madame Curie declared herself not unduly fatigued and ready to meet her dear American friends, once she had rested a wee bit.

One of the special dates planned, and marked by the woman scientist with a red cross, was the anniversary celebration of the jubilee of the incandescent light, in Detroit, October 21, 1929, honoring her friend and fellow-scientist, Thomas A. Edison. For two days Madame Curie rested quietly at the White House, the guest of President and Mrs. Hoover, and it was here that the second gift of radium was bestowed. Madame Curie's final public appearance in America was as the guest of honor at a dinner of the New York committee of the American Society for the Control of Cancer, October 31.

The closing years of Madame Curie's life were quiet ones, spent in her beloved laboratory. She passed away in Paris, July 4, 1934. Her workshop, now known as the Curie Laboratory of the Radium Institute, University of Paris, is still in charge of a Curie, her daughter, Irene, whose husband actively aids her in the research which still makes the institute famous.

MADAME CHIANG KAI-SHEK

In China there is an ancient legend about the girl Mulan, who went to war in her father's place. Wearing his helmet and his coat of mail, she fought for twelve years, and she fought so well that the soldiers by her very side never suspected. That is only a legend. During the four thousand years of Chinese history there have been powerful emperors and great philosophers, but women have had little part. The noble women have been like those described by Li Po and the other poets, highborn ladies who, with tears falling down like rain, mourned their husbands long absent at the wars, plied their embroidery needles behind silken screens, and watched the same sad moon that lighted the fighting men of Han. That, indeed, was the part they were expected to play.

A very old poem explains quite clearly the difference there between sons and daughters:

The son.
    He then shall have a son
    To sleep upon a couch,
    To wear a costly dress
    And play with toys of jade;
    Imperious, too, his cry;
    His pinafore of red; The house's lord he'll be.

The daughter.
    A daughter too he'll have
    To sleep upon the floor,
    A napkin for her gown,
    A potsherd (i. e. a piece of broken china) for her toy.
    No choice is hers to make

Save choose the food and drink
And spare her parents pain.

What the poet said so long ago has been true with scarcely
any change for centuries: The woman is inferior to the
man, and she must be obedient in three distinct ways.   In
childhood obedient to her father or elder brother.   In marriage obedient to her husband.   In old age obedient to her
son.

To us in America this seems almost impossible to understand, but it is almost impossible for us fully to understand
the Orient anyway.   We must realize that China is not
only a different country, it is almost a different world.

It was once said that the name *China* does not stand
for a country, but a civilization.   That civilization is a
thing which has grown by itself without paying the slight-
est attention to the rest of the world.   It is true that Christian missionaries visited the country during the seventh
century, and Marco Polo reached Peking in medieval times,
but this communication with the Occident had little more
effect than the visits of so many tourists.   Because of the
natural barriers the country was virtually cut off from the
world.   On one side is the Pacific, the greatest of the
oceans; on the other the Himalayas, the highest mountains
on the face of the earth.

Within that area are crowded 450,000,000 people, more
than three times the population of the United States.   Very
few of them can read or write, and about all they have to
go by is their complicated fabric of tradition, which reaches
back over the centuries.   It is no wonder that they have
developed a manner of living, and a mode of thought which
is altogether different from our own, and to us it can't but
seem strange.

In 1876 the first railway was built between Shanghai
and Wu-sung, but it was purchased by the authorities and

destroyed.   Recently, when an enterprising American set up an outdoor advertising sign, the citizens insisted that he furnish a supply of firecrackers with which to frighten away the devils which it would bring.   We think those things are funny, but they simply indicate how an old country must feel about the new-fangled devices of a modern one.

Besides, now it is different.

In 1912 the Emperor Süang-t'ung abdicated, and the Republic was established under Sun Yat-sen.   Since then the changes have been extraordinary.   Miles of macadam roads have been built, railroads have been constructed. Today China is struggling to adapt itself to the modern world.   It has what it calls its "New Culture," and from out of this new culture have flowered a few amazing personalities—many-sided, modern, and no less glamorous than the girl hero in the medieval legend.   No longer must the Chinese women lead their lives according to the patterns of female propriety, which are set down so exactly in the classical "Lessons for Women."

Of these personalities, by far the greatest is Madame Chiang Kai-shek—Mayling Soong.   She is wife, secretary and interpreter to China's Generalissimo, who has been for a decade both head of the Central Government and chief of all its military forces.   But she is also far more than that.   She is an educator, a social worker, chief of the relief and Red Cross services and the *working chief* (not just the honorary head) of the Chinese Army air force.   A woman of incredible energy, she travels largely by plane going constantly from one part of the country to the other.   She and General Chiang have been accustomed to toil together in the same room at National Army Headquarters for sixteen or more hours a day.   When the Japanese invaded China, she even became news reporter extraordinary to the Western World and, almost up to the

moment when they began to storm Nanking and she had
to flee, she filed daily news cables from the city, describing
the scenes of blood and fire.   Her future, like the future of
China, is in the hands of fate, but in the later months of the
year 1937, at any rate, Madame Chiang Kai-shek was by
common consent the most powerful woman in public life
anywhere in the world.   One day in January, 1938, a New
York newspaper said, "The most powerful woman the
modern world has known since Queen Victoria, this un-
crowned empress of 450,000,000 Chinese is playing a desperate game on which depends the destiny of the world.
She is really the Government, although nominally only the
wife of the Generalissimo."

Soong Mei-ling—or in the Shanghai rendering which
she prefers and the Americanized fashion of surname last,
Mayling Soong—was born into an extraordinary family,
a family sometimes dubbed the "Soong Dynasty."   It is
rich, but, first of all, rich in personalities.   In the drama
of China's political life, in which Mayling Soong was destined to play so spectacular a rôle, her two older sisters have
been hardly less influential :   In all likelihood these are the
most notable three sisters now alive in this third decade of
the twentieth century. Her three brothers, also, have taken
an active part in Chinese life.

It has been said of the Soong sisters and their brothers
that psychologically they are all Americans.   Perhaps they
could not easily help being so, since they spent much of their
childhood in the United States and were educated in American colleges.   Their father, Charles Jones Soong, had as-
sumed his Christian name on the occasion of his baptism,
which took place in the Fifth Street Methodist Church
South, of Wilmington, North Carolina.   He was, it is
thought, a native of the island of Hainan and came to the
United States in 1880, shipping, then or later, perhaps as a

cabin boy, on the revenue cutter, *Colfax,* the captain of
which was a man named Charles Jones. Having adopted
the Christian faith, with Captain Jones as his sponsor,
Charles Soong found benefactors to aid him in acquiring
Christian schooling. He first attended Trinity College
(now Duke University) and then studied at Vanderbilt
University, which conferred upon him a theological certifi-
cate. He is said to have followed the American custom of
earning a part of his college expenses in summer vacations.
In any case the Soong fortune was still to be made.

On his return to China as missionary and teacher of
English, Charles Soong met in Shanghai and married a
Miss Ni. She was a brilliant and attractive woman, and a
devout Christian, fervent in prayer, in whom, throughout
her long life, her children and friends recognized something
of greatness. Madame Chiang tells how she once asked
her mother, who lived to be ninety-two and was then very
old, "Why don't you pray that God will annihilate Japan—
by an earthquake or something?" The venerable Madame
Soong had transcended the human fault of bitterness and
rebuked her daughter sharply. Whether or not Madame
Chiang can still pray for the Japanese people, as she said she
had learned through her mother's saintliness to do, the influence of such a strong personality is not easily forgotten.

Not long after his return to Shanghai, Charles Soong,
who had more money making ability than he could be content to bury in a napkin, ventured into business in Shanghai. He printed, published and sold Bibles in the Chinese
language and became sufficiently prosperous to comply with
Madame Soong's wish that their children, girls as well as
boys, should be sent to college. As his fortune grew, he
contributed to various religious causes and also gave financial support to the revolutionary scheme in the interests of
which Sun Yat-sen traveled to and fro for fifteen years,
organizing Cantonese, particularly, all over the world, and

soliciting funds.   Later on, Charles Soong served Dr. Sun as secretary and treasurer and so was destined finally to bring his family into intimate relations with the Chinese revolutionaries.

Meanwhile the family was being educated.   Mayling, who was born in 1892 and since childhood had lived in the United States, first entered Wesleyan College, Macon, Georgia, the institution attended by her sisters.   In 1914 she registered at Wellesley, and from that college she was graduated three years later.   In dress and speech she was an American girl when she came there, but after her first year she began to wear Chinese costume and give time to study of the Chinese language, thus enhancing her personality, no doubt, and preparing somewhat for the adjustments to be made on her return to China.   As a student she did her best work in English, French and music.   She wrote verse, studied the piano and the violin and belonged to a sorority composed of girls chiefly interested in the fine arts.   She was being fitted, one might suppose, for a life of leisure or purely social career.   Yet she herself declared in a statement published during the session of the Nine-Power Treaty Conference in Brussels that she had gone home to her native land "full of American ideals."   She had investigated American welfare laws and methods, she said, had seen workers' homes, with children playing in spacious playgrounds, and had visited many health clinics. She added that, when marrying General Chiang Kai-shek, she understood that God had given her a great opportunity to realize her ambitions—which were centered in the colossal task of "transforming medieval China."

China's Revolution of 1911 overthrew the Empire and established the Republic but it did not change the country overnight.   Sun Yat-sen, widely revered as the Founder of the Republic, was years later still striving to realize his ideals, a weather-beaten and aging man.   He married the exquisite, shy Ching-ling, the second of the Soong sisters, and she threw herself at once into the cause of Nationalist China.   In 1924 Dr. Sun founded near Canton a military academy, and placed at its head an obscure general, unknown in China, who had received his military training in Japan.   His name was Chiang Kai-shek.

The choice was a good one, for this same obscure general, only two years later, led the Chinese Nationalist Army northward in a triumphant expedition.   Of course Mayling Soong was interested in current affairs, for her brother "T.V.," a Harvard graduate, was Finance Minister, and had set to work on a drastic reorganization of China's muddled finances.   But she may have watched this development with a special interest, for eventually she would be the wife of the expedition's leader.

Chiang Kai-shek was becoming more and more powerful, and as he became more powerful he became more independent.   At this time the existing government, the Hankow régime, had a peculiar kind of arrangement with communist Russia.   By this arrangement the Hankow government received much advice from Russia, and consulted Russia's advisers on political and military matters but did not commit itself to communism.   The plan worked very well; yet it was full of dynamite.

Chiang Kai-shek exploded the dynamite in the spring of 1927.   He suddenly decided to set up another government at Nanking and to drive out the Russians, lock, stock and barrel.   The result was that China was immediately split up into a number of bitter factions, which Chiang could not control.   In characteristic Chinese fashion he resigned all his offices and departed for Japan.   This was a very bad setback in his career.

At that moment of temporary eclipse Mayling joined her lot with his.   Her brother was very much opposed to the

match, but she had made up her mind.   On Chiang's return
from a tour of the Island Empire the wedding was celebrated, with the reading of a Christian service at the Soong
home, followed by a civil ceremony in the festively decorated ballroom of a Shanghai hotel.   The press gave much
space to the event and published the photograph of General
Chiang and his bride, in wedding costume of Western style,
elegant to the last detail of coiffure and bridal bouquet,
spats, gloves and boutonnière.

When he came back to China, General Chiang had said
to some Shanghai journalists who inquired about his plans,
"Marriage is a small matter, while matters concerning
Party and Nation are more important."   No doubt he was
showing both good taste and political discretion.   Also he
had told his interviewers that he would *not* resume the post
of Generalissimo.   But he was reëlected to it within a fortnight after his marriage, and he did not decline the honor.
"Marriage is a small matter."   Yet it may not be idle to see
a link between the two events or to ask whether without
this marriage, which has been in its public aspects a joint
dedication to the cause of China, General Chiang's efforts
would have been accorded so much success.

Having no children, Mme. Chiang has been free to devote her tremendous energies to the rôles of political help-
mate and spiritual counselor.   She attends to innumerable
official duties which would otherwise be entrusted to the
hands of hired secretaries and the Party henchmen who by
nature look upon every public crisis as an opportunity for
private gain.   She herself cooks her husband's food, because of his delicate health and his justifiable fear of being
poisoned.   She describes herself as gently reasoning with
him when political opposition makes him angry or un-
wisely stubborn.   When he is overwrought and cannot
sleep she reads to him, often from the Psalms.   At the time
of their marriage Chiang did not profess to be a Christian,

but afterward he became a church member and a student of the Bible.

Even as Generalissimo, Chiang had many powerful enemies, and transforming China turned out to be a slow process. When Japan seized control of Manchuria in 1931 and set up the puppet state of Manchoukuo, China, with all her other activities, was hardly in a position to resist Japan, and Japan knew it. The Central Government could not undertake a major war against Japan because all its physical resources were being used against the Chinese communists and in trying to cement the unity of the provinces.

In the next few years Chiang waged five very bloody "extermination campaigns" against the Chinese communists, who had succeeded in setting up governments, particularly in South China, and in winning over great masses of people through their communist "reforms." Mme. Chiang spent much of the time with her husband whenever he was at the front. Believing that the Chinese Reds were perhaps not really communistic at heart, many people blamed Chiang bitterly for not coming to terms with them and putting up a fight against Japan instead. His ruthless anti-communist campaigns were, they felt, a needless sacrifice of thousands of China's best youths. They wondered whether he were not on the way to becoming a dictator. These ideas were voiced less and less openly as the years passed, but Mayling's own gentle sister Ching-ling, who had returned from Moscow and was living in semi-retirement, sometimes issued statements that bore testimony to her courage and her deep-rooted conviction that she still best represented the ideals of her revered husband, Dr. Sun.

In reply to criticism, the Generalissimo and his wife pushed their own program more vigorously: modern roads, airplanes, rural rehabilitation. But "the most potent new broom was probably the spiritual one," Mme. Chiang says, and by this she means the New Life Movement which she and the Generalissimo launched in 1934 on a nation-wide scale. It combined a revival of Confucian ideals with Christian morals and modern conceptions of social service. Opium addicts were rounded up and "cured" in public hospitals, mass marriages were publicly encouraged to save burdensome family expense, villages were kept clean, laxness in dress was made subject to fine—all this and much more. Madame Chiang flew from place to place addressing scores of meetings; for she believed that, along with the things modern science had to give, China urgently needed "new life" in the individual before its transformation could take place.

Finally Chiang Kai-shek and his generals succeeded in routing the Reds, but the Reds were far from exterminated. In one of the most remarkable retreats of military history they made their way over mountains and deserts and turned up in Szechwan, several thousand miles away.

Some time before, these communists had issued a declaration of war against Japan, and called upon the Nanking government to join with them. Now it happened that the very person whom the Generalissimo had put in command of the Bandit Suppression Forces (that is, the forces for exterminating the communists) had a special grudge against Japan because they had driven him out of Manchuria. Chang Hsueh-liang was his name, and he was known as the "Young Marshal." Under these circumstances the communists were able to win him to their side, in spite of the fact that he was supposed to be their worst enemy. Before anyone knew what was happening, the Generalissimo had been kidnaped by this fellow, his own subordinate! Desperately Chiang Kai-shek, the most important man in China, had tried to make his getaway. In thin clothes, shivering from the cold, he climbed up over a craggy mountainside, amid the whizzing of bullets.   They caught him and threw him into captivity.

The whole world was shocked by such a thing.   Madame Chiang Kai-shek, anxiously waiting in Nanking, was beside herself with concern.   For days she telegraphed, over and over again, but it was impossible to accomplish anything.   She could not tell whether the messages were authentic or not, and there was no way of knowing if the Generalissimo were dead, alive, or whether he had been sentenced to die.

She decided that she must go to Sian and find out, even though it might mean stepping right into a trap.   She knew that if Chiang were dead, she would be killed too.   She knew that in any event she might be held for torture, an art in which the Chinese excel.   That was why, as the plane circled over Sian, she handed a revolver to the adviser who accompanied her, saying, "If the soldiers lay hands on me . . . then shoot me."   To herself she must have said when the plane gradually drew up to a stop on the field, "Which is it: Life or death?"

The Young Marshal met her himself.   He was courteous, half apologetic.   "Madame," he said, "this would not have happened at all, had you been here."

She was taken that day to the General's quarters, where he lay in bed, helpless from a wrenched back suffered during his attempted escape.   "Why have you come?" he said as she walked into the room.   "You have walked into a lion's den."   That is what he said, but he was so touched that later he admitted that he had wanted to cry.

With the arrival of Madame Chiang Kai-shek there began innumerable conferences and sessions.   Hour after hour during the day she conferred with the Young Marshal.   Then often they would talk the night through themselves.   Would they both be released?   On what terms would they be released?   And always Madame Chiang

Kai-shek held up before them her greatest ideal, the good of China.

At last it was concluded that permission to leave would be given Christmas morning. But tiffin time came and still no word. Orderlies were hurrying back and forth through the camp, and it was plain that something was afoot. Finally, late in the afternoon, official permission came for their departure. And even more—the Young Marshal insisted on going to Nanking for trial and proper punishment!

They took off in the Young Marshal's private plane, and as Sian faded behind them, Madame Chiang Kai-shek felt the exultation of having achieved one more step toward the unification of China.

THE END